Introduction to
BONSAI

The Complete Illustrated
Guide for Beginners

WITH MONTHLY GROWING SCHEDULES

By the Editors of
***Bonsai Sekai* Magazine**
Illustrated by Kyosuke Gun

TUTTLE Publishing

Tokyo | Rutland, Vermont | Singapore

Contents

The Power of Small Bonsai

Small bonsai trees impart a charming look and feel to your modern living space!

My bonsai trees are placed on a rack on a balcony that gets poor lighting, but I can enjoy the bonsai experience without depriving them. To make up for the lack of sunlight, I use a grow light. My wife also participates in caring for the bonsai. It is a very important aspect of our free time.

"Even though it's contained in a small pot, the bonsai maintains its vitality. I am especially drawn to the 'evergreenness' of the pine variety. I also appreciate experiencing the transition of seasons that I cannot enjoy from my workplace."

—HIROMU KUMANISHI, 10-year bonsai enthusiast in Minato Ward, Tokyo.

ABOVE LEFT AND RIGHT Even in small, sterile places such as the entrance to an apartment, bonsai cleanse the atmosphere and make the space seem brighter. (These trees are under 8 inches / 20 cm.)

RIGHT Hiromu Kumanishi says that though the bonsai are small, he enjoys having this little spot of life and greenery in the middle of his busy life in a bustling city.

Even in small spaces such as a window sill, having a bonsai makes for a relaxing environment that's very popular among my students. It's not surprising that the appreciation of bonsai has spread across the globe.

"Trees in nature emit power and 'ki' (vital energy). Bonsai, on the other hand, channel that power through small pots and wire. Nevertheless, even though their energy is contained, they present themselves in such an artistic way."

—JESSIE LEE PARKER, yoga instructor and 4-year bonsai enthusiast in Setagaya Ward, Tokyo.

LEFT Jessie Lee Parker says that bonsai play an important role in creating a tranquil atmosphere during meditation sessions at his yoga studio.

I work in an office and decided to add some plants to my apartment because they help me relax. That's how it all began. I started with typical houseplants, but slowly introduced bonsai. Now I have many varieties. I take pictures of the blooming plants every day to appreciate their blossoms and growth. For me now, having bonsai in my life has become essential.

"After all, these are plants that are meant to be observed and appreciated. With each bend of a branch or with each bonsai I plant, I can see the uniqueness of the individual bonsai. I find this very appealing."

—RUTSUKO KANEKO, **6-year bonsai enthusiast in**
  Suginami Ward, Tokyo.

ABOVE AND RIGHT Even in a cramped location, by placing a bonsai Rutsuko feels that she is bringing energy and vitality into her home. She says that being surrounded by her favorite plants is a spiritual aspect of her life.

Kaori Umezawa started attending classes at her local bonsai garden ten years ago. When she was in her twenties she moved into a well-lit apartment and started taking bonsai more seriously. Her garden, which is about 19.5 x 13 feet (6 x 4 meters), receives lots of sunlight.

The earlier you take on this hobby, the more trees you can care for and the longer you can enjoy the experience. In the art of bonsai, you are considered to be young and up-and-coming if you are in your fifties. In which case, you can still look forward to learning and achieving more for decades—maybe even another forty or fifty years.

"The ability to find good trees is important, but I would like to be able to propagate them myself as well."

—YOSHI UMEZAWA, **10-year bonsai enthusiast in Ichihara City,**
  Chiba Prefecture.

LEFT Living with bonsai allows one to truly take in the change of the seasons throughout the year. Mr. and Mrs. Umezawa begin and end each day by appreciating and talking about their bonsai. Sharing their observations and taking time to really enjoy their bonsai is a part of the passion for, and process of, caring for them.

Many Ways to Enjoy

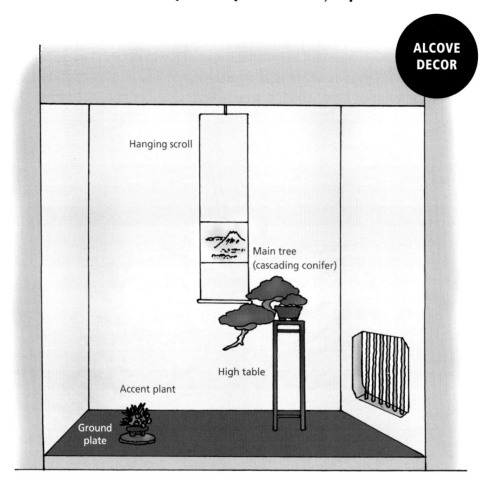

Here, a conifer cascading to the left is used as the main tree, and a hanging scroll is placed in such a way that branches superimpose the edge. Add grasses and flowers suitable for the season as a secondary bonsai or plant. The hanging scroll, main tree and the accent plant are placed in an irregular triangle. The depth elements here are the distant mountain in the scroll, the conifer in the middle, and undergrowth (grass or moss) on the floor in the foreground. This gives the alcove the sense of a full landscape.

A TRADITIONAL WAY OF DECORATING WITH THE MAGNIFICENCE OF NATURE

A traditional Japanese way to display bonsai is to create a harmonious arrangement in a confined space such as an alcove. The decoration of the alcove is called *tokokazari. Sekikazari*, which literally means "decorating a seat," pertains to the arrangement of bonsai in an area specifically for bonsai display.

As shown above, alcove decoration consists of three elements: the main tree, an accompanying bonsai (the accent), and a hanging scroll. When the main tree is a conifer, the flowers and grasses accompanying it should represent the season. The main tree is placed in such a way that it flows toward the hanging scroll, and a high table and a ground plate are laid beneath the bonsai. Choose a hanging scroll (or other wall hanging in a less traditional space) that complements the main tree well. The *sekikazari* is a two-part arrangement consisting of main tree and accent.

For the background, there are principles of harmony that have been in use for many generations. On the other hand, there are a variety of arrangements tailored to modern living spaces, such as apartments. You get beautiful results when you keep the basic principles in mind, but how you incorporate those ideas is up to you.

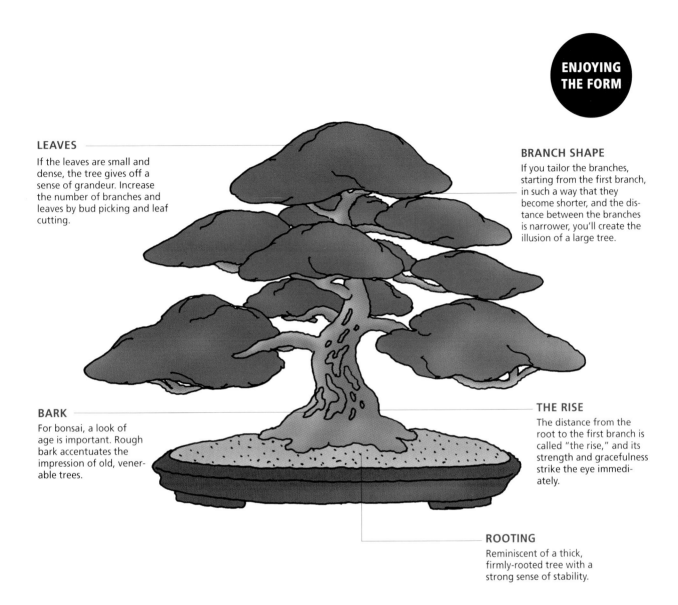

LEAVES

If the leaves are small and dense, the tree gives off a sense of grandeur. Increase the number of branches and leaves by bud picking and leaf cutting.

BRANCH SHAPE

If you tailor the branches, starting from the first branch, in such a way that they become shorter, and the distance between the branches is narrower, you'll create the illusion of a large tree.

BARK

For bonsai, a look of age is important. Rough bark accentuates the impression of old, venerable trees.

THE RISE

The distance from the root to the first branch is called "the rise," and its strength and gracefulness strike the eye immediately.

ROOTING

Reminiscent of a thick, firmly-rooted tree with a strong sense of stability.

TIPS FOR ENJOYING THE WHOLE AND EACH PART

When viewing a bonsai, stand in front of it and first take in the whole setting, including the pots and table, before moving on to the details. Then, scrutinize the middle of the tree height, and each part from the roots, the rise, the trunk, up to the branches, leaves and the flowers.

The illustration above suggests a large, old tree. The rise from the base to the first branch is a gentle curve that appears to have weathered many windy storms, the rough bark gives the impression of advanced age and the leaves convey a sense of vitality. The shape from the root to the rise is like a mountain ridge.

Bonsai are carefully cultivated and managed by human hands, and some have been trained for hundreds of years. The feeling of antiquity, sense of vitality and the skill that has gone into creating these things are already evident. If you have a young tree, you can visualize how, with care, its features will evolve. Bonsai is ideal when the tree is in its completed form (full season), so fall and winter are important times. Thus, the venerable bonsai is like an elderly person who feels long settled into the rhythms of life.

Basic Tree Forms

Slanted Trunk

The trunk grows diagonally to one side or the other. The branches do not grow in any particular direction, and there is not much organization in this type. It is most commonly found in growing in the wild.

Upright Trunk

The trunk grows straight toward the sky, the roots grow in all directions, and the symmetrical triangular shape is ideal for this type. It is the most basic form for bonsai. However, it requires a lot of experience to execute.

Pattern Tree

The expression "drawing a pattern" means the bending back and forth of the trunk and branches. The form is ideal if it undulates gently. The curvaceous shape is the most common form of bonsai.

Twin Trunk

This is a tree form in which two trunks spread from the same root. The taller, thicker trunk is the main trunk, whereas the thinner, shorter trunk is the secondary trunk. Some give them the nicknames of "parent" and "child."

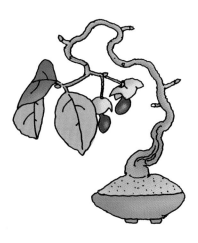

Literati Tree

The thin trunk stretches out in the absence of lower branches, and the whole tree creates a delicate silhouette. It was named for its popularity among authors in the Edo period.

Standing Trunk

This form exhibits several trunks extending from one root. The appeal is the harmony between the height and thickness of the main trunk and other trunks. The number of trunks is typically an odd number, such as three trunks, five trunks or seven trunks.

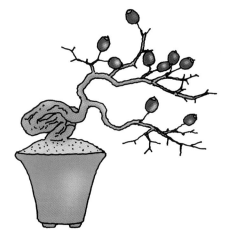

Windsock

This is a tree with a shape that makes it appear to have been exposed to high winds in mountainous or seaside regions and stretches in one direction from the trunk to the branches. Common to harsh environments in nature, conifers are the most suitable for this tree shape.

Root Over Rock

Similar to group planting (see right), this form mimics a natural landscape and is an ancient form of bonsai. It represents the character of a tree that lives on the cliffs of mountainous regions or on the rocks along a shoreline.

Cliff

This is a tree form that expresses a powerful stance, symbolizing persistence in the face of adversity. Those with trunks and branches hanging below the bottom of the bowl are called "overhanging cliffs," and those that do not fall below the bottom of the bowl are called "half-hanging cliffs."

Group Planting

Multiple roots of the same type planted in a single pot to form a group that looks like a forest. Although not covered in this book, there are several types of herbaceous bonsai that are grown in this arrangement.

Tools to Have on Hand

You can purchase these items at bonsai nurseries, garden shops and home centers, as well as online stores. Some items can be substituted with general gardening and household tools.

Basic Tools and Materials

Bonsai Tweezers

For bud-picking, bud-nipping, foliage trimming, weeding, etc. The curved blade on the back end is used for leveling the soil.

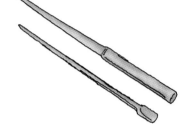

Bamboo Chopsticks

Use chopsticks to loosen toughened root clumps when planting and replanting, and to tamp soil into gaps between the roots.

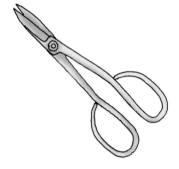

Pruning Scissors

Used for pruning fine branches and leaves. Because this tool has fine blade edges that are prone to blunting, do not use it for cutting roots. Use a root cutter instead (see facing page).

Wire

In addition to bending trunks and branches, wire is used to anchor the net and roots at the bottom of the pot. For gardening, 15 gauge (1.45 mm) and 9 gauge (2.9 mm) wires are best.

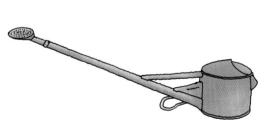

Watering Pot

Copper products have an antimicrobial effect. Professional gardeners and veteran bonsai enthusiasts alike seek out tools made, or plated with, copper.

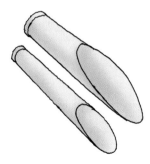

Soil Scoop

This tool is handy for distributing soil during planting and replanting. Use different sizes depending on the size of the pot being filled.

Fertilizer Basket

These plastic cages are used to anchor solid fertilizer to the pot soil. They also have the effect of preventing insect and bird feeding damage.

Branch Cutter

This robust tool will make short work of cleanly cutting the trunks, thick branches and roots.

Pot Netting

Prevents soil from spilling out of the bottom of the bowl, and also blocks entry for insects. Cut squares according to the size of the hole being covered.

Wire Cutter

An indispensable tool for preparing wire for anchors and for training branches and trunks. Cutters are also useful when the wires need to be removed.

Root Cutter

Root cutters are used to trim roots during replanting. They can also be used to cut thick branches.

Scissor Oil

This light oil keeps scissors sharp and rust free. Wash them after use, dry, and then apply lubricant each time.

Brush

When working with soil, a small brush is convenient for cleaning up messes.

Pliers

Pliers are used when twisting the wire that holds the roots or when removing wires installed when replanting.

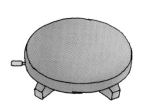

Turntable

This platform rotates 360 degrees, allowing you to see the tree from all directions without having to change positions.

Wound Dressing

This preparation is used to prevent microbes from entering wounds and grafts and to facilitate healing when branches are pruned.

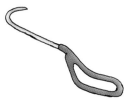

Root Pick

A useful tool for removing hardened roots during replanting.

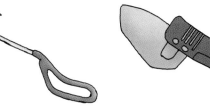

Soil Tamper

For use when replanting; this tool is used for flattening the soil in a pot containing a large area of topsoil before watering.

How Bonsai Use Air and Soil

PLANTS CONSUME NUTRIENTS AND BREATHE

Animals, including humans, take in nutrition essential for replenishing their bodies. Some of the nutrients are carbohydrates, which are refined into glucose through digestion. Glucose is then used as fuel to power daily activities. Plants use water and sunlight to produce their own glucose for growth and repair.

Respiration is another essential activity for terrestrial organisms. Oxygen-rich air enters the lungs, and the byproduct, carbon dioxide, is expelled. Plants do not have lungs, of course, but they also participate in respiration, exchanging oxygen for carbon dioxide.

Unlike the way animals metabolize food, plants can make the nutrients they need to sustain their lives. The process is called *photosynthesis*, and it takes place in the chloroplasts, which are located in the leaves. This is why plants are called "autotrophic organisms," whereas animals are called "heterotrophic organisms."

The quality of the soil is very important for optimal bonsai growth. Plant growth above the soil is determined by the plant's root growth below the soil. And root growth depends on the quality of the soil the roots occupy. Tree growth in the wild and bonsai growth both operate on the same principle.

But what conditions are necessary for roots to grow vigorously? Let's compare the conditions for trees in the wild and for bonsai.

Natural trees are not replanted, but bonsai must be replanted at regular intervals. This is because outdoor soil is constantly being renewed

naturally throughout the seasons, whereas the condition of bonsai pot soil gradually deteriorates without renewal.

In the case of natural trees, organic matter (compost), which is the nutrient source for plants, is constantly being supplied by fallen leaves, branches, fallen trees, dead roots, animal excrement and carcasses, and the dead bodies of microorganisms. Nitrogen is indispensable for protein synthesis in plants. However, plants cannot directly take in the nitrogen gas that is abundant in the atmosphere.

So, plants absorb this essential gas through the roots in the form of nitrogen-rich compounds such as ammonia and nitrates. Organic substances such as fallen leaves are the primary source of ammonia and nitrates. Microorganisms that proliferate in the soil act to break down this organic matter into ammonia and nitrates that are easy for plants to consume.

NECESSARY AIR IN THE SOIL

In agriculture, fields are plowed in the spring before planting seedlings. This tilling actually serves the purpose of aerating the soil. It is also necessary for bonsai soil to be relatively loose for good aeration. Aerated soil is the ideal medium for water to be supplied to the roots through precipitation or watering, while at the same time excess water is easily drained away by gravity. Plants take in carbon dioxide from the atmosphere only through the pores of their leaves, so no matter how loose the soil is, the roots do not absorb gases directly. However, part of the oxygen required for respiration is supplied by way of the element present in water absorbed by the roots.

WHY YOU NEED A GRANULAR SOIL

Bonsai soil should be granular. By using a granular soil, the naturally looser mix will facilitate the passage of water and nutrients to the roots. This kind of soil is called "granular structure soil." However, the quality of such soil gradually degrades as it compacts when smaller particles accumulate in the gaps between larger particles due to rainfall, daily irrigation, and root elongation. Replanting is how you reinvigorate the soil. Replanting is an indispensable task for improving the growing medium. Air and water shortages are likely to occur if it is neglected.

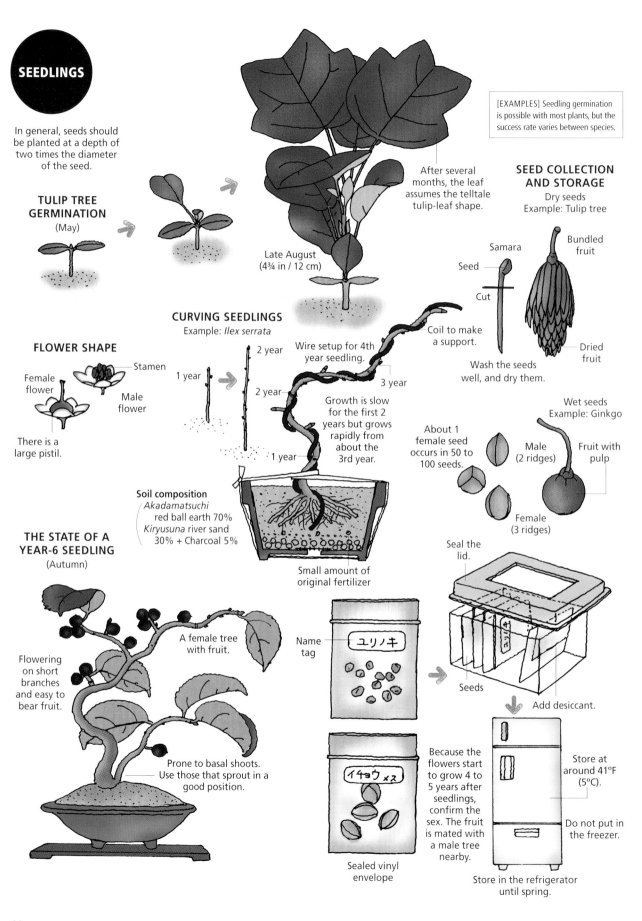

SEEDLINGS

In general, seeds should be planted at a depth of two times the diameter of the seed.

[EXAMPLES] Seedling germination is possible with most plants, but the success rate varies between species.

TULIP TREE GERMINATION
(May)

After several months, the leaf assumes the telltale tulip-leaf shape.

Late August
(4¾ in / 12 cm)

SEED COLLECTION AND STORAGE
Dry seeds
Example: Tulip tree

Samara
Bundled fruit
Seed
Cut
Coil to make a support.
Dried fruit

Wash the seeds well, and dry them.

CURVING SEEDLINGS
Example: *Ilex serrata*

2 year
Wire setup for 4th year seedling.
1 year
2 year
3 year
Growth is slow for the first 2 years but grows rapidly from about the 3rd year.
1 year

FLOWER SHAPE

Stamen
Female flower
Male flower

There is a large pistil.

Soil composition
Akadamatsuchi red ball earth 70%
Kiryusuna river sand 30% + Charcoal 5%

Small amount of original fertilizer

Wet seeds
Example: Ginkgo

About 1 female seed occurs in 50 to 100 seeds.

Male (2 ridges)
Fruit with pulp
Female (3 ridges)

THE STATE OF A YEAR-6 SEEDLING
(Autumn)

A female tree with fruit.

Flowering on short branches and easy to bear fruit.

Prone to basal shoots. Use those that sprout in a good position.

Name tag

ユリノキ

Seeds

Seal the lid.

Add desiccant.

Store at around 41°F (5°C).

イチョウ メス

Because the flowers start to grow 4 to 5 years after seedlings, confirm the sex. The fruit is mated with a male tree nearby.

Sealed vinyl envelope

Do not put in the freezer.

Store in the refrigerator until spring.

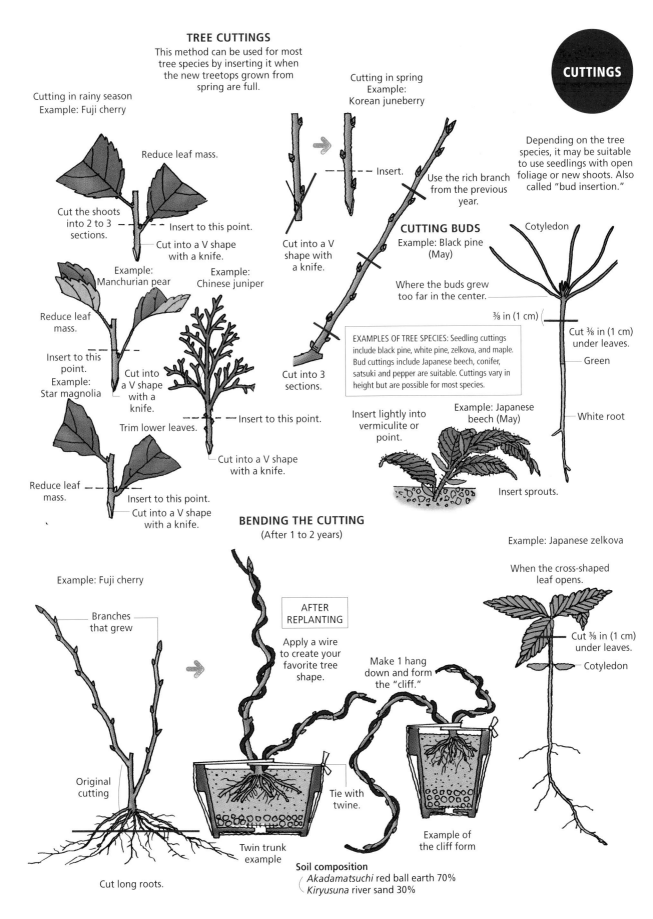

TREE CUTTINGS

This method can be used for most tree species by inserting it when the new treetops grown from spring are full.

Cutting in rainy season
Example: Fuji cherry

Reduce leaf mass.

Cut the shoots into 2 to 3 sections.

Insert to this point.

Cut into a V shape with a knife.

Example: Manchurian pear

Reduce leaf mass.

Insert to this point.
Example: Star magnolia

Cut into a V shape with a knife.

Trim lower leaves.

Reduce leaf mass.

Insert to this point.
Cut into a V shape with a knife.

Example: Chinese juniper

Insert to this point.

Cut into a V shape with a knife.

Cutting in spring
Example: Korean juneberry

Insert.

Cut into a V shape with a knife.

Use the rich branch from the previous year.

Cut into 3 sections.

CUTTING BUDS
Example: Black pine (May)

Where the buds grew too far in the center.

EXAMPLES OF TREE SPECIES: Seedling cuttings include black pine, white pine, zelkova, and maple. Bud cuttings include Japanese beech, conifer, satsuki and pepper are suitable. Cuttings vary in height but are possible for most species.

Insert lightly into vermiculite or point.

Example: Japanese beech (May)

Insert sprouts.

Depending on the tree species, it may be suitable to use seedlings with open foliage or new shoots. Also called "bud insertion."

Cotyledon

⅜ in (1 cm)

Cut ⅜ in (1 cm) under leaves.

Green

White root

Example: Japanese zelkova

When the cross-shaped leaf opens.

Cut ⅜ in (1 cm) under leaves.

Cotyledon

BENDING THE CUTTING
(After 1 to 2 years)

Example: Fuji cherry

Branches that grew

AFTER REPLANTING

Apply a wire to create your favorite tree shape.

Make 1 hang down and form the "cliff."

Original cutting

Tie with twine.

Example of the cliff form

Twin trunk example

Cut long roots.

Soil composition
Akadamatsuchi red ball earth 70%
Kiryusuna river sand 30%

Types of Bonsai Pots

Mud pot Red quince-style bowl—
5 × 4 × 2 in (12.6 × 10.2 × 4.9 cm)

Mud pot Rectangle cloud-foot pot—
6 × 4⅞ × 2¾ in (15 × 12.4 × 4.5 cm)

Mud pot Square cloud-foot pot—
3½ × 3½ × 2⅜ in (9 × 9 × 6 cm)

> Containers for bonsai come in various shapes and colors. If you start to worry about how the pot pairs with your plants, then you must be a bonsai enthusiast!

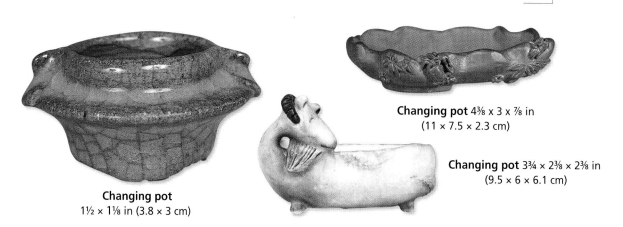

Changing pot
1½ × 1⅛ in (3.8 × 3 cm)

Changing pot 4⅜ × 3 × ⅞ in
(11 × 7.5 × 2.3 cm)

Changing pot 3¾ × 2⅜ × 2⅜ in
(9.5 × 6 × 6.1 cm)

A FUN WORLD OF SMALL POTS THAT BRING OUT THE CHARM OF TREES

What bonsai is to a person, the pot is to clothes. A tree becomes a bonsai only after planting in a bonsai pot. Furthermore, you create "good bonsai" by pairing pots with trees that complement each other. Bonsai is fascinating with its variety of expressions even if it is very small. But it's the pot that brings out the charm.

Small pots and bowls are classified as either "mud" or "glazed," as is the case with ordinary bonsai pots. In general, mud pots are used for conifers, and glazed bowls are used for other miscellaneous trees.

Mud pots are baked without glaze on the clay. They are also called baked pots." Glazed pots come in a variety of colors and designs. Just looking at the colorful glazed pots is already interesting, to say nothing of the bonsai!

Because the pots are small, it is easy to experiment with different sorts, as the shape of the containers vary. There are many "changing pots" that are unusual when compared to a conventional bonsai pot.

A bonsai connoisseur might mention that the pot looks good on the tree by saying "the pot pairing looks good." If you start to worry about how the pot pairs with your plants, then you must be a bonsai enthusiast!

Glazed pot Flower-type pot
2¾ × 1½ in (7 × 4 cm)

Glazed pot Porcelain round pot
3 × 1⅛ in (7.5 × 3 cm)

Glazed pot White vertical pot
5⅞ × 4½ × 1⅛ in (14.9 × 11.4 × 2.8 cm)

Glazed pot Long-type pot
3¼ × 2½ × 1 in (8.5 × 6.5 × 2.6 cm)

Glazed pot Hattori hexagon pot
3⅝ × 3⅛ × 1½ in (9.2 × 8.2 × 3.9 cm)

Glazed pot Chicken blood pot
2½ × 1⅛ in (6.5 × 3 cm)

Glazed pot Elliptical
4¾ × 3⅜ × 1 in (12 × 8.7 × 2.5 cm)

Glazed pot Yellow round pot
2 x 2¾ in (5 × 7 cm) base

Glazed pot (painting) Long pot
5⅞ x 4⅝ x 1¼ in (14.9 × 11.7 × 3.2 cm)

Glazed pot (painting) Hexagonal
3⅛ x 3⅛ x 1⅛ in (8 x 8 x 2.8 cm)

Glazed pot (painting) Long pot
4⅛ × 3½ x 1 in (10.5 × 9 × 2.5 cm)

Glazed pot (painting) Round pot
5 x 2 in (12.5 × 5 cm)

Planting in a Bonsai Pot

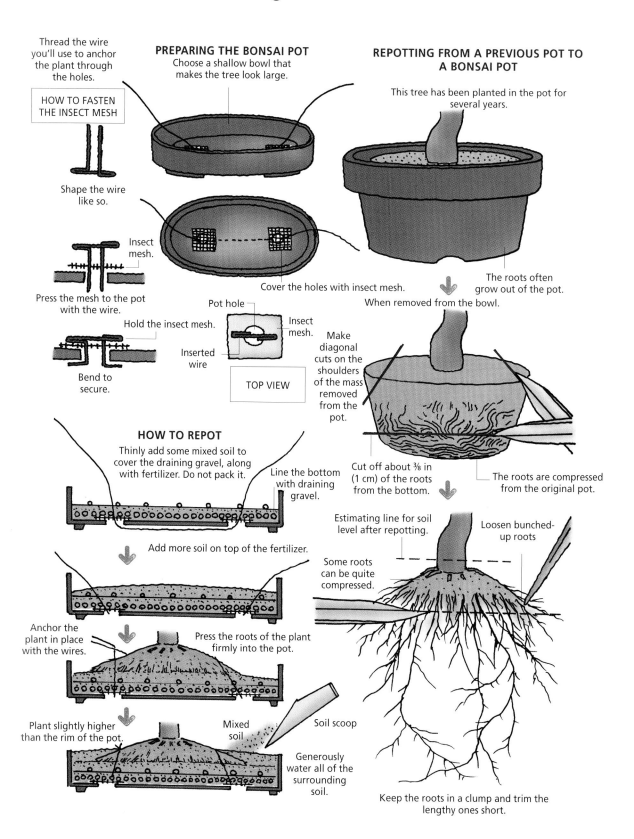

Thread the wire you'll use to anchor the plant through the holes.

HOW TO FASTEN THE INSECT MESH

Shape the wire like so.

Insect mesh.

Press the mesh to the pot with the wire.

Hold the insect mesh.

Bend to secure.

Pot hole

Insect mesh.

Inserted wire

TOP VIEW

PREPARING THE BONSAI POT
Choose a shallow bowl that makes the tree look large.

Cover the holes with insect mesh.

HOW TO REPOT
Thinly add some mixed soil to cover the draining gravel, along with fertilizer. Do not pack it.

Line the bottom with draining gravel.

Add more soil on top of the fertilizer.

Anchor the plant in place with the wires.

Press the roots of the plant firmly into the pot.

Plant slightly higher than the rim of the pot.

Mixed soil

Soil scoop

Generously water all of the surrounding soil.

REPOTTING FROM A PREVIOUS POT TO A BONSAI POT

This tree has been planted in the pot for several years.

The roots often grow out of the pot.

When removed from the bowl.

Make diagonal cuts on the shoulders of the mass removed from the pot.

The roots are compressed from the original pot.

Cut off about ⅜ in (1 cm) of the roots from the bottom.

Estimating line for soil level after repotting.

Loosen bunched-up roots

Some roots can be quite compressed.

Keep the roots in a clump and trim the lengthy ones short.

MONTHLY BONSAI CARE CALENDER
Sharing Our Lives with Bonsai

Plants create impressions that change from day to day, which can help you feel more in tune with the turning seasons. This book is based on the climate in the Kanto region of Japan. Be sure to tailor the instructions to the unique climate of the area you live in.

 January Examples of arrangement and ornamentation (indoors) / Various types of shelters / Managing and nurturing bonsai in their shelters / Cleaning used pots for re-use / Tree type and watering / Pruning and wiring

 February Pruning small, leafy trees I / Pruning small, leafy trees II / Second winter disinfection / Replanting / Wiring and guy-wiring / Managing and nurturing bonsai in their shelters / Pruning and propagating with cuttings / Preparing coarser material / Preparing the right soil mix / Pruning during the dormant period / Grafting

 March Opening bonsai shelters / Replanting preparation / Preparing pots for planting / Planting guide / Replanting guide / Preparing a mound of soil / Types of soil mixes / Preparing the soil mix (sieving) / Example of soil formulation / Soil composition

 April Flowering trees: Flowering and care / Fruiting trees: Flowering and cross-pollination / Leafy trees: Pinching off shoots / Replanting / Watering / Responding to aphids / Flowering trees: Pinching off shoots after flowering / Protecting against late frost

 May Pinching off conifer shoots / Leafy trees: Pinching off shoots / Fruiting trees: Managing bonsai flowering seasons / Disinfecting with pesticide / Flowering trees: Flowering / Leafy trees: Second bud picking / Fruiting trees: Flowering / Controlling shoots / Adding fertilizer

 June Leafy trees: Leaf trimming / Air-layering / Cross-pollinating *Ilex serrata* / Trimming shoots on black pine / Flowering trees: Pruning after flowering, managing and nurturing bonsai during flowering / Managing and nurturing bonsai during extended poor weather

 July Preparing bactericide and pesticide spray / Shading / Pest control / Managing and nurturing bonsai during extended poor weather / Wiring long branches / Bud trimming for black pine / Replanting stem-cutting shoots

 August Care & trimming of conifers / Pinching off shoots / Leafy bonsai: Care & trimming / Flowering and fruiting bonsai: Care & trimming / Leaf trimming / Protecting against summertime dehydration / Replanting Japanese white pine I / Replanting Japanese white pine II / Watering the needles / Protecting against storms / Treating leaf burn / Summer watering

 September Replanting in autumn / Removing the shade from your bonsai / Autumn fertilizer / Responding to gall disease / Transplanting / Removing a new cutting from its layering assembly / Replanting flowering quince / Flowering bonsai: Treating long branches / Fruiting bonsai: Leaf burn and flower buds / Leafy bonsai: Pinching off buds / Conifers: Removing old leaves

 October Care & trimming of bonsai on display at an exhibition / How to decide which bonsai to purchase / Seed collecting / Preserving seeds / Neutralizing acidified soil / Ripened fruit: Gathering and preserving seeds / Adding extra fertilizer / Disinfecting / Wiring

 November Gathering and preserving seeds / Protecting your bonsai from birds / Gathering seeds from parks / Care & trimming / Removing old needles on conifers / Citrus tree bonsai shelters / Care & trimming when leaves have fallen

 December Pruning and wiring / Disinfecting in winter / Broadening conifer candles: Wiring / Preparing bonsai shelters for winter / Black pine needle removal / Bonsai as New Year's decorations / Leafy bonsai: Light pruning

HEALTHY GROWTH COMES FROM DAILY CONVERSATIONS

Starting a bonsai and watching your favorite tree grow little by little is a great pleasure. However, to what extent it grows will require specific, prescribed care throughout the year.

To enjoy bonsai, it is important to consider your lifestyle and to what extent you can follow the monthly bonsai care calendar presented on the following pages without the situation becoming overwhelming.

Similar to caring for pets such as dogs and cats, bonsai will not thrive unless they are raised with careful attention. Because plants cannot clamor audibly for attention, you must have a keen eye and pay close attention to what you observe. To love a bonsai brings with it unspoken "conversations" with the tree as you concern yourself with its health.

The phrase "completed form" is used when discussing bonsai, but there is no true end to our efforts toward creating the ideal form of a bonsai.

January

Examples of arrangement and ornamentation (indoors)

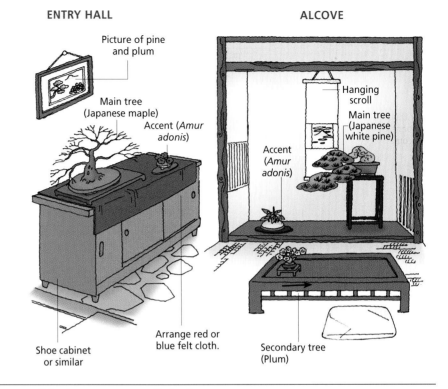

ENTRY HALL

Picture of pine and plum

Main tree (Japanese maple)

Accent (*Amur adonis*)

Shoe cabinet or similar

Arrange red or blue felt cloth.

ALCOVE

Hanging scroll

Main tree (Japanese white pine)

Accent (*Amur adonis*)

Secondary tree (Plum)

Various types of shelters

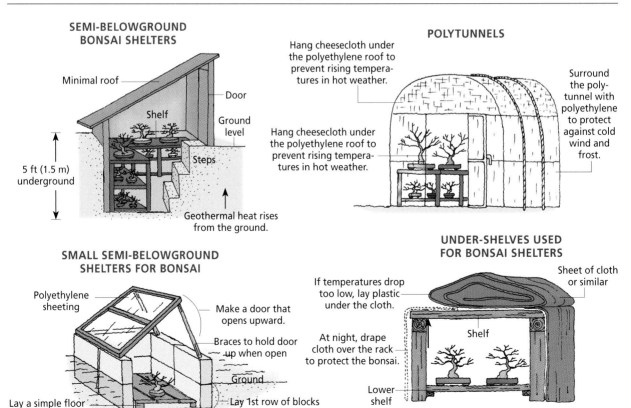

SEMI-BELOWGROUND BONSAI SHELTERS

Minimal roof

Door

Shelf

Ground level

Steps

5 ft (1.5 m) underground

Geothermal heat rises from the ground.

SMALL SEMI-BELOWGROUND SHELTERS FOR BONSAI

Polyethylene sheeting

Make a door that opens upward.

Braces to hold door up when open

Ground

Lay a simple floor for drainage.

Lay 1st row of blocks below ground level.

POLYTUNNELS

Hang cheesecloth under the polyethylene roof to prevent rising temperatures in hot weather.

Hang cheesecloth under the polyethylene roof to prevent rising temperatures in hot weather.

Surround the polytunnel with polyethylene to protect against cold wind and frost.

UNDER-SHELVES USED FOR BONSAI SHELTERS

Sheet of cloth or similar

If temperatures drop too low, lay plastic under the cloth.

Shelf

At night, drape cloth over the rack to protect the bonsai.

Lower shelf

Managing and nurturing bonsai in their shelters

Example: Polytunnels

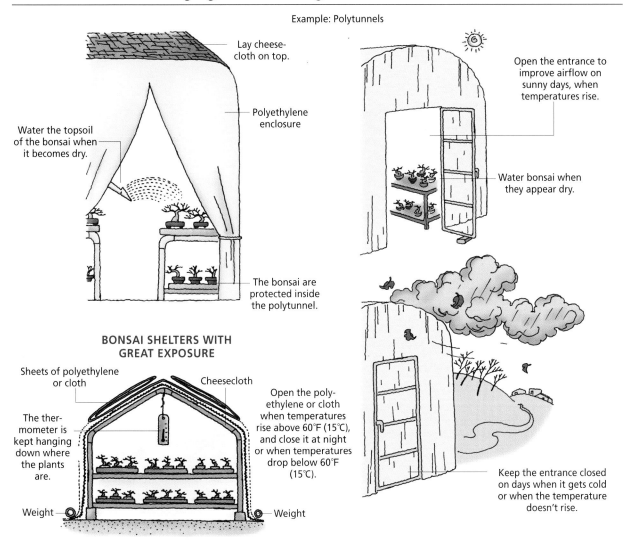

Lay cheese-cloth on top.

Polyethylene enclosure

Water the topsoil of the bonsai when it becomes dry.

The bonsai are protected inside the polytunnel.

Open the entrance to improve airflow on sunny days, when temperatures rise.

Water bonsai when they appear dry.

Keep the entrance closed on days when it gets cold or when the temperature doesn't rise.

BONSAI SHELTERS WITH GREAT EXPOSURE

Sheets of polyethylene or cloth

Cheesecloth

The thermometer is kept hanging down where the plants are.

Open the polyethylene or cloth when temperatures rise above 60°F (15°C), and close it at night or when temperatures drop below 60°F (15°C).

Weight

Weight

BONSAI SHELTERS WITH LITTLE EXPOSURE

Ideally, there should be no significant shifts in humidity and temperature.

Sheets of polyethylene or cloth

Until the soil becomes dry, it is fine to leave the bonsai in the shelter as they are.

Geothermal heat

Below 60°F (15°C)

Cheesecloth

Soil

Cleaning used pots for re-use

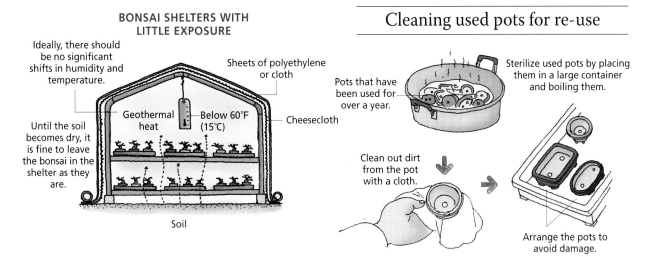

Pots that have been used for over a year.

Sterilize used pots by placing them in a large container and boiling them.

Clean out dirt from the pot with a cloth.

Arrange the pots to avoid damage.

Tree type and watering

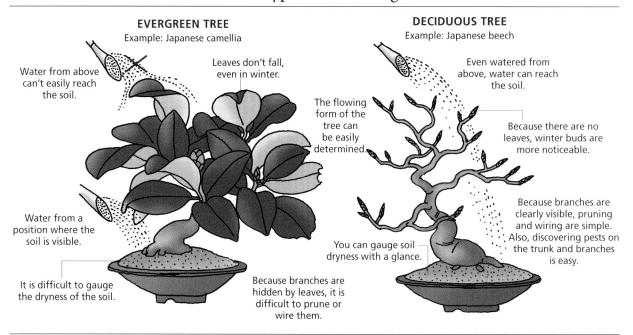

EVERGREEN TREE
Example: Japanese camellia

Water from above can't easily reach the soil.

Leaves don't fall, even in winter.

Water from a position where the soil is visible.

It is difficult to gauge the dryness of the soil.

Because branches are hidden by leaves, it is difficult to prune or wire them.

DECIDUOUS TREE
Example: Japanese beech

Even watered from above, water can reach the soil.

Because there are no leaves, winter buds are more noticeable.

The flowing form of the tree can be easily determined.

You can gauge soil dryness with a glance.

Because branches are clearly visible, pruning and wiring are simple. Also, discovering pests on the trunk and branches is easy.

Pruning and wiring

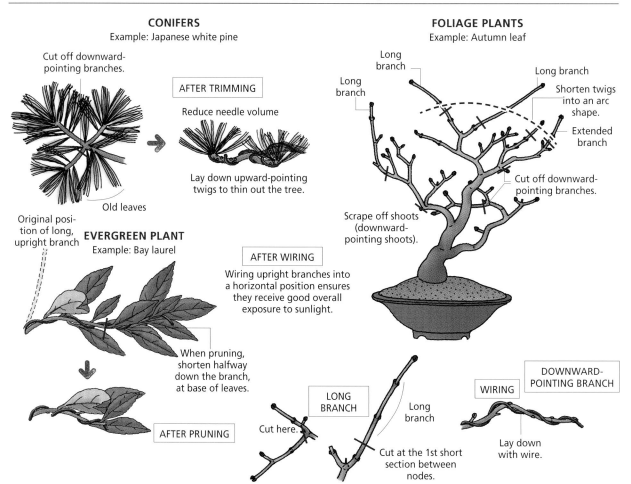

CONIFERS
Example: Japanese white pine

Cut off downward-pointing branches.

Old leaves

Original position of long, upright branch

AFTER TRIMMING

Reduce needle volume

Lay down upward-pointing twigs to thin out the tree.

EVERGREEN PLANT
Example: Bay laurel

When pruning, shorten halfway down the branch, at base of leaves.

AFTER PRUNING

AFTER WIRING

Wiring upright branches into a horizontal position ensures they receive good overall exposure to sunlight.

LONG BRANCH

Cut here.

Long branch

Cut at the 1st short section between nodes.

FOLIAGE PLANTS
Example: Autumn leaf

Long branch

Long branch

Long branch

Shorten twigs into an arc shape.

Extended branch

Cut off downward-pointing branches.

Scrape off shoots (downward-pointing shoots).

WIRING

DOWNWARD-POINTING BRANCH

Lay down with wire.

Pruning small, leafy trees I

Example: Japanese zelkova

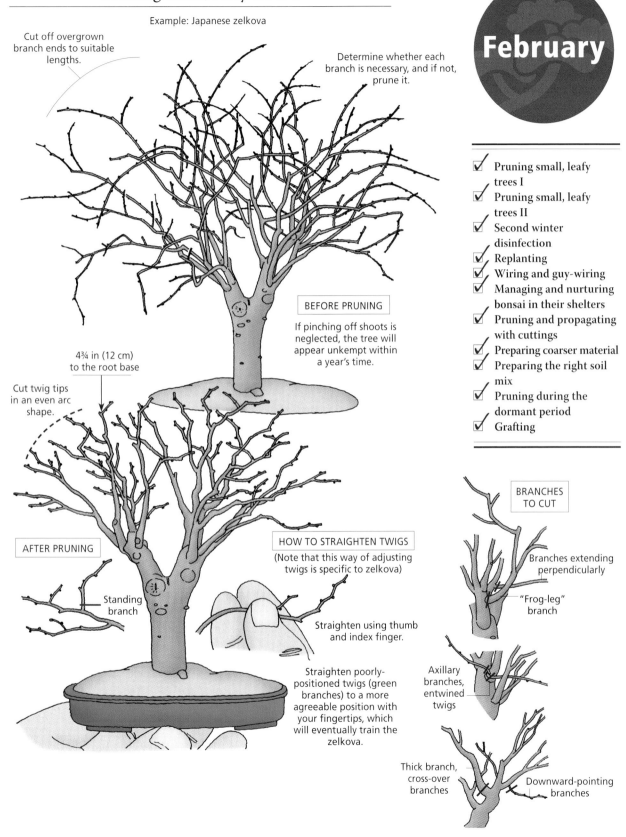

Cut off overgrown branch ends to suitable lengths.

Determine whether each branch is necessary, and if not, prune it.

☑ **Pruning small, leafy trees I**
☑ **Pruning small, leafy trees II**
☑ **Second winter disinfection**
☑ **Replanting**
☑ **Wiring and guy-wiring**
☑ **Managing and nurturing bonsai in their shelters**
☑ **Pruning and propagating with cuttings**
☑ **Preparing coarser material**
☑ **Preparing the right soil mix**
☑ **Pruning during the dormant period**
☑ **Grafting**

BEFORE PRUNING

If pinching off shoots is neglected, the tree will appear unkempt within a year's time.

4¾ in (12 cm) to the root base

Cut twig tips in an even arc shape.

AFTER PRUNING

Standing branch

HOW TO STRAIGHTEN TWIGS
(Note that this way of adjusting twigs is specific to zelkova)

Straighten using thumb and index finger.

Straighten poorly-positioned twigs (green branches) to a more agreeable position with your fingertips, which will eventually train the zelkova.

BRANCHES TO CUT

Branches extending perpendicularly

"Frog-leg" branch

Axillary branches, entwined twigs

Thick branch, cross-over branches

Downward-pointing branches

29

Pruning small, leafy trees II

Example: Japanese maple

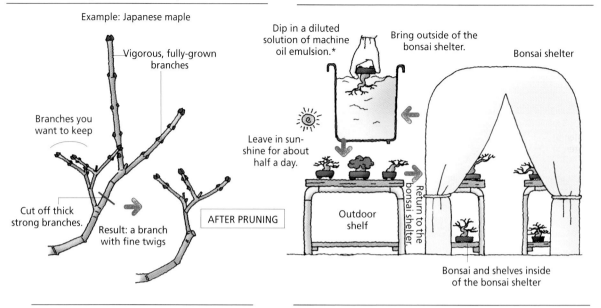

Vigorous, fully-grown branches

Branches you want to keep

Cut off thick strong branches.

Result: a branch with fine twigs

AFTER PRUNING

Second winter disinfection

Dip in a diluted solution of machine oil emulsion.*

Bring outside of the bonsai shelter.

Bonsai shelter

Leave in sunshine for about half a day.

Return to the bonsai shelter.

Outdoor shelf

Bonsai and shelves inside of the bonsai shelter

Replanting

Begin replanting toward the end of the month, still keeping bonsai in shelter.

Example: Privet

Replant yearly, because roots are especially likely to push out of the pot.

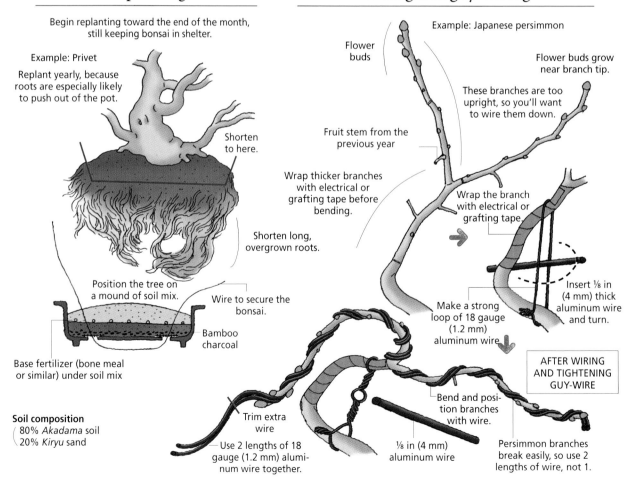

Shorten to here.

Shorten long, overgrown roots.

Position the tree on a mound of soil mix.

Wire to secure the bonsai.

Bamboo charcoal

Base fertilizer (bone meal or similar) under soil mix

Soil composition
80% *Akadama* soil
20% *Kiryu* sand

Wiring and guy-wiring

Example: Japanese persimmon

Flower buds

Flower buds grow near branch tip.

These branches are too upright, so you'll want to wire them down.

Fruit stem from the previous year

Wrap thicker branches with electrical or grafting tape before bending.

Wrap the branch with electrical or grafting tape.

Insert 1/8 in (4 mm) thick aluminum wire and turn.

Make a strong loop of 18 gauge (1.2 mm) aluminum wire

AFTER WIRING AND TIGHTENING GUY-WIRE

Trim extra wire

Use 2 lengths of 18 gauge (1.2 mm) aluminum wire together.

Bend and position branches with wire.

1/8 in (4 mm) aluminum wire

Persimmon branches break easily, so use 2 lengths of wire, not 1.

*Machine oil emulsion: In the past, "Lime sulfur" was frequently used, but it has become difficult to obtain from retail sources.

Managing and nurturing bonsai in their shelters

Conditions do vary, so knowing how to estimate dry conditions in your bonsai shelter is important.

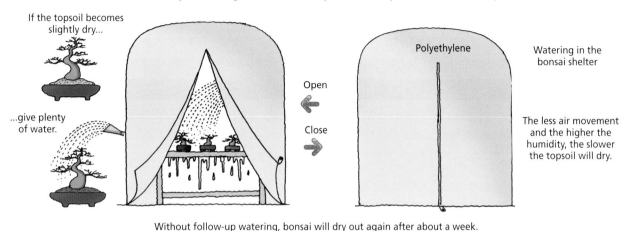

If the topsoil becomes slightly dry...

...give plenty of water.

Open

Close

Polyethylene

Watering in the bonsai shelter

The less air movement and the higher the humidity, the slower the topsoil will dry.

Without follow-up watering, bonsai will dry out again after about a week.

Pruning and propagating with cuttings

Make good use of overly-long twigs by cutting them off and propagating them as cuttings.

Fresh cuttings can be propagated in planters kept prepared for them.

Shelter is open (polyethylene or cloth sheets are folded away). Close the shelter when temperatures drop.

Airflow

When temperatures exceed 60°F (15°C), allow airflow through the bonsai shelter.

Cheesecloth

Airflow

Preparing the right soil mix

Keep soil prepared for replanting next year (refer to pages 16 and 17).

Kiryu sand

Hard *Akadama* soil

Soil mix sorted to ⅛ in (4 mm) or less can be used as is.

選別 KIRYUZUNA 桐生砂

AKADAMA 赤玉

¹/₃₂ to ⅛-in (1 to 4 mm) grains

Preparing coarser material

The coarser mixture spread in the bottom of the pot may be gravel, sand or mixed soil (⅛ to ¼-in / 4 to 6-mm grains).

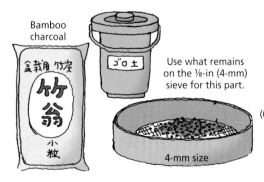

Bamboo charcoal

盆栽用 竹炭
竹
公翁
小粒

ゴロ土

Use what remains on the ⅛-in (4-mm) sieve for this part.

4-mm size

Mix bamboo charcoal with gravel or use as-is (⅛ to ¼-in / 4 to 6-mm grains)

Sift out *mijinko** with a ¹/₆₄-in (0.5-mm) sieve.

Sand and soil

0.5-mm size

Kiryu sand 20%

Akadama soil 80%

Mixing in a small amount of bamboo charcoal is fine.

Basic soil

Mix them well and keep stored in a labeled container.

*Mijinko: *Finely powdered volcanic ash particles*

Pruning during the dormant period

Example: Paniculous supplejack (fruiting)

If you wish to see their fruit, don't cut off long branches until after the viewing season.

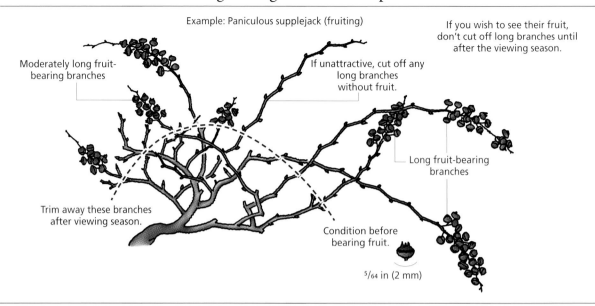

Moderately long fruit-bearing branches

If unattractive, cut off any long branches without fruit.

Long fruit-bearing branches

Trim away these branches after viewing season.

Condition before bearing fruit.

⁵/₆₄ in (2 mm)

Grafting

Even if there are female seedlings, female trees are virtually unknown, so grafting is essential.

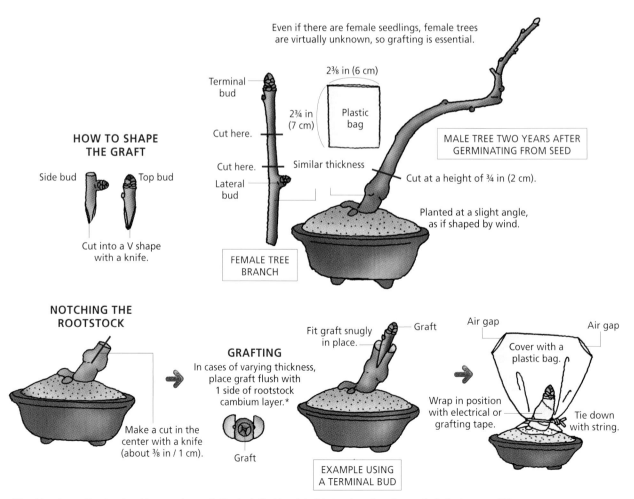

HOW TO SHAPE THE GRAFT

Side bud   Top bud

Cut into a V shape with a knife.

Terminal bud

Cut here.

Cut here.   Similar thickness

Lateral bud

2¾ in (7 cm)

2⅜ in (6 cm)

Plastic bag

MALE TREE TWO YEARS AFTER GERMINATING FROM SEED

Cut at a height of ¾ in (2 cm).

Planted at a slight angle, as if shaped by wind.

FEMALE TREE BRANCH

NOTCHING THE ROOTSTOCK

Make a cut in the center with a knife (about ⅜ in / 1 cm).

GRAFTING
In cases of varying thickness, place graft flush with 1 side of rootstock cambium layer.*

Graft

Fit graft snugly in place.   Graft

EXAMPLE USING A TERMINAL BUD

Air gap   Air gap

Cover with a plastic bag.

Wrap in position with electrical or grafting tape.

Tie down with string.

*Cambium layer: the structural layer underneath the bark that is related to trunk and root growth. Refer to page 180.

Opening bonsai shelters

POLYTUNNEL

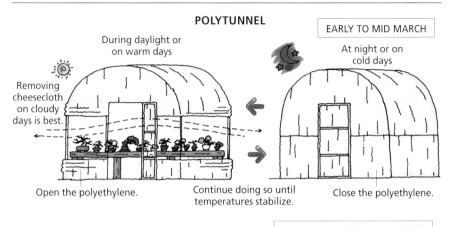

During daylight or on warm days

Removing cheesecloth on cloudy days is best.

At night or on cold days

Open the polyethylene.

Continue doing so until temperatures stabilize.

Close the polyethylene.

WHEN YOUNG SHOOTS ARE JUST BARELY STARTING TO OPEN

Remove the polyethylene.

Leave cheese-cloth in place.

New bud

Cloudy days or after sunset

Removing cheese-cloth on cloudy days is best.

Place the bonsai on an outdoor shelf.

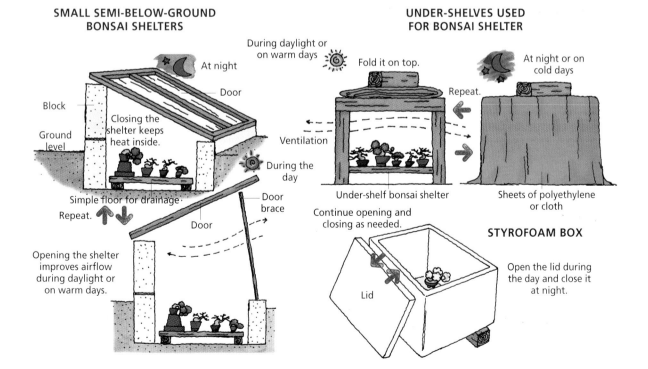

SMALL SEMI-BELOW-GROUND BONSAI SHELTERS

At night

Door

Block

Ground level

Closing the shelter keeps heat inside.

During the day

Simple floor for drainage

Repeat.

Door brace

Door

Opening the shelter improves airflow during daylight or on warm days.

UNDER-SHELVES USED FOR BONSAI SHELTER

During daylight or on warm days

Fold it on top.

At night or on cold days

Repeat.

Ventilation

Under-shelf bonsai shelter

Sheets of polyethylene or cloth

Continue opening and closing as needed.

STYROFOAM BOX

Lid

Open the lid during the day and close it at night.

Replanting preparation

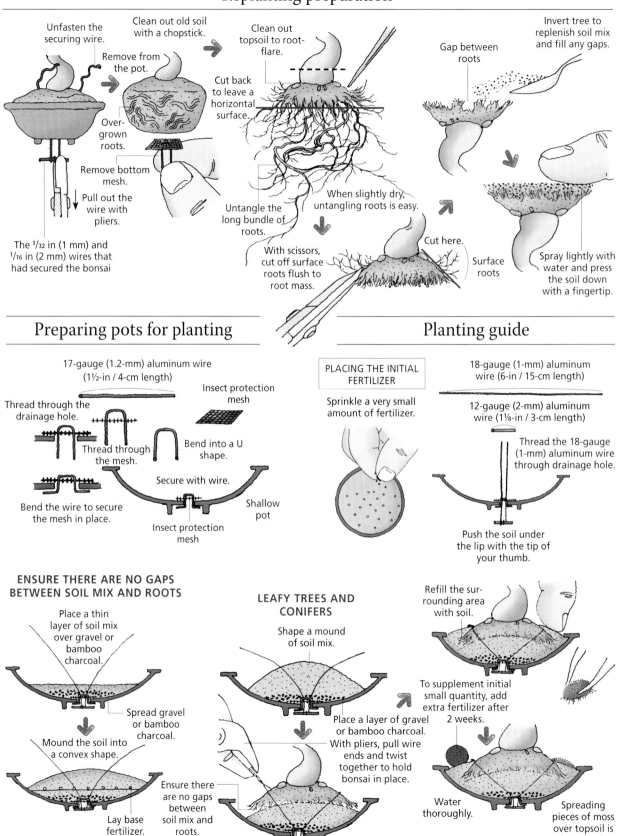

Unfasten the securing wire.

Clean out old soil with a chopstick.

Remove from the pot.

Over-grown roots.

Remove bottom mesh.

Pull out the wire with pliers.

The 1/32 in (1 mm) and 1/16 in (2 mm) wires that had secured the bonsai

Clean out topsoil to root-flare.

Cut back to leave a horizontal surface.

Untangle the long bundle of roots.

When slightly dry, untangling roots is easy.

With scissors, cut off surface roots flush to root mass.

Gap between roots

Invert tree to replenish soil mix and fill any gaps.

Cut here.

Surface roots

Spray lightly with water and press the soil down with a fingertip.

Preparing pots for planting

17-gauge (1.2-mm) aluminum wire (1½-in / 4-cm length)

Insect protection mesh

Thread through the drainage hole.

Thread through the mesh.

Bend into a U shape.

Bend the wire to secure the mesh in place.

Secure with wire.

Insect protection mesh

Shallow pot

Planting guide

PLACING THE INITIAL FERTILIZER

Sprinkle a very small amount of fertilizer.

18-gauge (1-mm) aluminum wire (6-in / 15-cm length)

12-gauge (2-mm) aluminum wire (1⅛-in / 3-cm length)

Thread the 18-gauge (1-mm) aluminum wire through drainage hole.

Push the soil under the lip with the tip of your thumb.

ENSURE THERE ARE NO GAPS BETWEEN SOIL MIX AND ROOTS

Place a thin layer of soil mix over gravel or bamboo charcoal.

Spread gravel or bamboo charcoal.

Mound the soil into a convex shape.

Lay base fertilizer.

LEAFY TREES AND CONIFERS

Shape a mound of soil mix.

Place a layer of gravel or bamboo charcoal.

With pliers, pull wire ends and twist together to hold bonsai in place.

Ensure there are no gaps between soil mix and roots.

Refill the sur-rounding area with soil.

To supplement initial small quantity, add extra fertilizer after 2 weeks.

Water thoroughly.

Spreading pieces of moss over topsoil is beneficial.

Replanting guide

Example: Replanting a maple from a no. 3 pot into a no. 4 pot

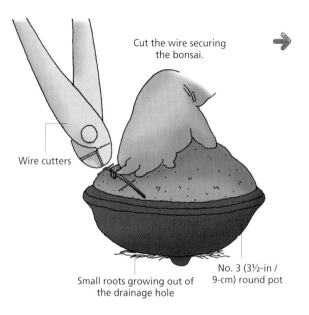

Cut the wire securing
the bonsai.

Wire cutters

Small roots growing out of
the drainage hole

No. 3 (3½-in /
9-cm) round pot

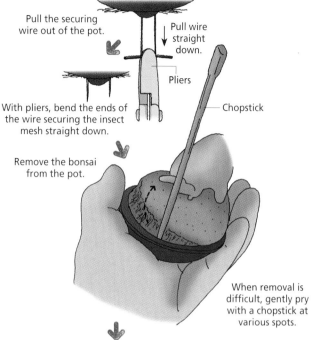

Pull the securing
wire out of the pot.

Pull wire
straight
down.

Pliers

With pliers, bend the ends of
the wire securing the insect
mesh straight down.

Chopstick

Remove the bonsai
from the pot.

When removal is
difficult, gently pry
with a chopstick at
various spots.

Preparing a mound of soil

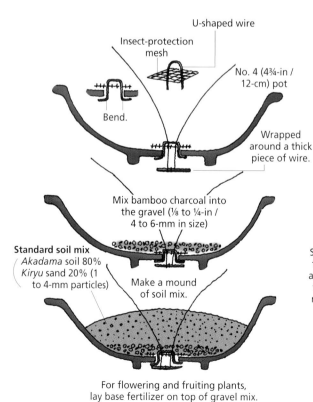

U-shaped wire

Insect-protection
mesh

Bend.

No. 4 (4¾-in /
12-cm) pot

Wrapped
around a thick
piece of wire.

Mix bamboo charcoal into
the gravel (⅛ to ¼-in /
4 to 6-mm in size)

Standard soil mix
Akadama soil 80%
Kiryu sand 20% (1
to 4-mm particles)

Make a mound
of soil mix.

For flowering and fruiting plants,
lay base fertilizer on top of gravel mix.

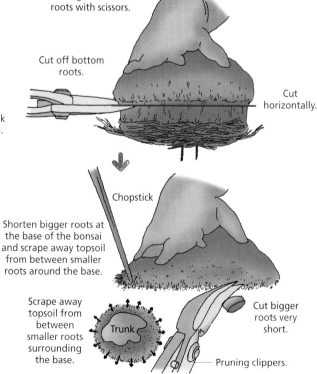

Cutting off bottom
roots with scissors.

Cut off bottom
roots.

Cut
horizontally.

Chopstick

Shorten bigger roots at
the base of the bonsai
and scrape away topsoil
from between smaller
roots around the base.

Scrape away
topsoil from
between
smaller roots
surrounding
the base.

Trunk

Cut bigger
roots very
short.

Pruning clippers.

Types of soil mixes

Kiryusuna river sand (others may include Fuji sand)

Charcoal or bamboo charcoal

くん炭

Sand

Akadama soil

Example of soil formulation

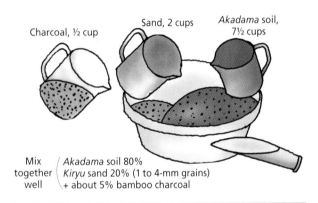

Charcoal, ½ cup

Sand, 2 cups

Akadama soil, 7½ cups

Mix together well
{ *Akadama* soil 80%
Kiryu sand 20% (1 to 4-mm grains)
+ about 5% bamboo charcoal }

Soil composition

NO. 1 POT

DIAMETER 1⅛ IN (3 CM)

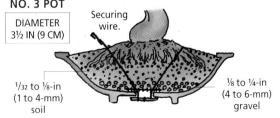

$1/64$ to $1/32$-in (0.5 to 1-mm) soil

$1/32$ to $1/16$-in (1 to 2.5-mm) gravel

NO. 2 POT

DIAMETER 2⅜ IN (6 CM)

$1/32$ to $1/16$-in (1 to 2.5-mm) soil

$1/32$ to $1/8$-in (1 to 4-mm) gravel

NO. 3 POT

DIAMETER 3½ IN (9 CM)

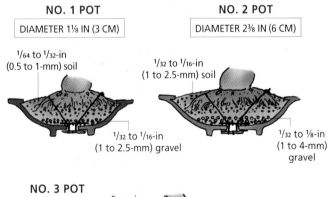

Securing wire.

$1/32$ to $1/8$-in (1 to 4-mm) soil

$1/8$ to $1/4$-in (4 to 6-mm) gravel

Preparing the soil mix (sieving)

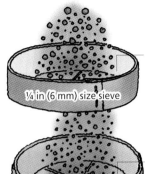
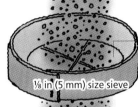

Particles (soil / sand) larger than ¼ in (6 mm) remain.

¼ in (6 mm) size sieve

Particles (soil / sand) from ⅛ to ¼ in (4 to 6 mm) in size remain (use as gravel).

⅛ in (5 mm) size sieve

Particles (soil / sand) from $1/16$ to ⅛ in (2.5 to 4 mm) in size remain (use as soil).

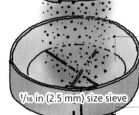

Particles (soil / sand) from $1/32$ to $1/16$ in (1 to 2.5 mm) in size remain (use as soil).

$1/16$ in (2.5 mm) size sieve

$1/32$ in (1 mm) size sieve

Baking sieves can be used in place of a $1/64$-in (0.5-mm) sieve.

$1/64$ in (0.5 mm) size sieve

Particles (soil / sand) from $1/64$ to $1/32$ in (0.5 to 1 mm) in size remain (used as soil in miniature bonsai pots).

Fine dust soil. Use mixed with *keto* soil ("peat clay" or "peat muck") for slab or rock bonsai

NO. 4 POT (TRAINING POT)

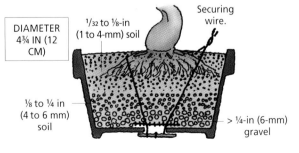

Securing wire.

$1/32$ to $1/8$-in (1 to 4-mm) soil

DIAMETER 4¾ IN (12 CM)

⅛ to ¼ in (4 to 6 mm) soil

> ¼-in (6-mm) gravel

Pot size is determined by a number of factors. A no. 1 pot is 1 ⅛ in (3 cm) in diameter.

Flowering trees: Flowering and care

Example: Flowering quince

Do not water flowers directly as they will be damaged.

Fertilizer is unnecessary during flowering.

- ☑ Flowering trees: Flowering and care
- ☑ Fruiting trees: Flowering and cross-pollination
- ☑ Leafy trees: Pinching off shoots
- ☑ Replanting
- ☑ Watering
- ☑ Responding to aphids
- ☑ Flowering trees: Pinching off shoots after flowering
- ☑ Protecting against late frost

CARE AFTER FLOWERING

Pick any withered flowers*, trim away long branches that create an unkempt appearance and add fertilizer.

Shorten long branches.

Fertilizer pellets placed at side of pot

FERTILIZING

Place fertilizer pellets 10 to 14 days after replanting.

This bonsai was replanted.

Place fertilizer pellets where young shoots had been growing.

This bonsai was not replanted.

Example: Fuji cherry

Avoid letting rain fall on the flowers.

Trim apical shoots of long branches that seem likely to grow well.

PRUNING

Place fertilizer after flowering.

Where flowers had bloomed

Short branch

Shorten long branches but keep 2 or 3 leaf buds.

Water at root base, not on the flowers.

Example: Japanese andromeda

White cocoon-shaped flowers hang from the tip of the branch. They may also appear in crimson.

Example: Japanese plum

Prune after 70 to 80% of the flowering has occurred.

PRUNING

Cut in an even arc shape.

Leaf buds

Terminal leaf buds

Shorten branches but keep leaf buds near base of branches.

AFTER PRUNING

*Withered flower picking: Removing remains of dead flowers that hadn't fallen off naturally. This protects against pests and weakening.

Fruiting trees: Flowering and cross-pollination

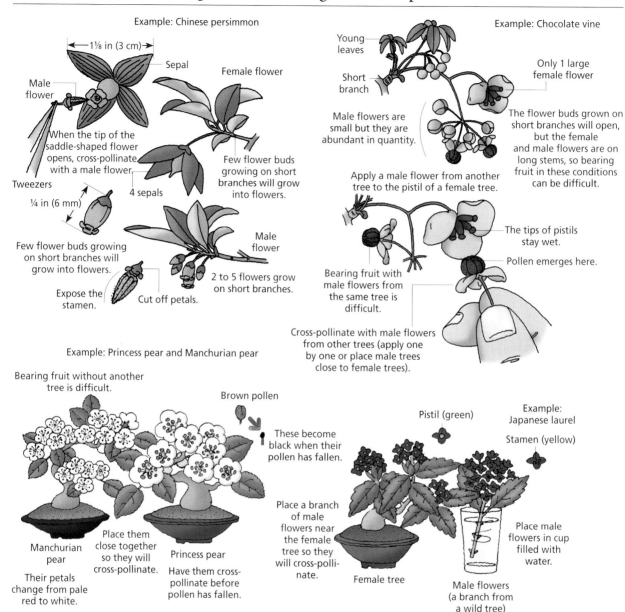

Example: Chinese persimmon

1⅛ in (3 cm)

Sepal

Male flower

Female flower

When the tip of the saddle-shaped flower opens, cross-pollinate with a male flower.

Tweezers

¼ in (6 mm)

Few flower buds growing on short branches will grow into flowers.

4 sepals

Expose the stamen.

Cut off petals.

Male flower

2 to 5 flowers grow on short branches.

Few flower buds growing on short branches will grow into flowers.

Example: Chocolate vine

Young leaves

Short branch

Only 1 large female flower

Male flowers are small but they are abundant in quantity.

The flower buds grown on short branches will open, but the female and male flowers are on long stems, so bearing fruit in these conditions can be difficult.

Apply a male flower from another tree to the pistil of a female tree.

The tips of pistils stay wet.

Pollen emerges here.

Bearing fruit with male flowers from the same tree is difficult.

Cross-pollinate with male flowers from other trees (apply one by one or place male trees close to female trees).

Example: Princess pear and Manchurian pear

Bearing fruit without another tree is difficult.

Brown pollen

These become black when their pollen has fallen.

Pistil (green)

Example: Japanese laurel

Stamen (yellow)

Place a branch of male flowers near the female tree so they will cross-pollinate.

Manchurian pear

Their petals change from pale red to white.

Place them close together so they will cross-pollinate.

Princess pear

Have them cross-pollinate before pollen has fallen.

Female tree

Place male flowers in cup filled with water.

Male flowers (a branch from a wild tree)

Example: Hall crabapple, Siebold's crab, Toringo crabapple, Pear-leaf crabapple

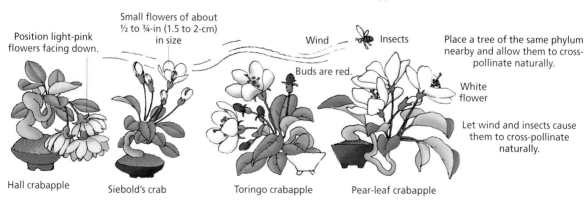

Position light-pink flowers facing down.

Small flowers of about ½ to ¾-in (1.5 to 2-cm) in size

Wind

Insects

Buds are red.

Place a tree of the same phylum nearby and allow them to cross-pollinate naturally.

White flower

Let wind and insects cause them to cross-pollinate naturally.

Hall crabapple

Siebold's crab

Toringo crabapple

Pear-leaf crabapple

Leafy trees: Pinching off shoots

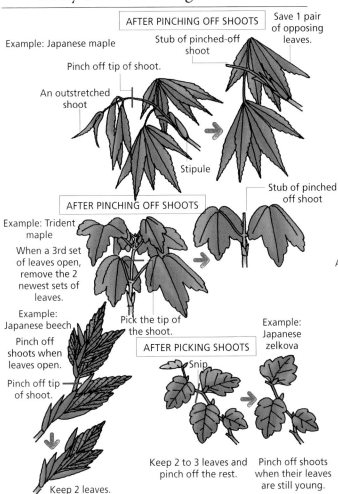

AFTER PINCHING OFF SHOOTS

Save 1 pair of opposing leaves.

Example: Japanese maple

Stub of pinched-off shoot

Pinch off tip of shoot.

An outstretched shoot

Stipule

Stub of pinched off shoot

AFTER PINCHING OFF SHOOTS

Example: Trident maple

When a 3rd set of leaves open, remove the 2 newest sets of leaves.

Example: Japanese beech

Pinch off shoots when leaves open.

Pinch off tip of shoot.

Pick the tip of the shoot.

AFTER PICKING SHOOTS

Snip

Example: Japanese zelkova

Keep 2 leaves.

Keep 2 to 3 leaves and pinch off the rest.

Pinch off shoots when their leaves are still young.

Flowering trees: Pinching off shoots after flowering

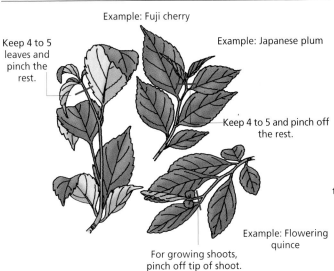

Example: Fuji cherry

Example: Japanese plum

Keep 4 to 5 leaves and pinch the rest.

Keep 4 to 5 and pinch off the rest.

For growing shoots, pinch off tip of shoot.

Example: Flowering quince

Replanting

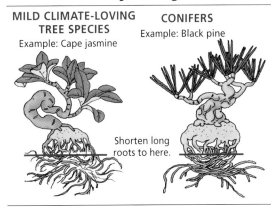

MILD CLIMATE-LOVING TREE SPECIES
Example: Cape jasmine

CONIFERS
Example: Black pine

Shorten long roots to here.

Watering

As a general rule, when topsoil becomes dry, provide plenty of water.

On a windy day, topsoil will dry out easily, so water as often as possible.

Responding to aphids

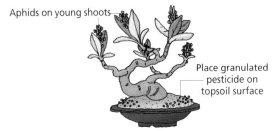

Aphids on young shoots

Place granulated pesticide on topsoil surface

Protecting against late frost

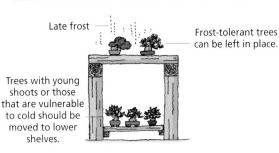

Late frost

Frost-tolerant trees can be left in place.

Trees with young shoots or those that are vulnerable to cold should be moved to lower shelves.

A stipule is an outgrowth produced on either side of the base of a leafstalk, or any small leaves or leaf parts.

May

- ✓ Pinching off conifer shoots
- ✓ Leafy trees: Pinching off shoots
- ✓ Fruiting trees: Managing bonsai flowering seasons
- ✓ Disinfecting with pesticide
- ✓ Flowering trees: Flowering
- ✓ Leafy trees: Second bud picking
- ✓ Fruiting trees: Flowering
- ✓ Controlling shoots
- ✓ Adding fertilizer

Pinching off conifer shoots

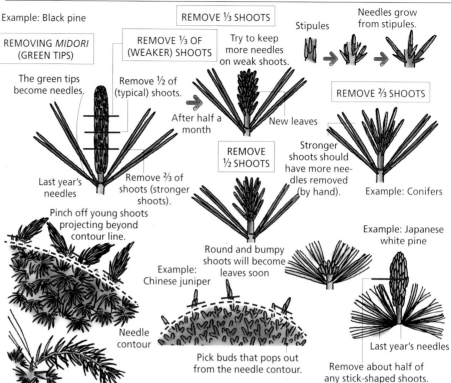

Example: Black pine

REMOVING MIDORI (GREEN TIPS)

The green tips become needles.

Last year's needles

REMOVE 1/3 OF (WEAKER) SHOOTS

Remove 1/2 of (typical) shoots.

After half a month

Remove 2/3 of shoots (stronger shoots).

Pinch off young shoots projecting beyond contour line.

Needle contour

REMOVE 1/3 SHOOTS

Try to keep more needles on weak shoots.

New leaves

REMOVE 1/2 SHOOTS

Round and bumpy shoots will become leaves soon

Example: Chinese juniper

Pick buds that pops out from the needle contour.

Stipules

Needles grow from stipules.

REMOVE 2/3 SHOOTS

Stronger shoots should have more needles removed (by hand).

Example: Conifers

Example: Japanese white pine

Last year's needles

Remove about half of any stick-shaped shoots.

While shaping a branch, pull out projecting *candles* (clusters of needles) for a moment and cut them off with scissors.

For details, refer to page 151, "How to Care for Coniferous Bonsai."

Leafy trees: Pinching off shoots

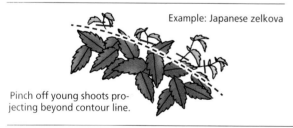

Example: Japanese zelkova

Pinch off young shoots projecting beyond contour line.

Fruiting trees: Managing bonsai flowering seasons

Be careful not to splash water on the flowers.

Remove fertilizer pellets and water with diluted liquid fertilizer.

Sprinkle water at the base to prevent flushing away pollen.

Move bonsai to a lower shelf during heavy rains.

Disinfecting with pesticide

If possible, preventative disinfection is preferable.

Aphids and other pests are found on young shoots.

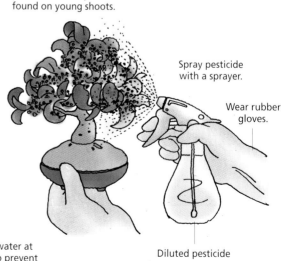

Spray pesticide with a sprayer.

Wear rubber gloves.

Diluted pesticide

Flowering trees: Flowering

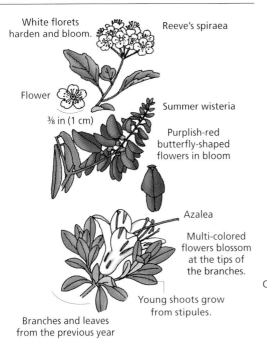

White florets harden and bloom.

Reeve's spiraea

Flower

3/8 in (1 cm)

Summer wisteria

Purplish-red butterfly-shaped flowers in bloom

Azalea

Multi-colored flowers blossom at the tips of the branches.

Young shoots grow from stipules.

Branches and leaves from the previous year

Leafy trees: Second bud picking

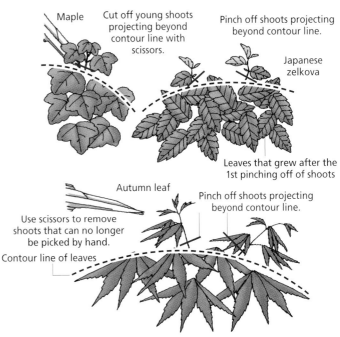

Maple

Cut off young shoots projecting beyond contour line with scissors.

Pinch off shoots projecting beyond contour line.

Japanese zelkova

Leaves that grew after the 1st pinching off of shoots

Autumn leaf

Pinch off shoots projecting beyond contour line.

Use scissors to remove shoots that can no longer be picked by hand.

Contour line of leaves

Fruiting trees: Flowering

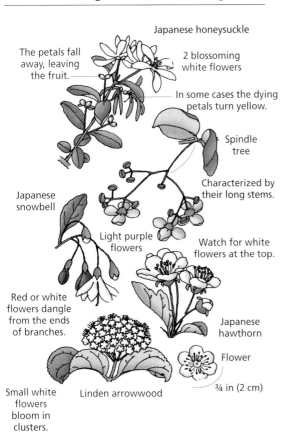

Japanese honeysuckle

The petals fall away, leaving the fruit.

2 blossoming white flowers

In some cases the dying petals turn yellow.

Spindle tree

Characterized by their long stems.

Japanese snowbell

Light purple flowers

Watch for white flowers at the top.

Red or white flowers dangle from the ends of branches.

Japanese hawthorn

Flower

3/4 in (2 cm)

Small white flowers bloom in clusters.

Linden arrowwood

Controlling shoots

Still growing and becoming stronger

Example: Persimmon

Example: Japanese plum

New branch tip

Keep upright branches laying down with wire.

Keep new branch tips down by wiring them in place.

Adding fertilizer

Fertilize around the edge of the pot (use fertilizer pellets).

June

- ☑ Leafy trees: Leaf trimming
- ☑ Air-layering
- ☑ Cross-pollinating *Ilex serrata*
- ☑ Trimming shoots on black pine
- ☑ Flowering trees: Pruning after flowering, managing and nurturing bonsai during flowering
- ☑ Managing and nurturing bonsai during extended poor weather

Leafy trees: Leaf trimming

BEFORE LEAF TRIMMING — Example: Maple — AFTER LEAF TRIMMING

Keep leaf stalks* (they will fall off naturally).

For long branches, shorten but keep 1 node of each.

Cut off with scissors.

Due to crowded leaves, interior airflow and exposure to sunlight are poor.

HOW TO CUT LEAVES

Example: Japanese zelkova

Cut twig tips in an even arc shape.

Interior airflow and exposure to sunlight have become poor.

Keep very small leaves.

BEFORE LEAF TRIMMING — AFTER LEAF TRIMMING

Air-layering

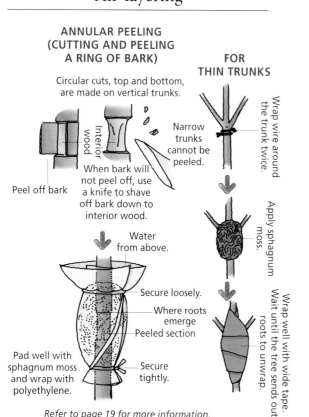

ANNULAR PEELING (CUTTING AND PEELING A RING OF BARK)

Circular cuts, top and bottom, are made on vertical trunks.

Interior wood

Peel off bark

When bark will not peel off, use a knife to shave off bark down to interior wood.

FOR THIN TRUNKS

Narrow trunks cannot be peeled.

Wrap wire around the trunk twice.

Apply sphagnum moss.

Wrap well with wide tape. Wait until the tree sends out roots to unwrap.

Water from above.

Secure loosely.

Where roots emerge

Peeled section

Pad well with sphagnum moss and wrap with polyethylene.

Secure tightly.

Refer to page 19 for more information.

Cross-pollinating *Ilex serrata*

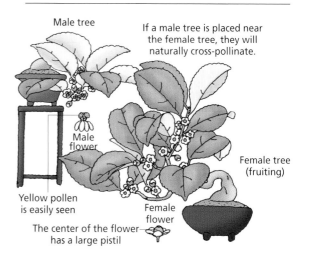

Male tree

If a male tree is placed near the female tree, they will naturally cross-pollinate.

Male flower

Yellow pollen is easily seen

Female tree (fruiting)

Female flower

The center of the flower has a large pistil

Leaf stalks or petioles: The stem attached to the leaf that serves as a conduit for sap. Refer to page 191.

Trimming shoots on black pine (late June)

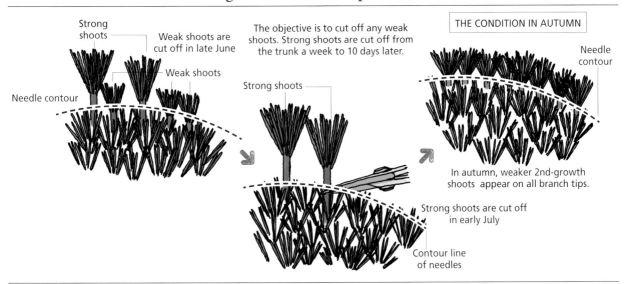

Strong shoots

Weak shoots are cut off in late June

Weak shoots

Needle contour

The objective is to cut off any weak shoots. Strong shoots are cut off from the trunk a week to 10 days later.

Strong shoots

THE CONDITION IN AUTUMN

Needle contour

In autumn, weaker 2nd-growth shoots appear on all branch tips.

Strong shoots are cut off in early July

Contour line of needles

Flowering trees: Pruning after flowering, managing and nurturing bonsai during flowering

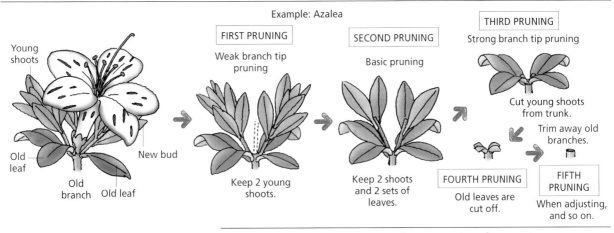

Example: Azalea

Young shoots

Old leaf

Old branch Old leaf

New bud

FIRST PRUNING

Weak branch tip pruning

Keep 2 young shoots.

SECOND PRUNING

Basic pruning

Keep 2 shoots and 2 sets of leaves.

THIRD PRUNING

Strong branch tip pruning

Cut young shoots from trunk.

Trim away old branches.

FOURTH PRUNING

Old leaves are cut off.

FIFTH PRUNING

When adjusting, and so on.

Avoid watering flowers directly, as they will be damaged.

Remove fertilizer.

Sprinkle water at root base.

Managing and nurturing bonsai during extended poor weather

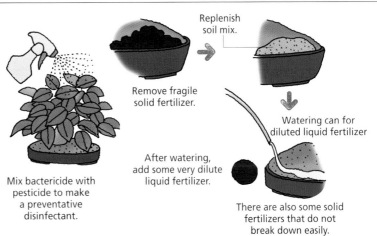

Replenish soil mix.

Remove fragile solid fertilizer.

After watering, add some very dilute liquid fertilizer.

Watering can for diluted liquid fertilizer

Mix bactericide with pesticide to make a preventative disinfectant.

There are also some solid fertilizers that do not break down easily.

July

- ✓ Preparing bactericide and pesticide spray
- ✓ Shading
- ✓ Pest control
- ✓ Managing and nurturing bonsai during extended poor weather
- ✓ Wiring long branches
- ✓ Bud trimming for black pine
- ✓ Replanting stem-cutting shoots

Preparing bactericide and pesticide spray

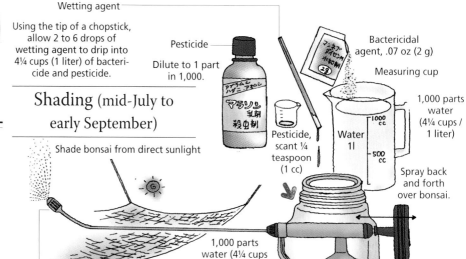

Wetting agent
Using the tip of a chopstick, allow 2 to 6 drops of wetting agent to drip into 4¼ cups (1 liter) of bactericide and pesticide.

Pesticide
Dilute to 1 part in 1,000.

Bactericidal agent, .07 oz (2 g)

Measuring cup

1,000 parts water (4¼ cups / 1 liter)

Pesticide, scant ¼ teaspoon (1 cc)

Water 1l

Spray back and forth over bonsai.

1,000 parts water (4¼ cups / 1 liter)

4¼ cups (1 liter) bactericide / insecticide solution

Dip tube intake

Shading (mid-July to early September)

Shade bonsai from direct sunlight

Shade your bonsai with cheesecloth or woven straw awning to protect them from summer heat.

Spray can be adjusted from full to fine mist by turning nozzle.

Pest control

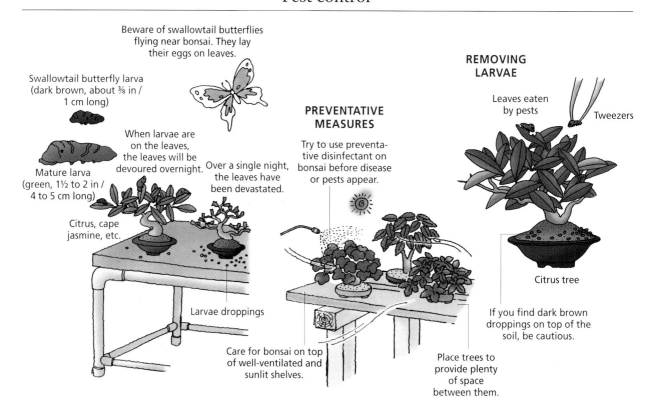

Beware of swallowtail butterflies flying near bonsai. They lay their eggs on leaves.

Swallowtail butterfly larva (dark brown, about ⅜ in / 1 cm long)

Mature larva (green, 1½ to 2 in / 4 to 5 cm long)

When larvae are on the leaves, the leaves will be devoured overnight. Over a single night, the leaves have been devastated.

Citrus, cape jasmine, etc.

Larvae droppings

PREVENTATIVE MEASURES

Try to use preventative disinfectant on bonsai before disease or pests appear.

Care for bonsai on top of well-ventilated and sunlit shelves.

Place trees to provide plenty of space between them.

REMOVING LARVAE

Leaves eaten by pests

Tweezers

Citrus tree

If you find dark brown droppings on top of the soil, be cautious.

Managing and nurturing bonsai during extended poor weather

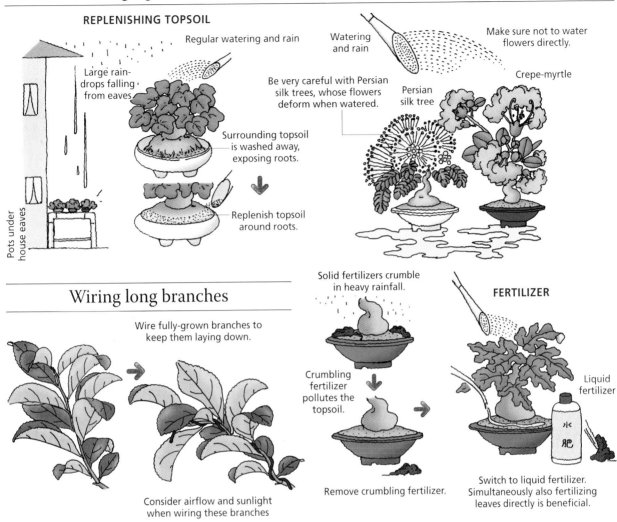

REPLENISHING TOPSOIL

Regular watering and rain

Large rain-drops falling from eaves

Pots under house eaves

Surrounding topsoil is washed away, exposing roots.

Replenish topsoil around roots.

Watering and rain

Make sure not to water flowers directly.

Be very careful with Persian silk trees, whose flowers deform when watered.

Persian silk tree

Crepe-myrtle

Wiring long branches

Wire fully-grown branches to keep them laying down.

Consider airflow and sunlight when wiring these branches

Solid fertilizers crumble in heavy rainfall.

Crumbling fertilizer pollutes the topsoil.

Remove crumbling fertilizer.

FERTILIZER

Liquid fertilizer

Switch to liquid fertilizer. Simultaneously also fertilizing leaves directly is beneficial.

Bud trimming for black pine
(Strong Bud)

Example: Black pine

Weak buds cut off 10 days prior

Cut off old needles from top of strong shoots.

2nd growth bud appears

Replanting stem-cutting shoots

Shorten both stems, keeping 4 or 5 leaves.

Cut here.

Example: Japanese zelkova

Do not remove 2nd set of true leaves until they fall off naturally.

AFTER PRUNING

AFTER REPLANTING

Keep ½
Keep ⅓
Keep ⅔

2nd set of true leaves (4-leaf type of leaf set)

Shorten long overgrown roots to here.

Position of planted stem-cutting shoot

Plant in a shallow pot.

Secure firmly in position with cord.

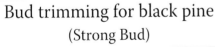

August

Care & trimming of conifers

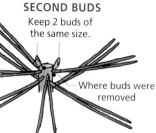

REMOVING BUDS (NEEDLES NOT SHOWN)

Example: Black pine

REMOVING SECOND BUDS

Remove buds growing too close to other buds.

Tweezers

Remove especially strong buds.

Keep the strong buds and remove the weak ones.

Remove buds that grow into each other's space.

Keep 2 buds of the same size.

Where buds were removed

• Removed buds

Pinching off shoots

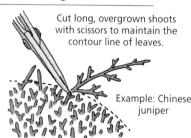

Cut long, overgrown shoots with scissors to maintain the contour line of leaves.

Example: Chinese juniper

Leafy bonsai: Care & trimming

PINCHING OFF SECOND GROWTH BUDS

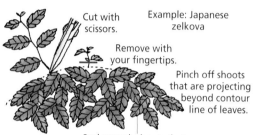

Cut with scissors.

Example: Japanese zelkova

Remove with your fingertips.

Pinch off shoots that are projecting beyond contour line of leaves.

2nd growth shoots that matured into leaves

Flowering and fruiting bonsai: Care & trimming

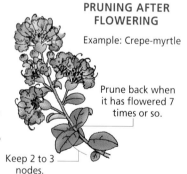

PRUNING AFTER FLOWERING

Example: Crepe-myrtle

Prune back when it has flowered 7 times or so.

Keep 2 to 3 nodes.

CROSS-POLLINATING WHEN FLOWERING

Example: Kadsura vine

Female flower (has light-green ovary). Bearing fruit is difficult without furnishing male flowers from another tree.

Furnish a male flower.

Leaf trimming

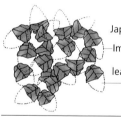

Example: Japanese beech

Improve airflow by trimming leaves when too crowded.

Protecting against summertime dehydration

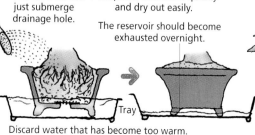

WATER TRAYS

Very beneficial for wisteria, *Mimosa albizia* and willow, tree species that drain quickly and dry out easily.

The reservoir should become exhausted overnight.

Water level should just submerge drainage hole.

Discard water that has become too warm.

Tray

DOUBLE POTTING

Setting the bonsai into a tall pot full of soil mix will reduce dehydration.

Filling a larger pot about half-full of soil mix and placing the bonsai on top will be just as effective as using a full tall pot.

In either situation, water the bonsai from above.

Cut off roots that grow out from the bottom.

Soil

Training pot

Replanting Japanese white pine I

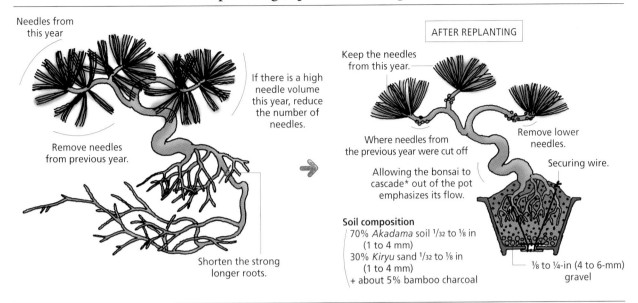

Needles from this year

If there is a high needle volume this year, reduce the number of needles.

Remove needles from previous year.

Shorten the strong longer roots.

AFTER REPLANTING

Keep the needles from this year.

Where needles from the previous year were cut off

Remove lower needles.

Allowing the bonsai to cascade* out of the pot emphasizes its flow.

Securing wire.

Soil composition
70% *Akadama* soil 1/32 to 1/8 in (1 to 4 mm)
30% *Kiryu* sand 1/32 to 1/8 in (1 to 4 mm)
+ about 5% bamboo charcoal

1/8 to 1/4-in (4 to 6-mm) gravel

Replanting Japanese white pine II

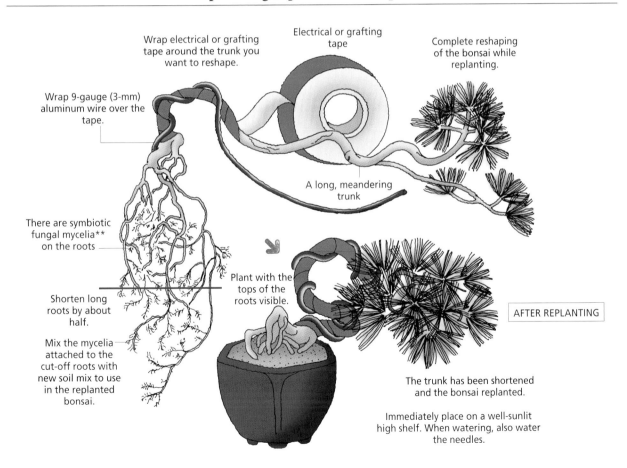

Wrap electrical or grafting tape around the trunk you want to reshape.

Electrical or grafting tape

Complete reshaping of the bonsai while replanting.

Wrap 9-gauge (3-mm) aluminum wire over the tape.

A long, meandering trunk

There are symbiotic fungal mycelia** on the roots

Shorten long roots by about half.

Mix the mycelia attached to the cut-off roots with new soil mix to use in the replanted bonsai.

Plant with the tops of the roots visible.

AFTER REPLANTING

The trunk has been shortened and the bonsai replanted.

Immediately place on a well-sunlit high shelf. When watering, also water the needles.

*A semi-cascade pot bonsai: A bonsai term for describing when the leaves and branches of a bonsai jut out and appear to be spilling out of the pot.
**Symbiotic fungal mycelia: Fungi that have a symbiotic relationship with trees and plants, propagating in the rhizosphere and root cells of plants, giving nitrogen to plants, and from trees, receiving carbohydrates and so on.

Watering the needles

Water the bonsai from above its needles.

This washes away any dirt on the needles.

This can help protect Needle juniper and other bonsai against mites.

Also effectively lowers pot temperature

Protecting against storms

Be cautious with strong winds and heavy rain.

Listen often to weather news and bulletins.

Remove bonsai from outdoor posts, stands, and other high places.

Move bonsai from top shelves to the shelves underneath.

If there is not enough time to move the plants, secure cheesecloth over bonsai.

Treating leaf burn

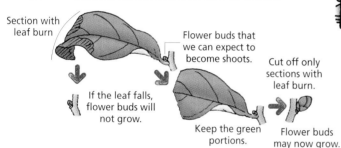

Section with leaf burn

Flower buds that we can expect to become shoots.

Cut off only sections with leaf burn.

If the leaf falls, flower buds will not grow.

Keep the green portions.

Flower buds may now grow.

Summer watering

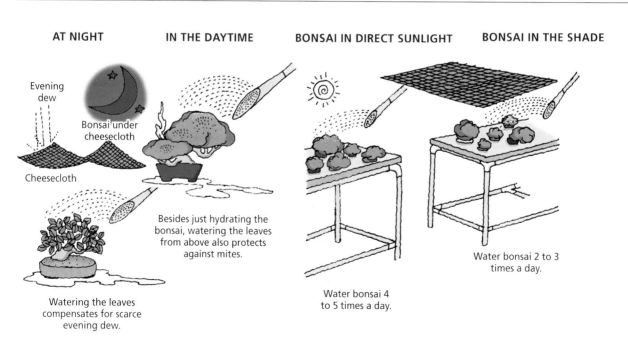

AT NIGHT

Evening dew

Bonsai under cheesecloth

Cheesecloth

Watering the leaves compensates for scarce evening dew.

IN THE DAYTIME

Besides just hydrating the bonsai, watering the leaves from above also protects against mites.

BONSAI IN DIRECT SUNLIGHT

Water bonsai 4 to 5 times a day.

BONSAI IN THE SHADE

Water bonsai 2 to 3 times a day.

Replanting in autumn (from around mid-September)

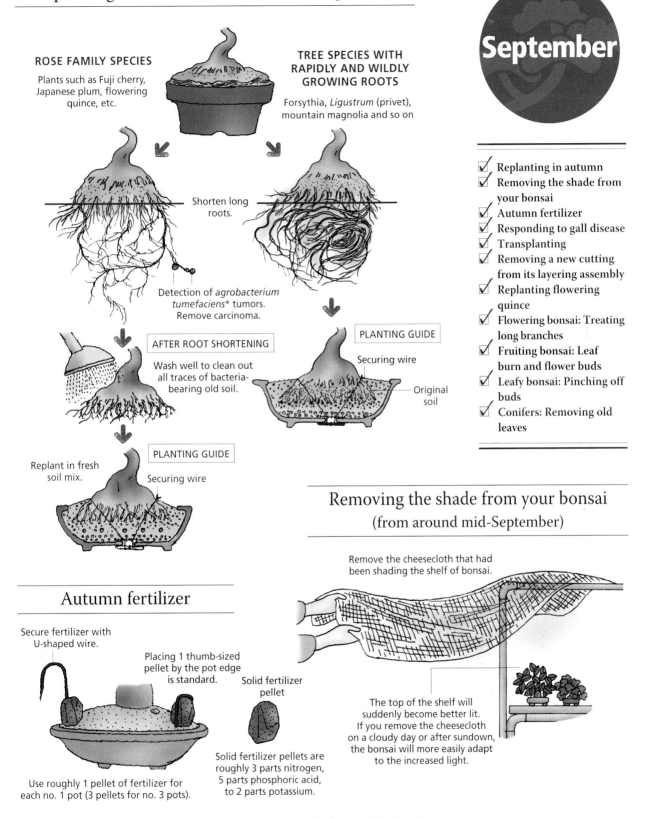

ROSE FAMILY SPECIES

Plants such as Fuji cherry, Japanese plum, flowering quince, etc.

TREE SPECIES WITH RAPIDLY AND WILDLY GROWING ROOTS

Forsythia, *Ligustrum* (privet), mountain magnolia and so on

Shorten long roots.

Detection of *agrobacterium tumefaciens** tumors. Remove carcinoma.

AFTER ROOT SHORTENING

Wash well to clean out all traces of bacteria-bearing old soil.

PLANTING GUIDE

Securing wire

Original soil

PLANTING GUIDE

Replant in fresh soil mix.

Securing wire

- ☑ Replanting in autumn
- ☑ Removing the shade from your bonsai
- ☑ Autumn fertilizer
- ☑ Responding to gall disease
- ☑ Transplanting
- ☑ Removing a new cutting from its layering assembly
- ☑ Replanting flowering quince
- ☑ Flowering bonsai: Treating long branches
- ☑ Fruiting bonsai: Leaf burn and flower buds
- ☑ Leafy bonsai: Pinching off buds
- ☑ Conifers: Removing old leaves

Autumn fertilizer

Secure fertilizer with U-shaped wire.

Placing 1 thumb-sized pellet by the pot edge is standard.

Solid fertilizer pellet

Solid fertilizer pellets are roughly 3 parts nitrogen, 5 parts phosphoric acid, to 2 parts potassium.

Use roughly 1 pellet of fertilizer for each no. 1 pot (3 pellets for no. 3 pots).

Removing the shade from your bonsai (from around mid-September)

Remove the cheesecloth that had been shading the shelf of bonsai.

The top of the shelf will suddenly become better lit. If you remove the cheesecloth on a cloudy day or after sundown, the bonsai will more easily adapt to the increased light.

*Agrobacterium tumefaciens *(or "gall disease"): Plant disease caused by bacteria living in soil. A carcinoma that can form on roots, often metastasizing and spreading, causing debilitation in plants.*

Responding to gall disease

TREATING BONSAI IS IMPOSSIBLE

Agrobacterium tumefaciens grown into the root base (becoming a solid mass)

Observe the progress of this condition.

Healthy roots should also be suspected of being cancerous.

Label to avoid confusing with healthy bonsai.

ガン腫病 A

Incinerate if withering continues.

TREATING BONSAI IS FEASIBLE

Cut off roots where *agrobacterium tumefaciens* appeared.

Cut here.

Soak in bactericidal agent (for about 10 minutes).

Bactericidal agent

Some tumors are quite small.

Agrobacterium tumefaciens grown into the root.

Remove old soil completely.

Replant in fresh soil mix.

ガン腫病 B

Confirm absence of *agrobacterium tumefaciens* while replanting the following year.

STERILIZING TOOLS

Sterilize tools that had contact with *agrobacterium tumefaciens* by soaking in alkaline (tri-sodium phosphate) solution.

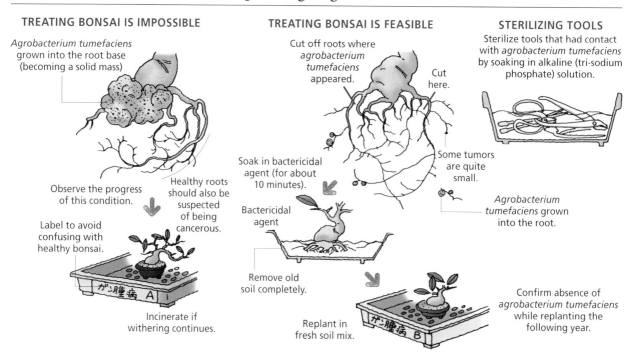

Transplanting

Example: Fuji cherry

Part that has grown since spring

Section planted in spring (February or March)

PLANTING GUIDE

Trim away long roots at this level.

Soil composition
- 70% *Akadama* soil
- 30% *Kiryu* sand
- + about 5% bamboo charcoal

Shape the rooted seedlings with wire and one by one transplant into training pots.

Removing a new cutting from its layering assembly

Remove polyethylene, and remove moss after confirming the presence of roots.

Remove cutting from layering.

Trim away long roots at this level.

To avoid damage, remove moss from roots with tweezers.

PLANTING GUIDE

Secure the cutting firmly in the pot with cord.

Soil composition
- 80% *Akadama* soil
- 20% *Kiryu* sand

Plant the cutting with its roots spread out.

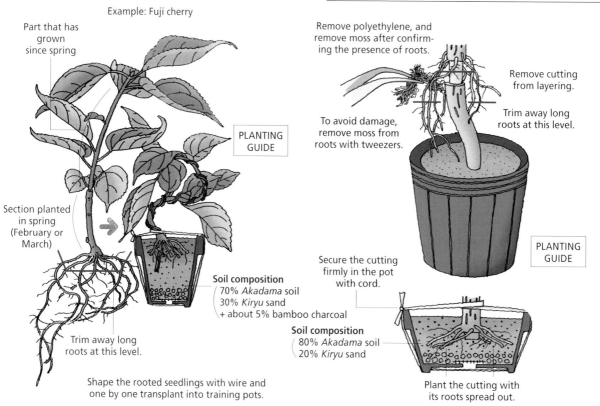

Replanting flowering quince

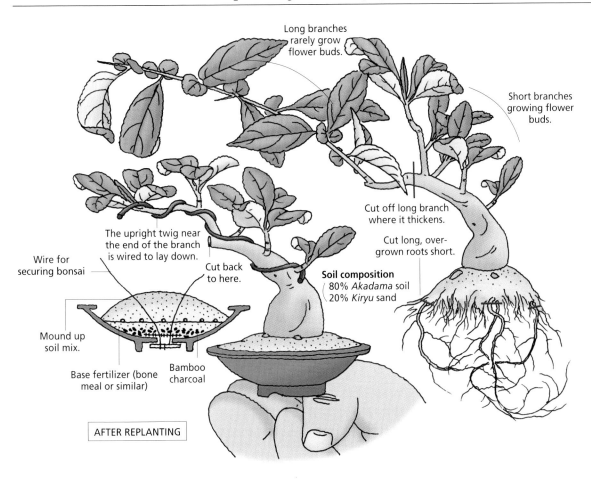

Long branches rarely grow flower buds.

Short branches growing flower buds.

Cut off long branch where it thickens.

Cut long, over-grown roots short.

The upright twig near the end of the branch is wired to lay down.

Wire for securing bonsai

Cut back to here.

Soil composition
80% *Akadama* soil
20% *Kiryu* sand

Mound up soil mix.

Base fertilizer (bone meal or similar)

Bamboo charcoal

AFTER REPLANTING

Flowering bonsai: Treating long branches

Example: Fuji cherry

Pinch off apical buds to avoid causing thicker branches.

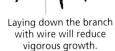

Laying down the branch with wire will reduce vigorous growth.

Fruiting bonsai: Leaf burn and flower buds

Example: Pear-leaf crabapple

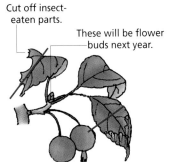

Cut off insect-eaten parts.

These will be flower buds next year.

Cut off burnt sections of leaves and leave green portions.

Leafy bonsai: Pinching off buds

Example: Maple

Pinch off.

Continue to snip off buds that project beyond contour line of leaves.

Conifers: Removing old leaves

Example: Chinese juniper

Old leaves

Use tweezers or similar to clean out old leaves that have turned brown.

October

- ☑ Care & trimming of bonsai on display at an exhibition
- ☑ How to decide which bonsai to purchase
- ☑ Seed collecting
- ☑ Preserving seeds
- ☑ Neutralizing acidified soil
- ☑ Ripened fruit: Gathering and preserving seeds
- ☑ Adding extra fertilizer
- ☑ Disinfecting
- ☑ Wiring

Care & trimming of bonsai on display at an exhibition

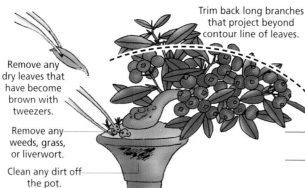

Trim back long branches that project beyond contour line of leaves.

Example: Firethorns

Remove any dry leaves that have become brown with tweezers.

Remove any weeds, grass, or liverwort.

Clean any dirt off the pot.

How to decide which bonsai to purchase

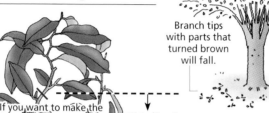

Select a bonsai with leaves and branches that can be trimmed and bearing robust buds.

Select the bonsai by assuming where it can be cut back.

Select a bonsai with a bend in its lower trunk.

Price is also a deciding factor, of course

If you want to make the bonsai even smaller, the branch could be cut off here also.

2⅜ in (6 cm) from here to the root base

Select a bonsai with solid rooting that is not shaky.

Seed collecting

Example: Japanese zelkova (around late October)

Trees with autumn colors in parks are good sources of seeds.

Depending on the year, there might be no seeds at all, but once every 3 to 4 years, there are many seeds on the branches.

Branch tips with parts that turned brown will fall.

Collect the seeds from the fallen branch tips.

⅛ in (5 mm)

The seeds are attached at the bases of leaves.

When storing seeds, keep in an envelope in a refrigerator until spring.

SORTING THE SEEDS

Floating seeds are infertile.

Plant only the seeds that sink to the bottom.

Water

SOWING THE SEEDS

Name tags

Seeds

Preserving seeds

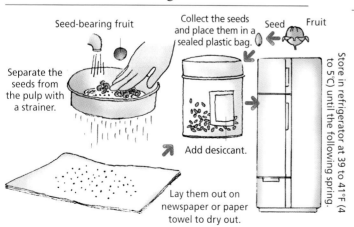

Seed-bearing fruit

Separate the seeds from the pulp with a strainer.

Collect the seeds and place them in a sealed plastic bag.

Seed   Fruit

Add desiccant.

Lay them out on newspaper or paper towel to dry out.

Store in refrigerator at 39 to 41°F (4 to 5°C) until the following spring.

Neutralizing acidified soil

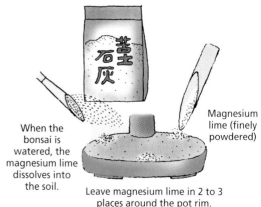

When the bonsai is watered, the magnesium lime dissolves into the soil.

Magnesium lime (finely powdered)

Leave magnesium lime in 2 to 3 places around the pot rim.

*Neutralizing: In terms of chemical conditions, a pH level of 7. Ideal pH depends on the bonsai species, but most plants and trees prefer a slightly acidic pH of between 5 and 7. With a pH that becomes higher than 7 and thus more alkaline, deficiencies of trace elements such as iron and manganese and decreased absorption of phosphoric acid are likely to occur.

Ripened fruit: Gathering and preserving seeds

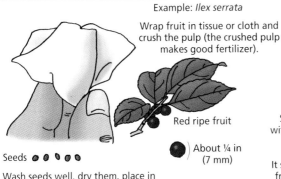

Example: *Ilex serrata*

Wrap fruit in tissue or cloth and crush the pulp (the crushed pulp makes good fertilizer).

Red ripe fruit

About ¼ in (7 mm)

Seeds

Wash seeds well, dry them, place in paper envelope (or similar), and store in refrigerator until spring.

Adding extra fertilizer

Current location (Place new fertilizers between previous locations.)

Previous location (Leave old fertilizer where it is.)

Previous location

Current location

Secure fertilizer with U-shaped wire.

It slowly fertilizes from where it is placed.

For no. 2.5 pots (3 in / 7.5 cm), 2 or so solid fertilizer pellets per pot is standard.

Each ⅜ in (1 cm) solid fertilizer pellet contains 35% nitrogen, 50% phosphoric acid, and 15% potassium.

Disinfecting

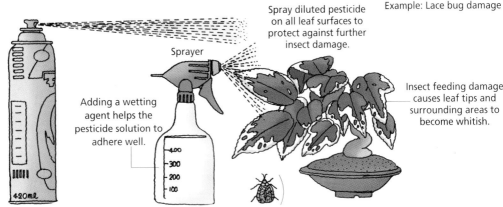

Use aerosol disinfectant solutions at least 12 in (30 cm) away from bonsai.

Spray diluted pesticide on all leaf surfaces to protect against further insect damage.

Example: Lace bug damage

Sprayer

Adding a wetting agent helps the pesticide solution to adhere well.

Insect feeding damage causes leaf tips and surrounding areas to become whitish.

Lace bug (about ⅛ in / 3 mm)

Wiring

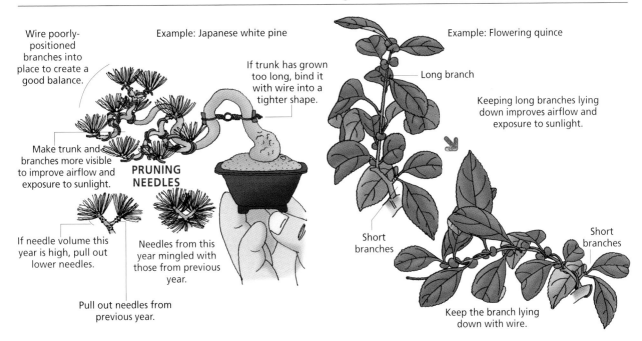

Wire poorly-positioned branches into place to create a good balance.

Example: Japanese white pine

If trunk has grown too long, bind it with wire into a tighter shape.

Example: Flowering quince

Long branch

Keeping long branches lying down improves airflow and exposure to sunlight.

Make trunk and branches more visible to improve airflow and exposure to sunlight.

PRUNING NEEDLES

If needle volume this year is high, pull out lower needles.

Needles from this year mingled with those from previous year.

Short branches

Short branches

Pull out needles from previous year.

Keep the branch lying down with wire.

November

- ☑ Gathering and preserving seeds
- ☑ Protecting your bonsai from birds
- ☑ Gathering seeds from parks
- ☑ Care & trimming
- ☑ Removing old needles on conifers
- ☑ Citrus tree bonsai shelters
- ☑ Care & trimming when leaves have fallen

Gathering and preserving seeds (from trees in public parks and so on)

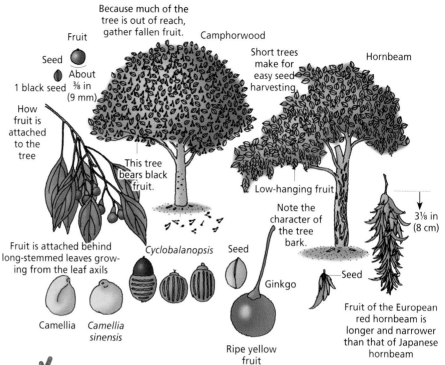

Because much of the tree is out of reach, gather fallen fruit.

Fruit

Seed

About ⅜ in (9 mm)

1 black seed

How fruit is attached to the tree

This tree bears black fruit.

Camphorwood

Short trees make for easy seed harvesting.

Hornbeam

Low-hanging fruit

Note the character of the tree bark.

3⅛ in (8 cm)

Seed

Fruit is attached behind long-stemmed leaves growing from the leaf axils

Cyclobalanopsis

Seed

Ginkgo

Camellia   *Camellia sinensis*

Ripe yellow fruit

Fruit of the European red hornbeam is longer and narrower than that of Japanese hornbeam

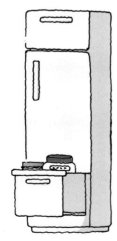

Canister

Plastic bag

ウメモドキ

ロウヤガキ

Desiccant

Desiccant   Seeds   Seeds

Store in refrigerator until spring

Protecting your bonsai from birds

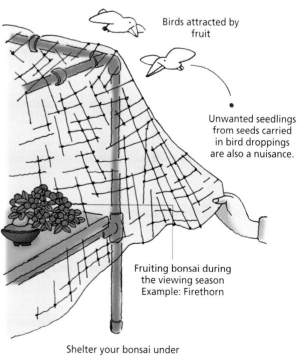

Birds attracted by fruit

Unwanted seedlings from seeds carried in bird droppings are also a nuisance.

Fruiting bonsai during the viewing season
Example: Firethorn

Shelter your bonsai under a coarsely-woven net to protect from bird predation.

Gathering seeds from parks

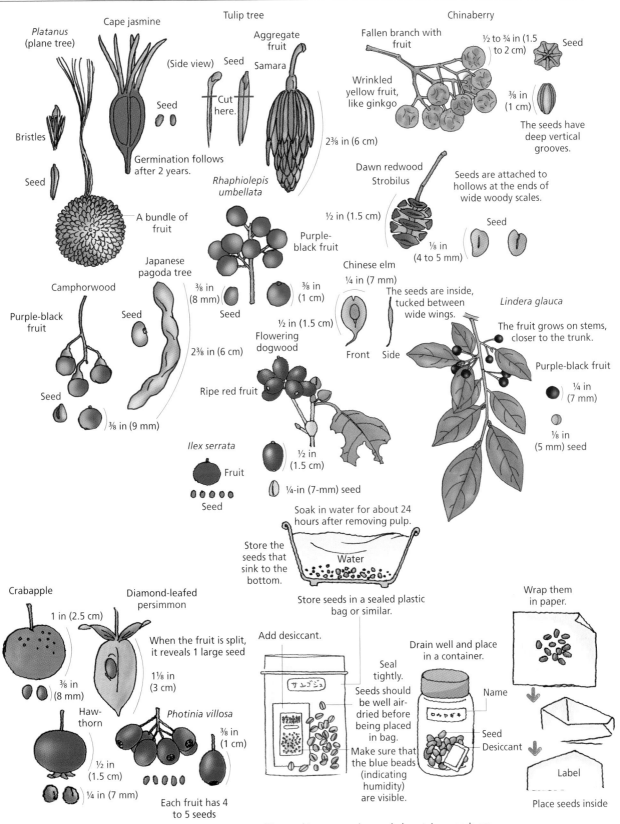

Platanus (plane tree)
Bristles
Seed
A bundle of fruit
Germination follows after 2 years.

Cape jasmine
Seed

Tulip tree
(Side view) Seed
Samara
Aggregate fruit
Cut here.
2⅜ in (6 cm)

Chinaberry
Fallen branch with fruit
Wrinkled yellow fruit, like ginkgo
½ to ¾ in (1.5 to 2 cm)
Seed
⅜ in (1 cm)
The seeds have deep vertical grooves.

Rhaphiolepis umbellata
Purple-black fruit
⅜ in (8 mm) Seed
⅜ in (1 cm) Seed
½ in (1.5 cm)

Dawn redwood
Strobilus
½ in (1.5 cm)
⅛ in (4 to 5 mm)
Seeds are attached to hollows at the ends of wide woody scales.
Seed

Japanese pagoda tree
Seed
2⅜ in (6 cm)

Camphorwood
Purple-black fruit
Seed
⅜ in (9 mm)

Flowering dogwood
Ripe red fruit
½ in (1.5 cm)
¼-in (7-mm) seed

Chinese elm
¼ in (7 mm)
The seeds are inside, tucked between wide wings.
Front   Side

Lindera glauca
The fruit grows on stems, closer to the trunk.
Purple-black fruit
¼ in (7 mm)
⅛ in (5 mm) seed

Ilex serrata
Fruit
Seed

Soak in water for about 24 hours after removing pulp.
Store the seeds that sink to the bottom.
Water

Store seeds in a sealed plastic bag or similar.

Crabapple
1 in (2.5 cm)
⅜ in (8 mm)

Diamond-leafed persimmon
When the fruit is split, it reveals 1 large seed
1⅛ in (3 cm)

Hawthorn
½ in (1.5 cm)
¼ in (7 mm)

Photinia villosa
⅜ in (1 cm)
Each fruit has 4 to 5 seeds

Add desiccant.
Seal tightly.
Seeds should be well air-dried before being placed in bag.
Make sure that the blue beads (indicating humidity) are visible.

Drain well and place in a container.
Name
Seed
Desiccant

Wrap them in paper.
Label
Place seeds inside

Wrapped in paper or in a sealed container, seeds are stored in a refrigerator (at around 60°F / 5°C) until spring.

Care & trimming

FLOWERING BONSAI
Example: Japanese plum

Short branches growing flower buds.

Trim back long branches.

FRUITING PLANTS
Example: Diamond-leafed persimmon

Flower buds attached to the short branches

Trim back long branches.

Preserve an arc shape.

PRUNING

Debranch halfway up the branch

Trim downward-pointing branches

LEAFY BONSAI
Example: Japanese maple

Cut upraised sprouts short

Citrus tree bonsai shelters

STYROFOAM BOX

Opening the cooler during daylight hours ensures that the bonsai receive adequate sunlight.

Close the cooler at night to protect the bonsai from frost.

Hong Kong kumquat or other citrus bonsai.

Move temperate climate trees, evergreens, and cold-intolerant bonsai into the shelter.

SIMPLE SHELTER
Move bonsai into shelters or green-houses before frost arrives.

Glass or polyethylene

Opening end

Hinge

Wood beam

Block

Ground level

Sheltering citrus bonsai

Lay a simple floor for drainage.

SEMI-BELOWGROUND BONSAI SHELTER

Removing old needles on conifers

Example: Black pine

Example: Japanese white pine

Old needles

Old needles

Pull out needles by grasping their bases with strong tweezers.

Pull out old brown needles by grasping the bases with strong tweezers.

AFTER REMOVING OLD NEEDLES

Area where old needles were removed.

Removing needles

Places where old needles were removed.

Branching is easily seen and airflow has improved.

Being able to clearly differentiate between the green and brown needles is evidence of the excellent development of the bonsai.

Branching is well-defined.

It is beneficial to also remove lower needles from branches with a high needle volume.

Care & trimming when leaves have fallen

(Wiring removal, wiring into position, weeding and fertilizing)

Wire any upright shoots down into position shown by the dotted line.

Take off the wiring that was placed in June.

Remove the wire by pinching the end and unwinding.

Use pliers for unwinding thick wire or working in hard-to-access areas.

Pull any weeds.

If you placed fertilizer pellets in your bonsai in early November, you have finished fertilizing for this year.

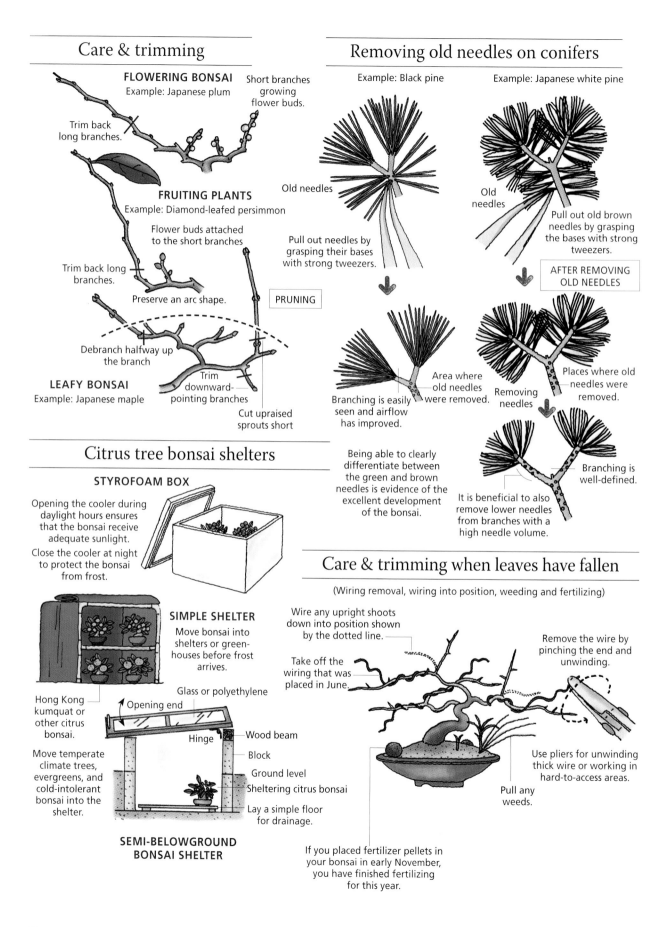

Pruning and wiring

- ☑ Pruning and wiring
- ☑ Disinfecting in winter
- ☑ Broadening conifer candles: Wiring
- ☑ Preparing bonsai shelters for winter
- ☑ Black pine needle removal
- ☑ Bonsai as New Year's decorations
- ☑ Leafy bonsai: Light pruning

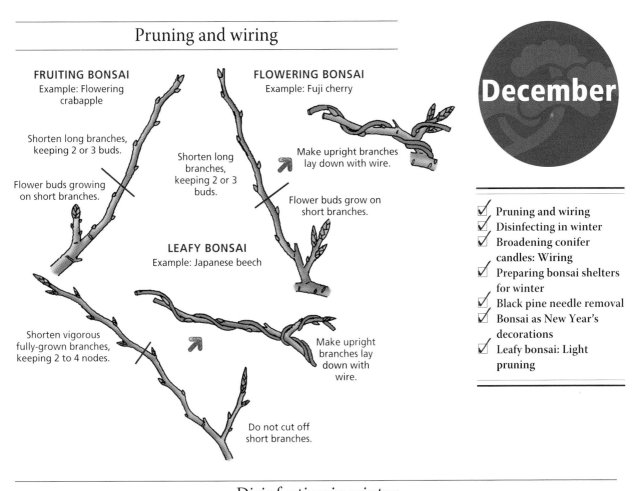

FRUITING BONSAI
Example: Flowering crabapple

Shorten long branches, keeping 2 or 3 buds.

Flower buds growing on short branches.

Shorten vigorous fully-grown branches, keeping 2 to 4 nodes.

FLOWERING BONSAI
Example: Fuji cherry

Shorten long branches, keeping 2 or 3 buds.

Make upright branches lay down with wire.

Flower buds grow on short branches.

LEAFY BONSAI
Example: Japanese beech

Make upright branches lay down with wire.

Do not cut off short branches.

Disinfecting in winter

DISINFECTANT SPRAYING

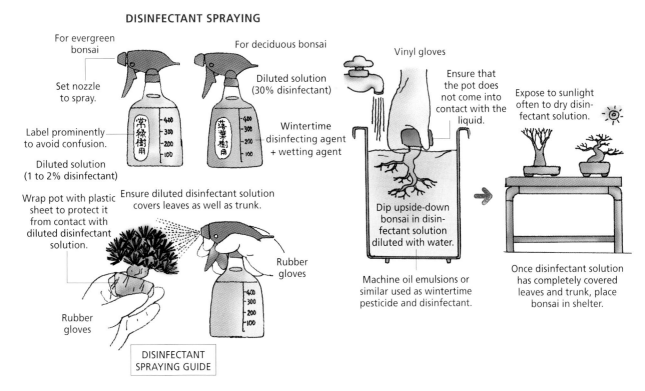

For evergreen bonsai

Set nozzle to spray.

Label prominently to avoid confusion.

Diluted solution (1 to 2% disinfectant)

常緑樹用

For deciduous bonsai

Diluted solution (30% disinfectant)

Wintertime disinfecting agent + wetting agent

落葉樹用

Vinyl gloves

Ensure that the pot does not come into contact with the liquid.

Expose to sunlight often to dry disinfectant solution.

Wrap pot with plastic sheet to protect it from contact with diluted disinfectant solution.

Ensure diluted disinfectant solution covers leaves as well as trunk.

Rubber gloves

Rubber gloves

DISINFECTANT SPRAYING GUIDE

Dip upside-down bonsai in disinfectant solution diluted with water.

Machine oil emulsions or similar used as wintertime pesticide and disinfectant.

Once disinfectant solution has completely covered leaves and trunk, place bonsai in shelter.

Broadening conifer candles: Wiring

Example: Black Pine

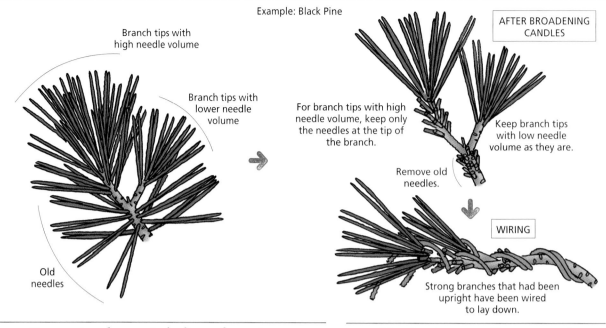

Branch tips with high needle volume

Branch tips with lower needle volume

Old needles

AFTER BROADENING CANDLES

For branch tips with high needle volume, keep only the needles at the tip of the branch.

Remove old needles.

Keep branch tips with low needle volume as they are.

WIRING

Strong branches that had been upright have been wired to lay down.

Preparing bonsai shelters for winter

Example: Polytunnels

Draping cheesecloth over the exterior will prevent interior temperatures from spiking.

Plastic / Polyethylene

Prepare shelf inside

Doorway

Bonsai as New Year's decorations

Example: Entry hall

Cascading conifer bonsai

Arrange red or blue felt cloth.

Accompanying accent plant

Shoe cabinet

Refer to page 8.

Leafy bonsai: Light pruning

Example: Japanese zelkova

Trim overgrown branches.

Black pine needle removal

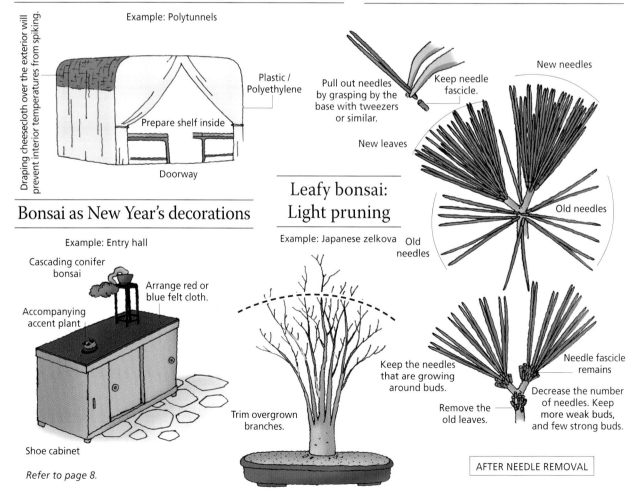

Pull out needles by grasping by the base with tweezers or similar.

Keep needle fascicle.

New leaves

New needles

Old needles

Old needles

Keep the needles that are growing around buds.

Remove the old leaves.

Needle fascicle remains

Decrease the number of needles. Keep more weak buds, and few strong buds.

AFTER NEEDLE REMOVAL

THE POPULARITY OF BONSAI TREES IS DUE IN PART
TO THE PROMISE OF THEIR FLORAL GLORY
How to Care for Flowering Bonsai

Of course, these bonsai are noteworthy for their flowering, but the personality of their root-flare, trunks and so on are also fascinating. To begin, let's prepare some specific popular varieties.

LET'S BEGIN BY SELECTING AND NURTURING ATTRACTIVE BONSAI SPECIES

Charming and lustrous flowers made to bloom on small trees, these "flowering" bonsai herald the arrival of another season, imbuing the entire space with their festive atmosphere. This book puts aside such philosophical discussions as "What is a bonsai?" and rather, it will provide a foundation of instructions and tips on raising and caring for them. Illustrator Gun Kyosuke uses his vast experience with small bonsai (under 8 inches / 20 cm) to show you how to nurture them. And naturally, this foundation applies to raising larger bonsai as well. First, you choose a tree you really like, and use the monthly bonsai care calendar (pages 25–58) as a guide. Don't be afraid of making mistakes—let yourself enjoy the tradition of bonsai that Japan has shown to the world.

Caring for bonsai is a way of life, and the presence of bonsai can transform your lifestyle. And part of this transformation is in making time to train and care for the bonsai every day.

In addition, basic information about bonsai begins with "How to Appreciate Bonsai" on page 7, and to help improve your understanding of the more technical language of this art, refer to the Glossary, which begins on page 176.

Plum

JAPANESE NAME
Ume

ALTERNATIVE NAMES
Koubun Bun Kiboku

SCIENTIFIC NAME
Prunus mume

CLASSIFICATION
Rose

SYMBOLIC OF
Independence, Strength

FLOWERING
February to March

This tree was brought to Japan by Chinese ambassadors during the Nara period. The flowers provided enjoyment, and the fruit was used as food and medicine. With fragrant five-petaled flowers, the flowering of this bonsai is an indication of early spring. The flowers can be various colors, such as white, pink or red. The dormant period is a good time for pruning.

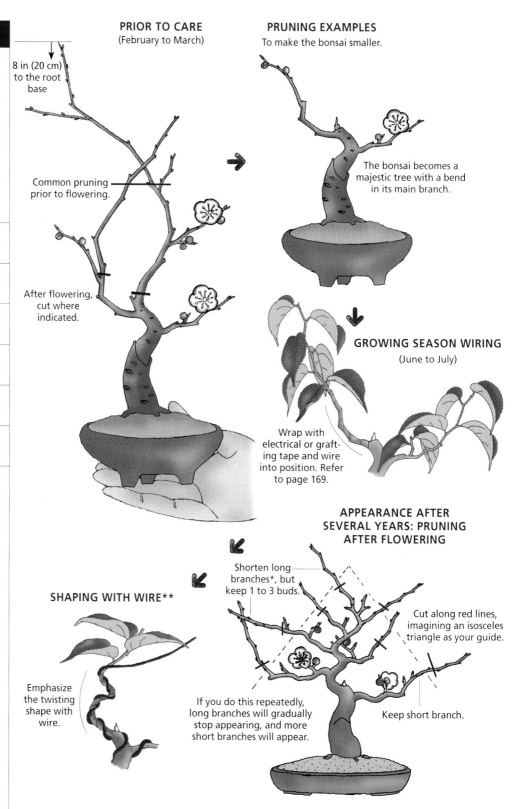

PRIOR TO CARE
(February to March)

8 in (20 cm) to the root base

Common pruning prior to flowering.

After flowering, cut where indicated.

PRUNING EXAMPLES
To make the bonsai smaller.

The bonsai becomes a majestic tree with a bend in its main branch.

GROWING SEASON WIRING
(June to July)

Wrap with electrical or grafting tape and wire into position. Refer to page 169.

APPEARANCE AFTER SEVERAL YEARS: PRUNING AFTER FLOWERING

Shorten long branches*, but keep 1 to 3 buds.

Cut along red lines, imagining an isosceles triangle as your guide.

If you do this repeatedly, long branches will gradually stop appearing, and more short branches will appear.

Keep short branch.

SHAPING WITH WIRE**

Emphasize the twisting shape with wire.

*Long branches: The situation where a vigorous branch has grown to a length that seems discordant. Many adventitious buds grow and often become branches that give the tree an unkempt shape and appearance.
**Shape with wire: Bending with wire: The situation where a branch or trunk is shaped with wire to cause it to bend. On their own, branches have a tendency to grow upward, and training them is an art that all bonsai practitioners must develop. Pruning and bending will promote the health and training of the bonsai by improving airflow and sunlight. Refer to page 169.

Cut off the twig just above the leaf buds near the branch base

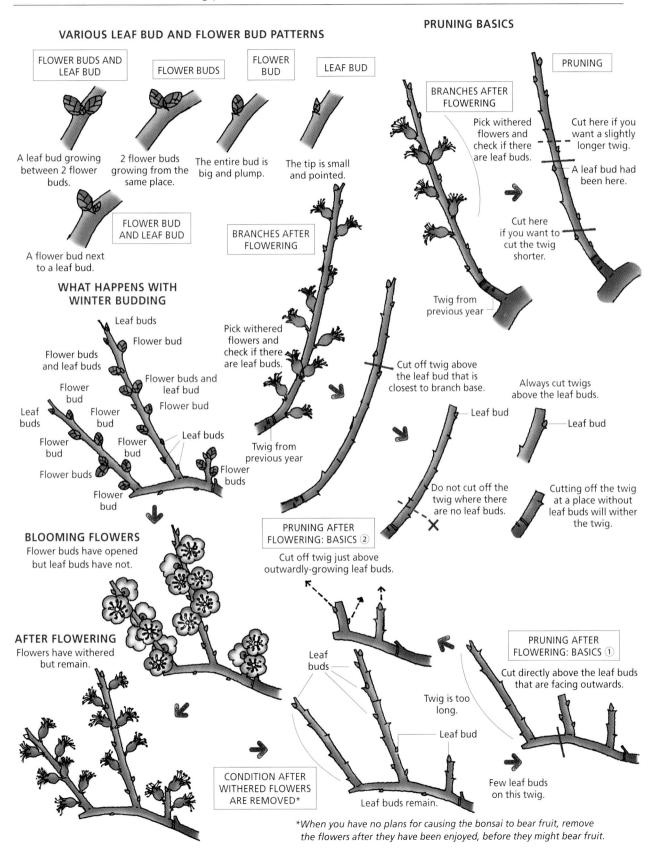

VARIOUS LEAF BUD AND FLOWER BUD PATTERNS

FLOWER BUDS AND LEAF BUD

A leaf bud growing between 2 flower buds.

FLOWER BUDS

2 flower buds growing from the same place.

FLOWER BUD

The entire bud is big and plump.

LEAF BUD

The tip is small and pointed.

FLOWER BUD AND LEAF BUD

A flower bud next to a leaf bud.

WHAT HAPPENS WITH WINTER BUDDING

Leaf buds
Flower bud
Flower buds and leaf buds
Flower buds and leaf bud
Flower bud
Flower bud
Flower bud
Leaf buds
Flower bud
Flower bud
Leaf buds
Flower bud
Flower buds
Flower bud
Flower buds

BLOOMING FLOWERS

Flower buds have opened but leaf buds have not.

AFTER FLOWERING

Flowers have withered but remain.

BRANCHES AFTER FLOWERING

Pick withered flowers and check if there are leaf buds.

Twig from previous year

Cut off twig above the leaf bud that is closest to branch base.

Leaf bud

Do not cut off the twig where there are no leaf buds.

PRUNING AFTER FLOWERING: BASICS ②

Cut off twig just above outwardly-growing leaf buds.

Leaf buds

CONDITION AFTER WITHERED FLOWERS ARE REMOVED*

Leaf buds remain.

PRUNING BASICS

PRUNING

BRANCHES AFTER FLOWERING

Pick withered flowers and check if there are leaf buds.

Cut here if you want a slightly longer twig.

A leaf bud had been here.

Cut here if you want to cut the twig shorter.

Twig from previous year

Always cut twigs above the leaf buds.

Leaf bud

Cutting off the twig at a place without leaf buds will wither the twig.

Twig is too long.

Leaf bud

PRUNING AFTER FLOWERING: BASICS ①

Cut directly above the leaf buds that are facing outwards.

Few leaf buds on this twig.

When you have no plans for causing the bonsai to bear fruit, remove the flowers after they have been enjoyed, before they might bear fruit.

SCHEDULE

Month	Propagating	Watering	Fertilizing	Protection	Shaping	Sterilization	Transplanting	Growth State
January	Grafting	1–2 times / week		Protection room				Dormancy period • Flowering (February–March)
February	Grafting / Seeding	1–2 times / week		Protection room	Pruning	Winter		Dormancy period • Flowering (February–March)
March	Seeding	1–2 times / week		Protection room	Pruning			Dormancy period • Flowering (February–March)
April		2–3 times / day	Add fertilizer		Bud picking (April–May) • Wiring			Growth period
May		2–3 times / day	Add fertilizer		Bud picking (April–May) • Wiring / Growth period			Growth period
June	Cutting	3–4 times / day	Water & fertilizer		Growth period			Growth period • Sprout separating (June–August)
July	Cutting	3–4 times / day	Water & fertilizer	Shading	Growth period			Growth period • Sprout separating (June–August)
August		3–4 times / day	Water & fertilizer	Shading				Growth period • Sprout separating (June–August)
September		2–3 times / day	Add fertilizer					
October		2–3 times / day	Add fertilizer					Prime
November								
December						Winter		

Growth Period Work
(Laying down new branch tips & folding down unneeded branches)

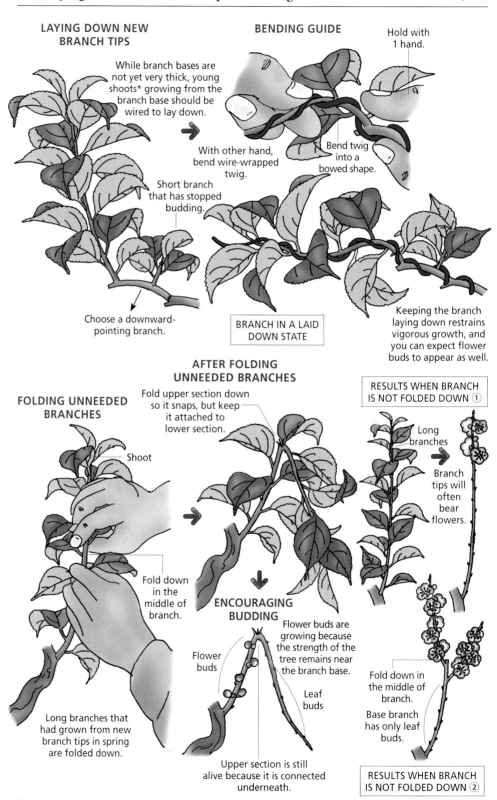

LAYING DOWN NEW BRANCH TIPS

While branch bases are not yet very thick, young shoots* growing from the branch base should be wired to lay down.

With other hand, bend wire-wrapped twig.

Short branch that has stopped budding.

Choose a downward-pointing branch.

BENDING GUIDE

Hold with 1 hand.

Bend twig into a bowed shape.

BRANCH IN A LAID DOWN STATE

Keeping the branch laying down restrains vigorous growth, and you can expect flower buds to appear as well.

FOLDING UNNEEDED BRANCHES

Shoot

Fold down in the middle of branch.

Long branches that had grown from new branch tips in spring are folded down.

AFTER FOLDING UNNEEDED BRANCHES

Fold upper section down so it snaps, but keep it attached to lower section.

Upper section is still alive because it is connected underneath.

ENCOURAGING BUDDING

Flower buds are growing because the strength of the tree remains near the branch base.

Flower buds

Leaf buds

RESULTS WHEN BRANCH IS NOT FOLDED DOWN ①

Long branches

Branch tips will often bear flowers.

RESULTS WHEN BRANCH IS NOT FOLDED DOWN ②

Fold down in the middle of branch.

Base branch has only leaf buds.

*Young shoots: branches that have grown this year. The spring buds that grew into branches are known as one-year branches. They will be two-year branches in the following year.

Siberian Peashrub

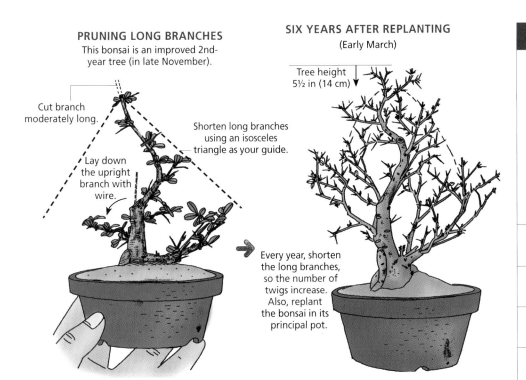

PRUNING LONG BRANCHES

This bonsai is an improved 2nd-year tree (in late November).

Cut branch moderately long.

Lay down the upright branch with wire.

Shorten long branches using an isosceles triangle as your guide.

SIX YEARS AFTER REPLANTING
(Early March)

Tree height 5½ in (14 cm)

Every year, shorten the long branches, so the number of twigs increase. Also, replant the bonsai in its principal pot.

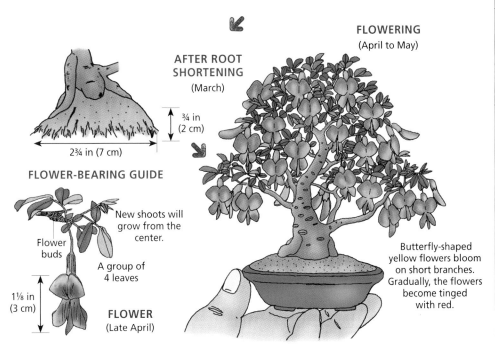

AFTER ROOT SHORTENING
(March)

¾ in (2 cm)

2¾ in (7 cm)

FLOWER-BEARING GUIDE

Flower buds

New shoots will grow from the center.

A group of 4 leaves

1⅛ in (3 cm)

FLOWER
(Late April)

FLOWERING
(April to May)

Butterfly-shaped yellow flowers bloom on short branches. Gradually, the flowers become tinged with red.

JAPANESE NAME
Muresuzume

ALTERNATIVE NAMES
Enishida, Caragana

SCIENTIFIC NAME
Caragana chamlagu

CLASSIFICATION
Legume

SYMBOLIC OF
Community, Abundance

FLOWERING
April to May

In full bloom, its flowers resemble a flock of sparrows perched among the branches. These flowers are butter-fly-shaped, about 1 inch (2.5 cm) long and gradually take on a reddish tinge. Pruning should be done during dormant period or after flowering, and laying down roots is effective for propagation. Keep a trimmed-off thick root in a pot buried in soil and it will sprout.

SCHEDULE		January	February	March	April	May	June	July	August	September	October	November	December
	Propagating			Grafting			Cutting • Layering						
	Watering		1–2 times / day			2–3 times / day		3–4 times / day			2–3 times / day		
	Fertilizing					Add fertilizer		Water & fertilizer			Add fertilizer		
	Protection		Protection room						Shading				
	Shaping			Pruning			Wiring						
	Sterilization		Winter			Growth stage							Winter
	Transplanting												
	Growth State		Dormancy period			Growth period • Flowering (April–June)					Prime		

Japanese Quince

JAPANESE NAME
Choujubai

ALTERNATIVE NAMES
Yodoboke, Chojubai

SCIENTIFIC NAME
Chaenomeles specios

CLASSIFICATION
Rose

SYMBOLIC OF
n/a

FLOWERING
March to April

These trees are year-round bloomers*, and may flower three to five times a year. Its flowers are brilliant reds and oranges, and even after flowering, we can enjoy its beautiful leaves. Although its leaves fall several times a year, before long, new buds will appear. After flowering, plucking the withered blossoms and adding extra fertilizer are essential to encourage the next flowering.

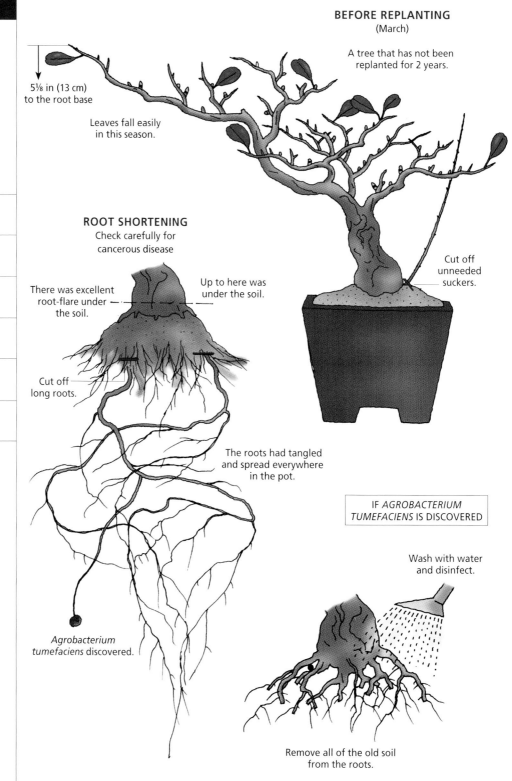

BEFORE REPLANTING
(March)

A tree that has not been replanted for 2 years.

5⅛ in (13 cm) to the root base

Leaves fall easily in this season.

Cut off unneeded suckers.

ROOT SHORTENING
Check carefully for cancerous disease

There was excellent root-flare under the soil.

Up to here was under the soil.

Cut off long roots.

The roots had tangled and spread everywhere in the pot.

Agrobacterium tumefaciens discovered.

IF *AGROBACTERIUM TUMEFACIENS* IS DISCOVERED

Wash with water and disinfect.

Remove all of the old soil from the roots.

**Year-round bloomer: When in peak condition, flowers can bloom year-round as long as the tree is main tained at minimum temperatures required for growth. Many trees only bloom in the spring and autumn.*

PLANTING GUIDE

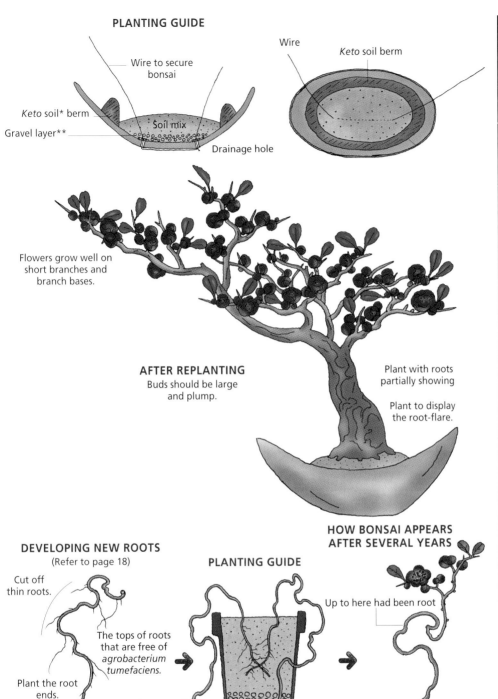

Wire to secure bonsai

Keto soil* berm

Gravel layer**

Soil mix

Drainage hole

Wire

Keto soil berm

Flowers grow well on short branches and branch bases.

AFTER REPLANTING
Buds should be large and plump.

Plant with roots partially showing

Plant to display the root-flare.

HOW BONSAI APPEARS AFTER SEVERAL YEARS

Up to here had been root

DEVELOPING NEW ROOTS
(Refer to page 18)

Cut off thin roots.

The tops of roots that are free of *agrobacterium tumefaciens*.

Plant the root ends.

Make good use of roots with interesting bends.

PLANTING GUIDE

Keep roots dangling outside of the pot.

With a slender, bent trunk, a tree in the Literati style can be created. Refer to page 13.

*Keto soil: A sticky soil formed by plant compost (primarily common reeds that grow wild in rivers and wetlands. Composed largely of fiber, keto soil is used to make moss balls and is in the soil mix for root-in-rock bonsai.
**Gravel layer: Also known as the bottom layer, it is the coarsest part (with particles being about ¼ to 7/16 in / 7 to 10 mm in diameter) of a soil mix in bonsai. Used to improve drainage through the bottom of pots.

SCHEDULE

Month	Growth State	Transplanting	Sterilization	Shaping	Protection	Fertilizing	Watering	Propagating
January	Dormancy period • Flowering (March-April)						1–2 times / week	
February			Winter	Pruning	Protection room			Cutting
March								
April								
May						Add fertilizer	2–3 times / day	
June	Growth period			Wiring				Cutting
July				Growth period		Water & fertilizer	3–4 times / day	
August			Shading • Pruning (September)					
September								
October	Prime					Add fertilizer	2–3 times / day	
November								
December	Winter	Winter						

Fuji Cherry

JAPANESE NAME
Sakura

ALTERNATIVE NAMES
Fuji Sakura, Hakone Sakura

SCIENTIFIC NAME
Cerasus insica Thunb. ex Murray

CLASSIFICATION
Rose (deciduous hardwood / shrub)

SYMBOLIC OF
Excellent beauty

FLOWERING
April

Flowers open, revealing small white or pale red petals. This iconic tree grows wild around Hakone and Mount Fuji, and in the mountains of Honshu and Chubu regions. The debranching* of cherry trees is standard, because if branches are cut mid-way up, they wither easily, and wiring branches to lay them down is recommended to restrain their otherwise vigorous growth.

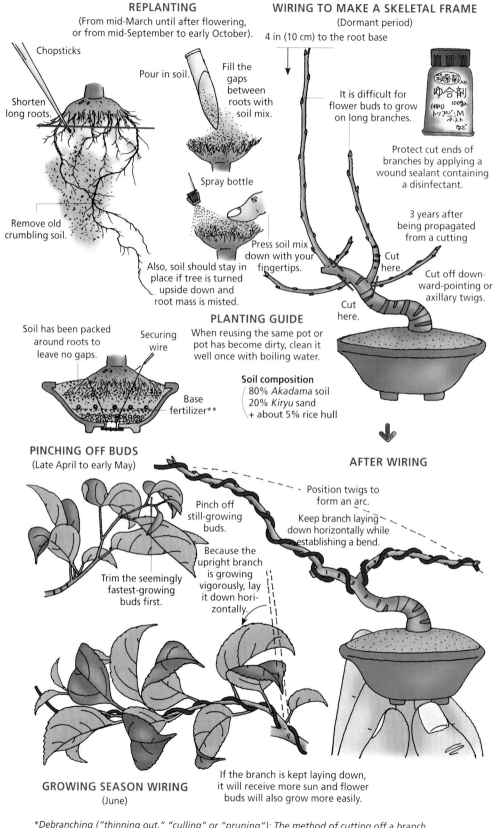

REPLANTING
(From mid-March until after flowering, or from mid-September to early October).

Chopsticks

Shorten long roots.

Pour in soil.

Fill the gaps between roots with soil mix.

Remove old crumbling soil.

Spray bottle

Also, soil should stay in place if tree is turned upside down and root mass is misted.

Press soil mix down with your fingertips.

Soil has been packed around roots to leave no gaps.

Securing wire

Base fertilizer**

WIRING TO MAKE A SKELETAL FRAME
(Dormant period)

4 in (10 cm) to the root base

It is difficult for flower buds to grow on long branches.

Protect cut ends of branches by applying a wound sealant containing a disinfectant.

3 years after being propagated from a cutting

Cut here.

Cut off downward-pointing or axillary twigs.

Cut here.

PLANTING GUIDE
When reusing the same pot or pot has become dirty, clean it well once with boiling water.

Soil composition
80% *Akadama* soil
20% *Kiryu* sand
+ about 5% rice hull

PINCHING OFF BUDS
(Late April to early May)

Pinch off still-growing buds.

Trim the seemingly fastest-growing buds first.

Because the upright branch is growing vigorously, lay it down horizontally.

AFTER WIRING

Position twigs to form an arc.

Keep branch laying down horizontally while establishing a bend.

If the branch is kept laying down, it will receive more sun and flower buds will also grow more easily.

GROWING SEASON WIRING
(June)

*Debranching ("thinning out," "culling" or "pruning"): The method of cutting off a branch above the base of a smaller branch (the section at the base of the smaller branch).
**Base fertilizer: Before planting, fertilizers are needed in advance for growth, and slow-acting organic fertilizers are often employed.

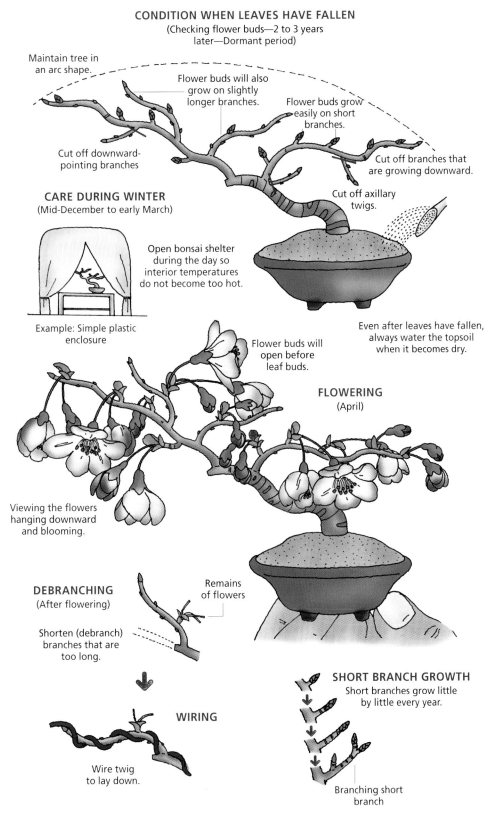

CONDITION WHEN LEAVES HAVE FALLEN
(Checking flower buds—2 to 3 years later—Dormant period)

Maintain tree in an arc shape.

Flower buds will also grow on slightly longer branches.

Flower buds grow easily on short branches.

Cut off downward-pointing branches

Cut off branches that are growing downward.

Cut off axillary twigs.

CARE DURING WINTER
(Mid-December to early March)

Open bonsai shelter during the day so interior temperatures do not become too hot.

Example: Simple plastic enclosure

Even after leaves have fallen, always water the topsoil when it becomes dry.

Flower buds will open before leaf buds.

FLOWERING
(April)

Viewing the flowers hanging downward and blooming.

DEBRANCHING
(After flowering)

Shorten (debranch) branches that are too long.

Remains of flowers

WIRING

Wire twig to lay down.

SHORT BRANCH GROWTH
Short branches grow little by little every year.

Branching short branch

SCHEDULE								
	Propagating	Watering	Fertilizing	Protection	Shaping	Sterilization	Transplanting	Growth State
January								
February	Cutting	1–2 times / week		Protection room		Winter		Dormancy period
March								
April					Pruning			
May		2–3 times / day	Add fertilizer					Growth period • Flowering (April) • Sprout separating (July–August)
June	Layering • Cutting		Growth period		Wiring			
July		3–4 times / day	Water & fertilizer	Shading				
August								
September								
October		2–3 times / day	Add fertilizer					
November	Prime							
December						Winter		

Japanese Andromeda

JAPANESE NAME
Asebi

ALTERNATIVE NAMES
Asebo, Umagoroshi

SCIENTIFIC NAME
Pieris japonica

CLASSIFICATION
Azalea (evergreen hard-wood / shrub)

SYMBOLIC OF
Dedication, Pure heart

FLOWERING
March to April

Resembling lily of the valley, small white or pink flowers bloom in clusters on drooping branches. A shrub of the family *ericaceae*, it grows wild in the mountains of Japan and is popular in gardens. It grows reliably, and because it is entirely toxic, animals and insects cannot feed on it.

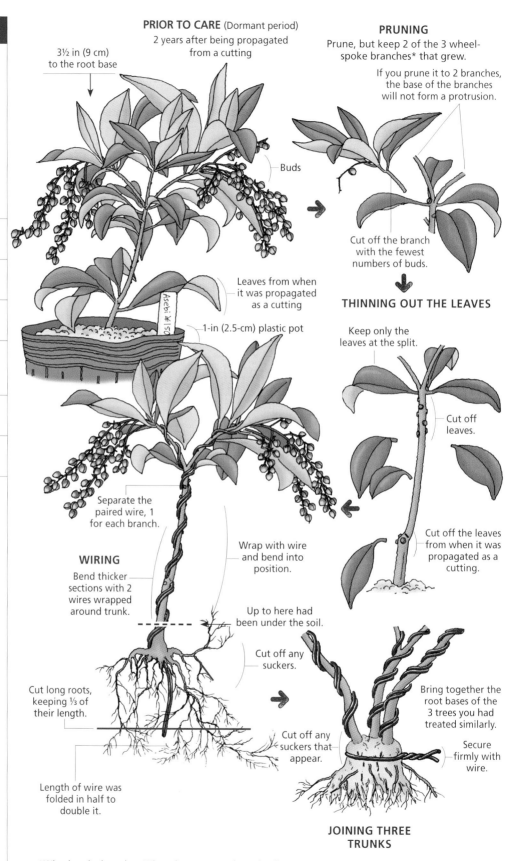

PRIOR TO CARE (Dormant period)
2 years after being propagated from a cutting

3½ in (9 cm) to the root base

Buds

Leaves from when it was propagated as a cutting

1-in (2.5-cm) plastic pot

PRUNING
Prune, but keep 2 of the 3 wheel-spoke branches* that grew.

If you prune it to 2 branches, the base of the branches will not form a protrusion.

Cut off the branch with the fewest numbers of buds.

THINNING OUT THE LEAVES

Keep only the leaves at the split.

Cut off leaves.

Cut off the leaves from when it was propagated as a cutting.

Separate the paired wire, 1 for each branch.

WIRING
Bend thicker sections with 2 wires wrapped around trunk.

Wrap with wire and bend into position.

Up to here had been under the soil.

Cut off any suckers.

Cut long roots, keeping ⅓ of their length.

Cut off any suckers that appear.

Length of wire was folded in half to double it.

Bring together the root bases of the 3 trees you had treated similarly.

Secure firmly with wire.

JOINING THREE TRUNKS

Wheel-spoke branches: When three or more branches have grown from one spot on a trunk in a spoke-like configuration.

PREPARING THE MOUND OF SOIL MIX

Make a mound* of soil mix and plant the tree high** on the mound.

Wire to secure bonsai

Base fertilizer (bone meal or similar)

Wrapped around thick piece of wire

Arrange bamboo charcoal over bottom of pot.

PLANTING GUIDE

Fill in surrounding gaps with soil mix.

Secure firmly with wire.

Soil composition
(80% *Akadama* soil
  20% *Kiryu* sand)

AFTER PLANTING

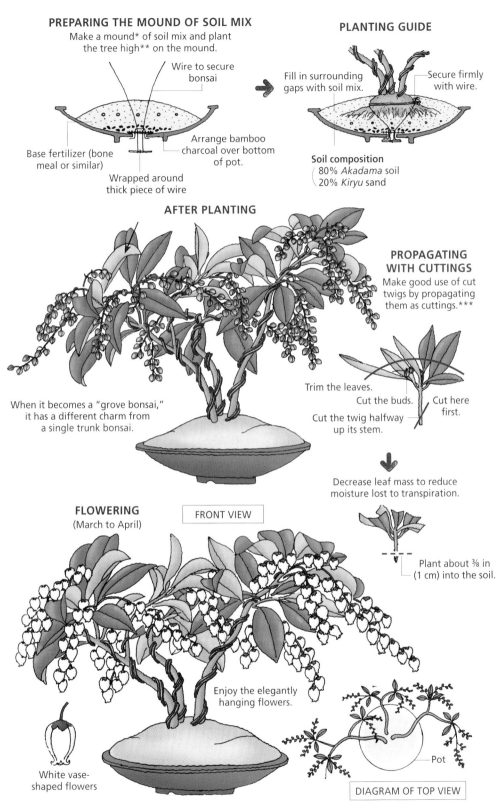

When it becomes a "grove bonsai," it has a different charm from a single trunk bonsai.

FRONT VIEW

PROPAGATING WITH CUTTINGS

Make good use of cut twigs by propagating them as cuttings.***

Trim the leaves.

Cut the buds.

Cut here first.

Cut the twig halfway up its stem.

Decrease leaf mass to reduce moisture lost to transpiration.

Plant about ⅜ in (1 cm) into the soil.

FLOWERING
(March to April)

Enjoy the elegantly hanging flowers.

White vase-shaped flowers

Pot

DIAGRAM OF TOP VIEW

*Mound: When a bonsai pot is filled with soil mix, the soil in the center is higher than the rim.
**Plant high: When the tree is planted on a mound so the entire surface of topsoil is higher than the rim.
***Propagating with cuttings: A method of propagation in which tree twigs lacking roots are cut off and planted into soil, causing them to put out new roots. Refer to page 21.

SCHEDULE

Month	Propagating	Watering	Fertilizing	Protection	Shaping	Sterilization	Transplanting	Growth State
January	Grafting / Seedling • Split stock	1–2 times / week						
February				Protection room	Pruning		Winter	Dormancy period
March								Growth period • Flowering (March–April)
April	Cutting	2–3 times / day						
May			Add fertilizer		Wiring		Growth period	Growth period
June								
July		3–4 times / day		Shading		Water & fertilizer		
August								
September			Add fertilizer					
October		2–3 times / day						Prime
November								
December							Winter	

Japanese Rose

JAPANESE NAME
Noibara

ALTERNATIVE NAMES
Multiflora rose, Baby rose

SCIENTIFIC NAME
Rosa multiflora

CLASSIFICATION
Rose (deciduous broad-leaved tree / shrub)

SYMBOLIC OF
Simple love

FLOWERING
May to June

Flowers are white or pale red and carry a faint scent upon blooming. Each flower is about ¾ in (2 cm) in diameter and has five petals. Representative of wild roses, the Japanese rose grows wild on sunny rural hillsides and mountainous areas. Only existing as a wild species, it is a resilient tree, and propagating with cuttings is recommended.

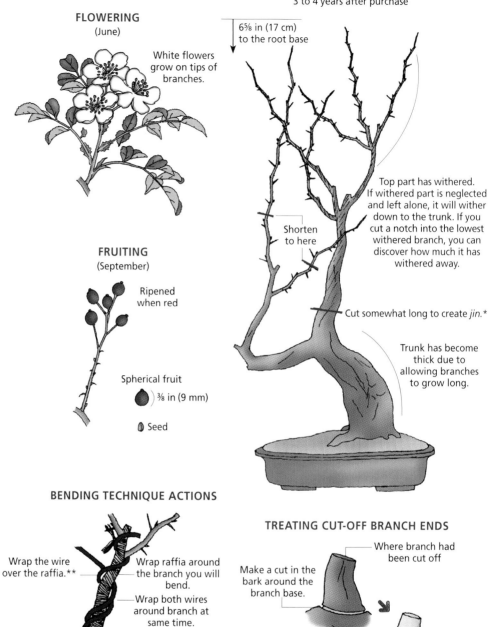

FLOWERING
(June)

White flowers grow on tips of branches.

FRUITING
(September)

Ripened when red

Spherical fruit

⅜ in (9 mm)

Seed

CURRENT CONDITION (February to March)
3 to 4 years after purchase

6⅝ in (17 cm) to the root base

Top part has withered. If withered part is neglected and left alone, it will wither down to the trunk. If you cut a notch into the lowest withered branch, you can discover how much it has withered away.

Shorten to here

Cut somewhat long to create *jin*.*

Trunk has become thick due to allowing branches to grow long.

BENDING TECHNIQUE ACTIONS

Wrap the wire over the raffia.**

Wrap raffia around the branch you will bend.

Wrap both wires around branch at same time.

Spread raffia flat before wrapping.

TREATING CUT-OFF BRANCH ENDS

Where branch had been cut off

Make a cut in the bark around the branch base.

Peel off the bark.

Sharpen to a point

This will become the *jin*.

*Jin: A branch that was withered, causing it to become bleached white. To produce the impression of an old tree in coniferous bonsai, the bark of its main branch and other branches can be peeled off and removed to artificially create an age-withered branch. Also, when cutting off unneeded branches, keep a short section of branch base to make into a jin, to convey that impression of an older tree. Furthermore, a bleached white section of trunk is known as shari. Refer to page 172.
**Raffia: A cord for gardening made from a kind of soft (leaf) fiber.*

REPLANTING
(September)

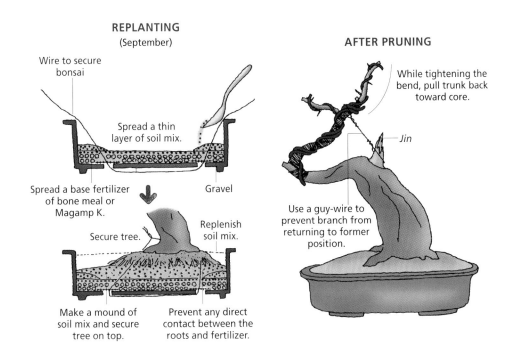

Wire to secure bonsai

Spread a thin layer of soil mix.

Spread a base fertilizer of bone meal or Magamp K.

Gravel

Secure tree.

Replenish soil mix.

Make a mound of soil mix and secure tree on top.

Prevent any direct contact between the roots and fertilizer.

AFTER PRUNING

While tightening the bend, pull trunk back toward core.

Jin

Use a guy-wire to prevent branch from returning to former position.

WIRING
(June)

Fix any bends with wire while the branch is still flexible.

Pluck.

Because adventitious buds from the branch base will become strong, pinch them off.

Shorten to here, keeping 2 to 3 leaves.

Where a bend was made during the growing season.

Part that was bent during the growth period.

PRUNING
Falling leaves (wintering)

HOW THE BONSAI APPEARS IN THE FUTURE
(June)

Flowers are blooming near the tips of new shoots.

Axillary twigs should be removed as soon as they are discovered.

If this section fattens, the flow of the bonsai will appear more natural.

Remove suckers* as soon as you discover them.

*Suckers: Adventitious shoots that emerge from tree root bases and tend to become long branches.

	Growth State	Transplanting	Sterilization	Shaping	Protection	Fertilizing	Watering	Propagating
January							1–2 times / week	Grafting
February	Dormancy period		Winter	Pruning	Protection room			
March								
April						Add fertilizer	2–3 times / day	Layering & Cutting
May	Growth period • Flowering (May–June)							
June				Wiring				
July	Growth period				Shading	Water & fertilizer	3–4 times / day	
August								
September								
October	Prime • Fruiting (October–November)					Add fertilizer	2–3 times / day	
November								Seeding
December					Winter			

SCHEDULE

71

Chinese Quince

JAPANESE NAME
Boke

ALTERNATIVE NAMES
Karaboke, Moke

SCIENTIFIC NAME
Chaenomeles japonica

CLASSIFICATION
Flowering quince, Rose (deciduous broad-leaved tree / shrub)

SYMBOLIC OF
Health, Enthusiasm

FLOWERING
March to May

Blossoming while the chill of winter remains, reminding us that spring is close. Flowers of red, pink, white and so on open before leaves appear. These flowers have five petals and diameters of around 1 or 2 inches (2 to 5 cm), and bloom in every season. Varieties with scarlet flowers are called *hi-boke*, and those with white flowers are called *shiro-boke*.

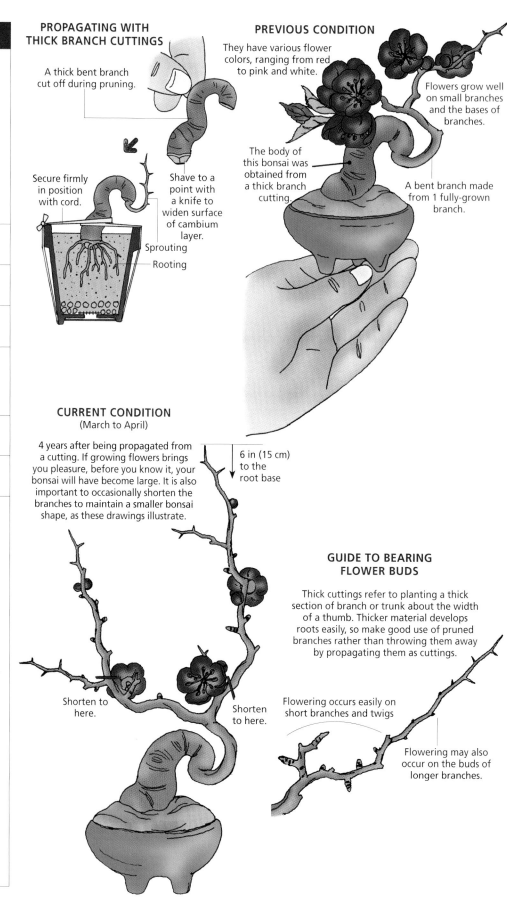

PROPAGATING WITH THICK BRANCH CUTTINGS

A thick bent branch cut off during pruning.

Shave to a point with a knife to widen surface of cambium layer.

Secure firmly in position with cord.

Sprouting

Rooting

PREVIOUS CONDITION

They have various flower colors, ranging from red to pink and white.

Flowers grow well on small branches and the bases of branches.

The body of this bonsai was obtained from a thick branch cutting.

A bent branch made from 1 fully-grown branch.

CURRENT CONDITION
(March to April)

4 years after being propagated from a cutting. If growing flowers brings you pleasure, before you know it, your bonsai will have become large. It is also important to occasionally shorten the branches to maintain a smaller bonsai shape, as these drawings illustrate.

6 in (15 cm) to the root base

Shorten to here.

Shorten to here.

GUIDE TO BEARING FLOWER BUDS

Thick cuttings refer to planting a thick section of branch or trunk about the width of a thumb. Thicker material develops roots easily, so make good use of pruned branches rather than throwing them away by propagating them as cuttings.

Flowering occurs easily on short branches and twigs

Flowering may also occur on the buds of longer branches.

REPLANTING

Remove all old soil and replant in clean soil mix.

Cut off small roots below this line.

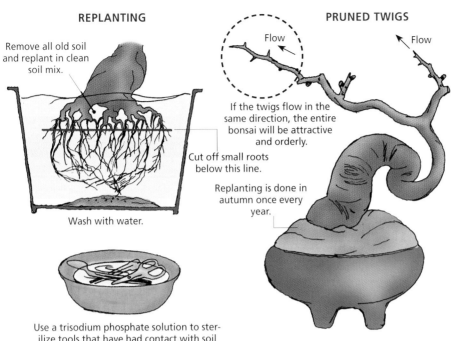

Wash with water.

Use a trisodium phosphate solution to sterilize tools that have had contact with soil with *agrobacterium tumefaciens*. Refer to page 50.

PRUNED TWIGS

Flow

Flow

If the twigs flow in the same direction, the entire bonsai will be attractive and orderly.

Replanting is done in autumn once every year.

TWIG SHAPING

Cut off long twigs, keeping 1 or 2 buds.

AFTER PRUNING

Keep bonsai positioned with wire during growing season.

1 year later

Cut off here, keeping 2 buds.

This will become a flower bud.

1 year later

Leave 2 buds and cut off the rest.

HOW THE BONSAI APPEARS AFTER FIVE YEARS

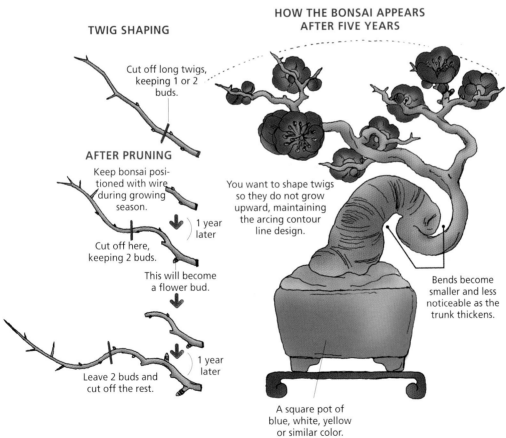

You want to shape twigs so they do not grow upward, maintaining the arcing contour line design.

Bends become smaller and less noticeable as the trunk thickens.

A square pot of blue, white, yellow or similar color.

SCHEDULE

Month	Growth State	Transplanting	Sterilization	Shaping	Protection	Fertilizing	Watering	Propagating
January							1-2 times / week	Cutting
February	Dormancy period		Winter	Pruning	Protection room		1-2 times / week	Cutting
March							1-2 times / week	Cutting
April				Pruning			1-2 times / week	
May	Growth period • Flowering (March-April)			Wiring		Add fertilizer	2-3 times / day	Layering & Cutting
June	Growth period					Add fertilizer	2-3 times / day	Layering & Cutting
July					Growing stage	Water & fertilizer	3-4 times / day	
August					Growing stage	Water & fertilizer	3-4 times / day	
September					Growing stage		2-3 times / day	
October	Prime					Add fertilizer	2-3 times / day	
November	Prime							
December							Winter	

Reeve's Spiraea

JAPANESE NAME
Kodemari

ALTERNATIVE NAMES
Bridalwreath spirea,
Double White May,
Cape May or May Bush

SCIENTIFIC NAME
Spiraea cantoniensis

CLASSIFICATION
Meadowsweets / Rose

SYMBOLIC OF
Elegance, Hard work

FLOWERING
April to May

Little, five-petal white flowers grow and bloom in hemispherical clusters. The source of the Japanese name is due to the way the shape and appearance of the clusters of flowers on some parts of the branches are similar to *temari*, the small handmade fabric and thread balls used for playing a traditional children's game. As it is a resilient tree, propagating with cuttings is recommended.

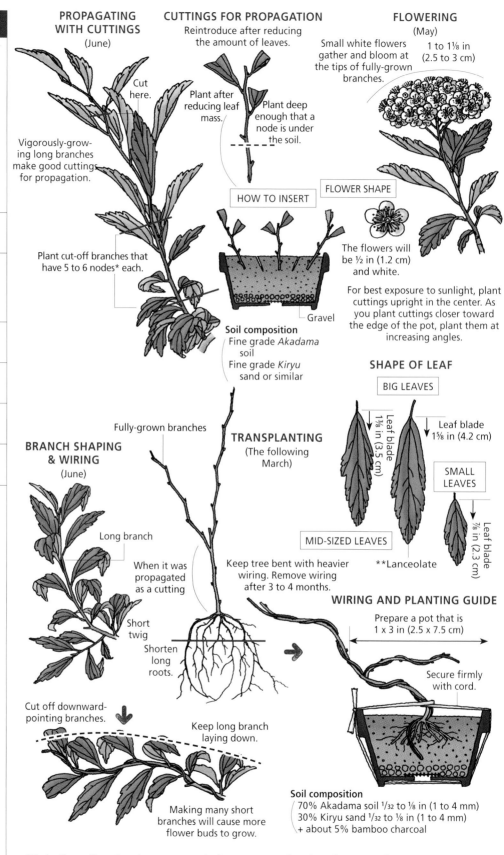

PROPAGATING WITH CUTTINGS
(June)

Cut here.

Vigorously-growing long branches make good cuttings for propagation.

Plant cut-off branches that have 5 to 6 nodes* each.

CUTTINGS FOR PROPAGATION
Reintroduce after reducing the amount of leaves.

Plant after reducing leaf mass.

Plant deep enough that a node is under the soil.

HOW TO INSERT

Gravel

Soil composition
Fine grade *Akadama* soil
Fine grade *Kiryu* sand or similar

FLOWERING
(May)
1 to 1⅛ in (2.5 to 3 cm)
Small white flowers gather and bloom at the tips of fully-grown branches.

FLOWER SHAPE

The flowers will be ½ in (1.2 cm) and white.

For best exposure to sunlight, plant cuttings upright in the center. As you plant cuttings closer toward the edge of the pot, plant them at increasing angles.

SHAPE OF LEAF

BIG LEAVES

Leaf blade 1⅜ in (3.5 cm)

Leaf blade 1⅝ in (4.2 cm)

SMALL LEAVES

Leaf blade ⅞ in (2.3 cm)

MID-SIZED LEAVES

**Lanceolate

BRANCH SHAPING & WIRING
(June)

Long branch

Short twig

Cut off downward-pointing branches.

Making many short branches will cause more flower buds to grow.

Fully-grown branches

When it was propagated as a cutting

Shorten long roots.

TRANSPLANTING
(The following March)

Keep tree bent with heavier wiring. Remove wiring after 3 to 4 months.

Keep long branch laying down.

WIRING AND PLANTING GUIDE

Prepare a pot that is 1 x 3 in (2.5 x 7.5 cm)

Secure firmly with cord.

Soil composition
70% Akadama soil 1/32 to ⅛ in (1 to 4 mm)
30% Kiryu sand 1/32 to ⅛ in (1 to 4 mm)
+ about 5% bamboo charcoal

*Node: The section where leaves are attached to a stem, or where branches extend from the trunk.
**Lanceolate: Shaped like a lozenge or spear tip. Refer to "Various Shapes of Leaves" on page 191.

PROPAGATING WITH CUTTINGS
(Dormant period)

Plant the branches you cut off during pruning.

To mitigate freezing topsoil, sprinkle gravel on top.

Plant cuttings so 2 to 3 buds are in the soil.

Cut into a V shape with a knife.

Develops roots nicely even during dormant period

Keeping more branch length means less energy for budding.

PRUNING

DORMANT PERIOD

Shorten to here but keep 2 to 3 top and side buds.

The point of shortening the long branches is to channel their energy into buds. Make good use of trimmed twigs by propagating them as cuttings.

A long branch that was laid down with wire in June.

Shorten to here.

Short twig

FOLLOWING YEAR

If there are any downward-pointing twigs, remove them.

Gradually, long branches will stop growing.

YEAR AFTER NEXT

Ensure that branches do not grow beyond this line.

Shorten to here if too long.

Short branches become flowering branches.

Flowering

PLANTING GUIDE

Securing wire

Soil composition
- 80% *Akadama* soil
- 20% *Kiryu* sand ¹/₃₂ to ⅛ in (1 to 4 mm)
- + 5% bamboo charcoal

Base fertilizer (bone meal or similar) under soil mix

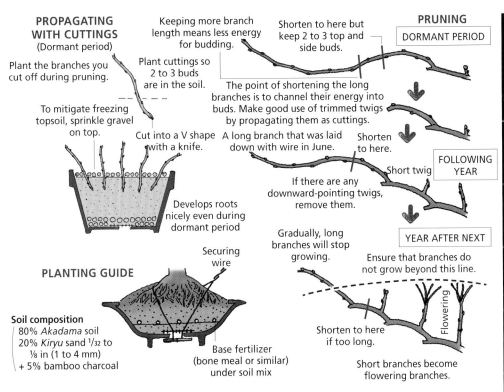

How bonsai appears after several years

Train the bonsai to form an arc shape, without any protruding twigs.

FLOWER VIEWING (May)

Spherical inflorescences* grow from short branch tips.

Surface of trunk is rough and has many small bumps.

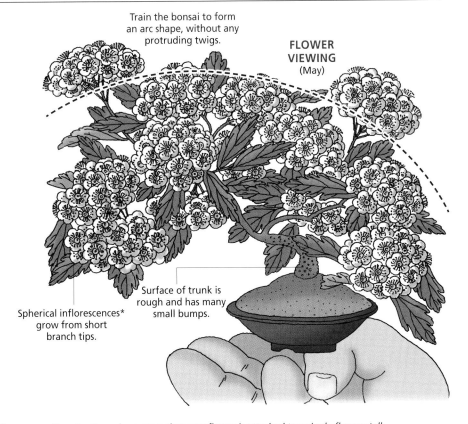

* Inflorescence: The situation where more than one flower is attached to a single flower stalk.
**Flower bud differentiation: After germinating, plants grow buds that become large leaves and stems, and eventually, for the purposes of propagation, via differentiation, some buds become flowers.

Growth State	Transplanting	Sterilization	Shaping	Protection	Fertilizing	Watering	Propagating
SCHEDULE							
January	Dormancy period	Winter	Pruning	Protection room		1–2 times / week	Split stock • Cutting
February							
March							
April						2–3 times / day	Layering & Cutting
May	Growth period • Flowering (April–May)		Pruning • Wiring		Add fertilizer		
June							
July			Growth period			3–4 times / day	
August				Shading	Water & fertilizer		
September							
October	Peak condition phase and flower bud differentiation** (October)				Add fertilizer	2–3 times / day	
November							
December		Winter					

Azalea
Rhododendron

JAPANESE NAME
Satsuki

ALTERNATIVE NAMES
Tsutsusi

SCIENTIFIC NAME
Rhododendron indicum

CLASSIFICATION
Azalea (evergreen
hardwood / shrub)

SYMBOLIC
Shyness

FLOWERING
May to June

Named after the
month of *satsuki* in
the Japanese lunar
calendar (roughly falling
between late May and
early July), when they
bloom. While azalea
flowers typically bloom
before their leaves
unfold, the small flowers
of *satsuki* open after
new shoots unfurl and
are a deep magenta.
Propagating with cut-
tings is recommended.

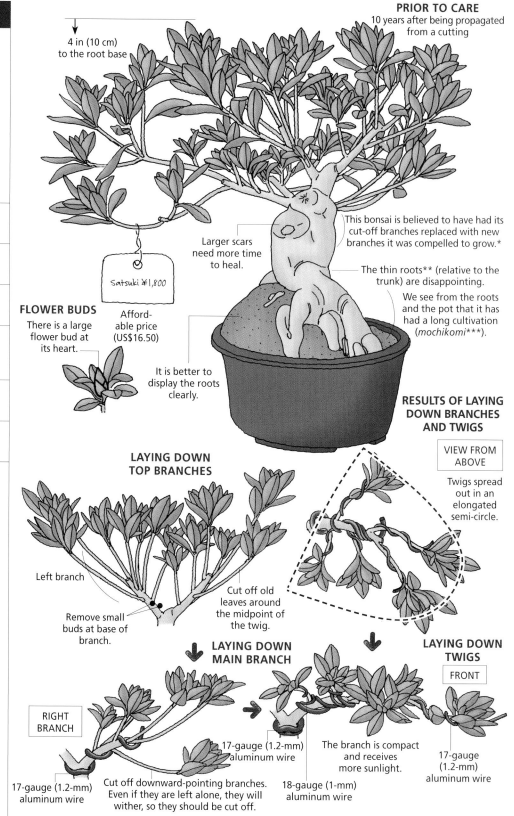

PRIOR TO CARE
10 years after being propagated
from a cutting

4 in (10 cm)
to the root base

This bonsai is believed to have had its
cut-off branches replaced with new
branches it was compelled to grow.*

Larger scars
need more time
to heal.

The thin roots** (relative to the
trunk) are disappointing.

We see from the roots
and the pot that it has
had a long cultivation
(mochikomi***).

Satsuki ¥1,800

FLOWER BUDS
There is a large
flower bud at
its heart.

Afford-
able price
(US$16.50)

It is better to
display the roots
clearly.

**RESULTS OF LAYING
DOWN BRANCHES
AND TWIGS**

VIEW FROM
ABOVE

Twigs spread
out in an
elongated
semi-circle.

**LAYING DOWN
TOP BRANCHES**

Left branch

Remove small
buds at base of
branch.

Cut off old
leaves around
the midpoint of
the twig.

**LAYING DOWN
MAIN BRANCH**

**LAYING DOWN
TWIGS**

FRONT

RIGHT
BRANCH

17-gauge (1.2-mm)
aluminum wire

The branch is compact
and receives
more sunlight.

17-gauge
(1.2-mm)
aluminum wire

17-gauge (1.2-mm)
aluminum wire

Cut off downward-pointing branches.
Even if they are left alone, they will
wither, so they should be cut off.

18-gauge (1-mm)
aluminum wire

*Compulsory growth: When a tree is forced to produce new branches from due to the condition of having no branches.
**Thin roots: When roots are extremely thin compared to the root base.
***Mochikomi: The length of time the bonsai has been cultivated, often meaning how old the bonsai appears
to be, but occasionally its actual physical age.

PRUNING AFTER *SATSUKI* HAS FLOWERED

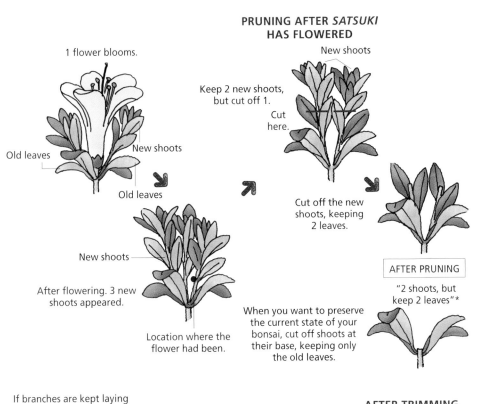

1 flower blooms.

Old leaves

New shoots

Old leaves

New shoots

After flowering. 3 new shoots appeared.

Location where the flower had been.

New shoots

Keep 2 new shoots, but cut off 1.

Cut here.

Cut off the new shoots, keeping 2 leaves.

When you want to preserve the current state of your bonsai, cut off shoots at their base, keeping only the old leaves.

AFTER PRUNING

"2 shoots, but keep 2 leaves"*

If branches are kept laying down horizontally, you can expect every branch to get better airflow and exposure to sunlight.

AFTER TRIMMING

Adjust twigs so entire bonsai forms an arc shape.

Lower branch

With 3 branches, you should keep 2 branches with good orientation. The remainder is an auxiliary branch.

IMPORTANT POINTS ABOUT PRUNING

Keep as many uncut branches as you can, and arrange to lay them down to make the best use of them.

Front view

SCHEMATIC OF LOWER TWIGS, VIEWED FROM ABOVE

(Leaves and wiring not shown)

"(Prune) two shoots, but keep two leaves": This is an expression related to satsuki *bonsai.*
To prune without harming the tree, beginners are reminded to keep two leaves when they cut off shoots.

SCHEDULE

Month	Growth State	Transplanting	Sterilization	Shaping	Protection	Fertilizing	Watering	Propagating
January							1–2 times / week	Cutting
February	Dormancy period	Winter		Pruning	Protection room			Cutting
March								
April						Add fertilizer	2–3 times / day	
May	Growth period • Flowering (May-June) • Sprout separating (July-August)							Layering • Cutting
June				Pruning • Wiring			Growth period	
July						Water & fertilizer	3–4 times / day	
August						Shading		
September								
October	Prime					Add fertilizer	2–3 times / day	
November								
December		Winter						

Stachyurus Praecox

JAPANESE NAME
Kibushi

ALTERNATIVE NAMES
Early *stachyurus*

SCIENTIFIC NAME
Stachyurus praecox

CLASSIFICATION
Stachyuraceae (deciduous broad-leaved tree / shrub)

SYMBOLIC OF
Meeting

FLOWERING
March to April

In early spring, before there are leaves, there are the male flowers, whose pale yellow florets hang down like beaded door curtains. A dioecious* tree, the female flowers are a lush green with four petals. Growing wild in the mountains of rural Japan, their flowers bloom in much the same the way as Japanese wisteria. The male tree is characterized by dense clusters of bright yellow flowers.

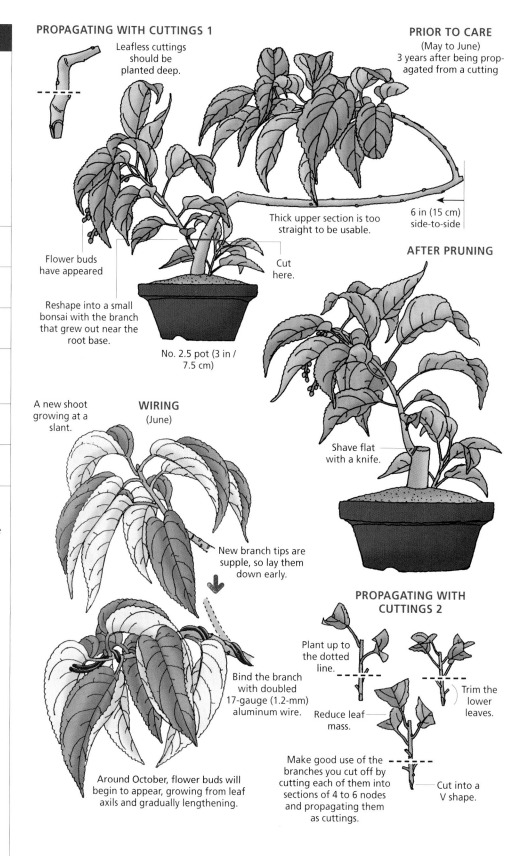

PROPAGATING WITH CUTTINGS 1

Leafless cuttings should be planted deep.

PRIOR TO CARE
(May to June)
3 years after being propagated from a cutting

Thick upper section is too straight to be usable.

6 in (15 cm) side-to-side

Flower buds have appeared

Cut here.

AFTER PRUNING

Reshape into a small bonsai with the branch that grew out near the root base.

No. 2.5 pot (3 in / 7.5 cm)

Shave flat with a knife.

A new shoot growing at a slant.

WIRING
(June)

New branch tips are supple, so lay them down early.

PROPAGATING WITH CUTTINGS 2

Plant up to the dotted line.

Trim the lower leaves.

Reduce leaf mass.

Bind the branch with doubled 17-gauge (1.2-mm) aluminum wire.

Around October, flower buds will begin to appear, growing from leaf axils and gradually lengthening.

Make good use of the branches you cut off by cutting each of them into sections of 4 to 6 nodes and propagating them as cuttings.

Cut into a V shape.

*Dioecious: Any type of plant where the male and female flowers are produced on different trees, dividing them into male and female trees. For example, ginkgo biloba, Ilex serrata and so on.

AFTER ROOT SHORTENING

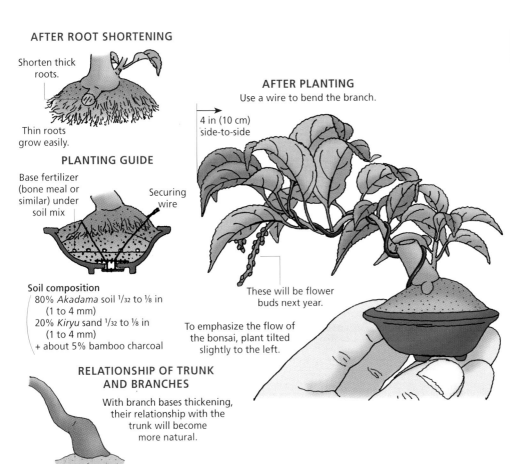

Shorten thick roots.

Thin roots grow easily.

PLANTING GUIDE

Base fertilizer (bone meal or similar) under soil mix

Securing wire

Soil composition
- 80% *Akadama* soil 1/32 to 1/8 in (1 to 4 mm)
- 20% *Kiryu* sand 1/32 to 1/8 in (1 to 4 mm)
- + about 5% bamboo charcoal

RELATIONSHIP OF TRUNK AND BRANCHES

With branch bases thickening, their relationship with the trunk will become more natural.

AFTER PLANTING

Use a wire to bend the branch.

4 in (10 cm) side-to-side

These will be flower buds next year.

To emphasize the flow of the bonsai, plant tilted slightly to the left.

How the bonsai appears after several years

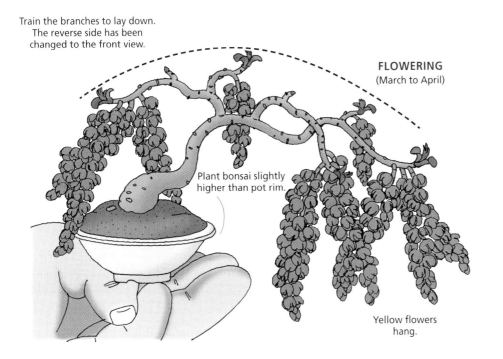

Train the branches to lay down. The reverse side has been changed to the front view.

FLOWERING
(March to April)

Plant bonsai slightly higher than pot rim.

Yellow flowers hang.

SCHEDULE

Month	Growth State	Transplanting	Shaping	Sterilization	Protection	Fertilizing	Watering	Propagating
January							1–2 times / week	Grafting
February	Dormancy period		Pruning	Winter	Protection room			Cutting
March								
April						Add fertilizer		
May	Growth period	Growth period	Wiring				2–3 times / day	Layering • Cutting
June	Growth period • Flowering (March–April)							
July						Water & fertilizer	3–4 times / day	
August					Shading			
September							2–3 times / day	
October						Add fertilizer		
November	Prime							
December							Winter	

79

Kousa Dogwood

JAPANESE NAME
Yamaboushi

ALTERNATIVE NAMES
Chinese dogwood, Korean dogwood and Japanese dogwood

SCIENTIFIC NAME
Cornus kousa

CLASSIFICATION
Dogwood (deciduous broad-leaved tree / *takagi*)

SYMBOLIC OF
Friendship

FLOWERING
June to July

With flowers clustered in the center section, the four white petal-shaped objects are petaloid bract* leaves at the base of the inflorescence. Many spherical pale yellow-green florets are attached in the center. Their durability is excellent, and they can be viewed for a long time. Propagation can be done with cuttings, seed-grown seedlings, air-layering and so on.

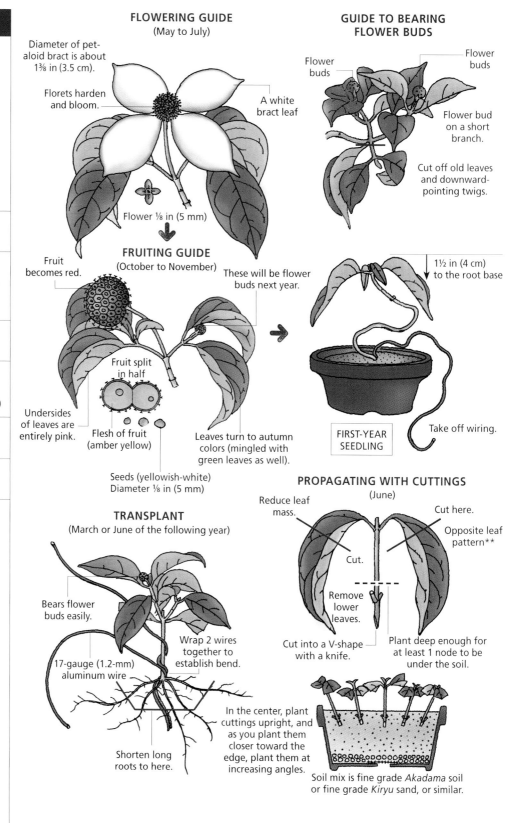

FLOWERING GUIDE
(May to July)

Diameter of petaloid bract is about 1⅜ in (3.5 cm).

Florets harden and bloom.

A white bract leaf

Flower ⅛ in (5 mm)

FRUITING GUIDE
(October to November)

Fruit becomes red.

These will be flower buds next year.

Fruit split in half

Undersides of leaves are entirely pink.

Flesh of fruit (amber yellow)

Leaves turn to autumn colors (mingled with green leaves as well).

Seeds (yellowish-white) Diameter ⅛ in (5 mm)

GUIDE TO BEARING FLOWER BUDS

Flower buds

Flower buds

Flower bud on a short branch.

Cut off old leaves and downward-pointing twigs.

1½ in (4 cm) to the root base

Take off wiring.

FIRST-YEAR SEEDLING

TRANSPLANT
(March or June of the following year)

Bears flower buds easily.

17-gauge (1.2-mm) aluminum wire

Wrap 2 wires together to establish bend.

Shorten long roots to here.

PROPAGATING WITH CUTTINGS
(June)

Reduce leaf mass.

Cut here.

Opposite leaf pattern**

Cut.

Remove lower leaves.

Cut into a V-shape with a knife.

Plant deep enough for at least 1 node to be under the soil.

In the center, plant cuttings upright, and as you plant them closer toward the edge, plant them at increasing angles.

Soil mix is fine grade *Akadama* soil or fine grade *Kiryu* sand, or similar.

*Petaloid bracts: Bracts are leaves that had concealed flower buds. Every bract that is a bract leaf which conceals the entire base of an inflorescence is a petaloid bract. The individual whole bracts are called petaloid bract leaves.

**Opposite leaf pattern: Refer to page 191, "Names of Leaf Parts and How They are Attached."

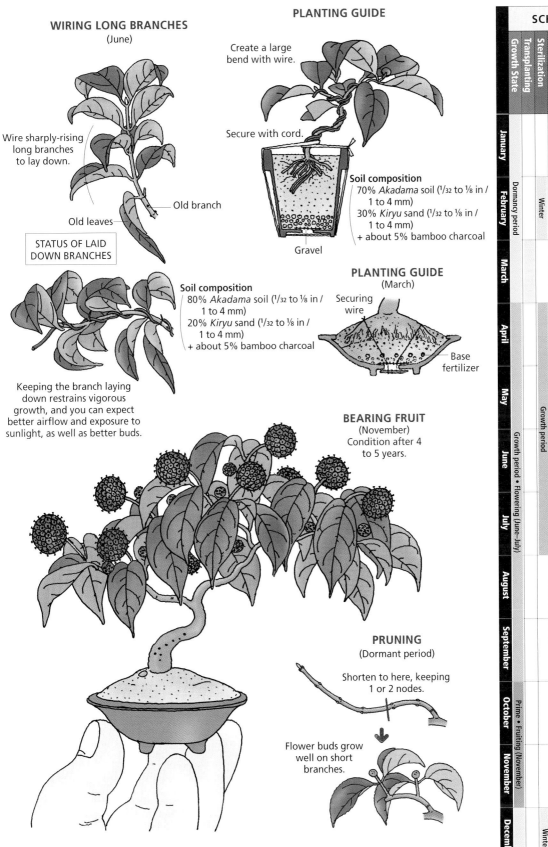

WIRING LONG BRANCHES
(June)

Wire sharply-rising long branches to lay down.

Old branch

Old leaves

STATUS OF LAID DOWN BRANCHES

Soil composition
80% *Akadama* soil (¹/₃₂ to ¹/₈ in / 1 to 4 mm)
20% *Kiryu* sand (¹/₃₂ to ¹/₈ in / 1 to 4 mm)
+ about 5% bamboo charcoal

Keeping the branch laying down restrains vigorous growth, and you can expect better airflow and exposure to sunlight, as well as better buds.

PLANTING GUIDE

Create a large bend with wire.

Secure with cord.

Soil composition
70% *Akadama* soil (¹/₃₂ to ¹/₈ in / 1 to 4 mm)
30% *Kiryu* sand (¹/₃₂ to ¹/₈ in / 1 to 4 mm)
+ about 5% bamboo charcoal

Gravel

PLANTING GUIDE
(March)

Securing wire

Base fertilizer

BEARING FRUIT
(November)
Condition after 4 to 5 years.

PRUNING
(Dormant period)

Shorten to here, keeping 1 or 2 nodes.

Flower buds grow well on short branches.

SCHEDULE

Growth State	Transplanting	Sterilization	Shaping	Protection	Fertilizing	Watering	Propagating
January	Dormancy period	Winter	Pruning	Protection room		1–2 times / week	Grafting
February							
March							Seedling
April	Growth period • Flowering (June–July)		Growth period		Add fertilizer	2–3 times / day	Cutting
May							
June			Wiring				
July					Water & fertilizer	3–4 times / day	
August					Shading		
September							
October	Prime • Fruiting (November)				Add fertilizer	2–3 times / day	Seedling
November							
December		Winter					

81

Pomegranate

JAPANESE NAME
Zakuro

ALTERNATIVE NAMES
n/a

SCIENTIFIC NAME
Punica granatum

CLASSIFICATION
Pomegranate (deciduous hardwood / *kotakagi*)

SYMBOLIC OF
Maturity, Grace, Nurturing

FLOWERING
June to July

On the tips of new branches, 6 roughly 2-in (5-cm) wrinkled cylindrical petals emerge from a cylindrical vermilion calyx.* As if crowding around them, the blooming petals surround countless yellow stamens in the center. Some cultivars are also double flowered. Propagating with cuttings is recommended.

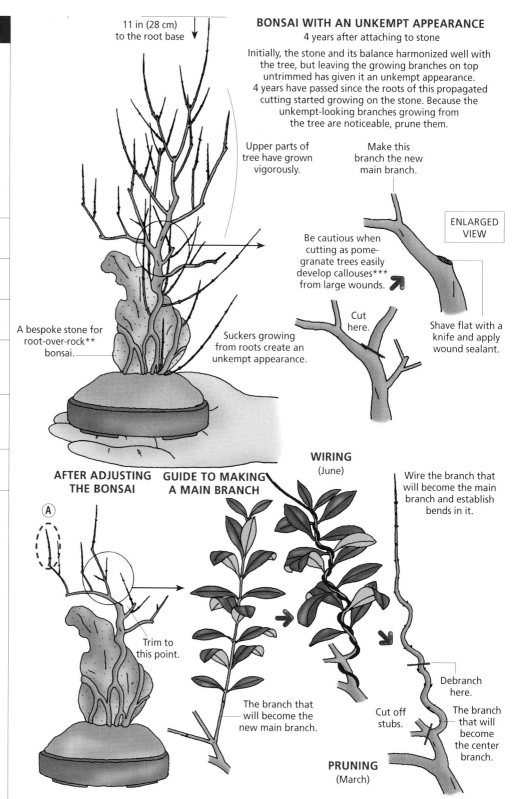

11 in (28 cm) to the root base

BONSAI WITH AN UNKEMPT APPEARANCE
4 years after attaching to stone

Initially, the stone and its balance harmonized well with the tree, but leaving the growing branches on top untrimmed has given it an unkempt appearance. 4 years have passed since the roots of this propagated cutting started growing on the stone. Because the unkempt-looking branches growing from the tree are noticeable, prune them.

Upper parts of tree have grown vigorously.

Make this branch the new main branch.

ENLARGED VIEW

Be cautious when cutting as pomegranate trees easily develop callouses*** from large wounds.

Cut here.

Shave flat with a knife and apply wound sealant.

A bespoke stone for root-over-rock** bonsai.

Suckers growing from roots create an unkempt appearance.

AFTER ADJUSTING THE BONSAI

A

Trim to this point.

GUIDE TO MAKING A MAIN BRANCH

WIRING
(June)

Wire the branch that will become the main branch and establish bends in it.

The branch that will become the new main branch.

Debranch here.

Cut off stubs.

The branch that will become the center branch.

PRUNING
(March)

*Calyx: The calyx is a modified leaf, and the outermost part of the flower. In cases where the calyx separates at the base of the flower, each of these is known as a sepal.

**Root-over-rock bonsai: One form of bonsai where the tree has been planted on a stone to enhance its feeling of natural rustic beauty.

***Callous: The phenomenon where the tree dries out at the place where a branch was cut off and the cells die. To prevent this from happening, do not cut deep.

BRANCH RESHAPING GUIDE

SECTION A
(from previous page)

Lengthen.

Develop this into a branch.

Allow base of branch to grow fuller.

WIRING
Lay down branch base.

A single flower will bear fruit.

Ovary

PRUNING
Shorten to here.

Debranch here.

PRUNING

LEAF TRIMMING
(June to July)

Trim the leaves on vigorous twigs.

Shorten to here.

Keep some of the bases of the leaves.

This can increase the number of leaves.

PINCHING OFF BUDS
(April to May)

Pinch off tip of shoot.

Keep 3 nodes or so.

UTILIZING SUCKERS
(ADVENTITIOUS SHOOTS)
(June to July)

Cut off here once sucker has taken root.

The stone

Whittle off the bark of the root and the sucker, and glue them together.

The root   Use sucker as a root.

SEEDLING
(November to December)
Planting harvested seeds.

Seed

The fruit is edible.

July

HOW BONSAI APPEARS
IN THE FUTURE

6 in (15 cm) to the root base

The hanging ripe red fruit is wonderful.

The roots will also thicken.

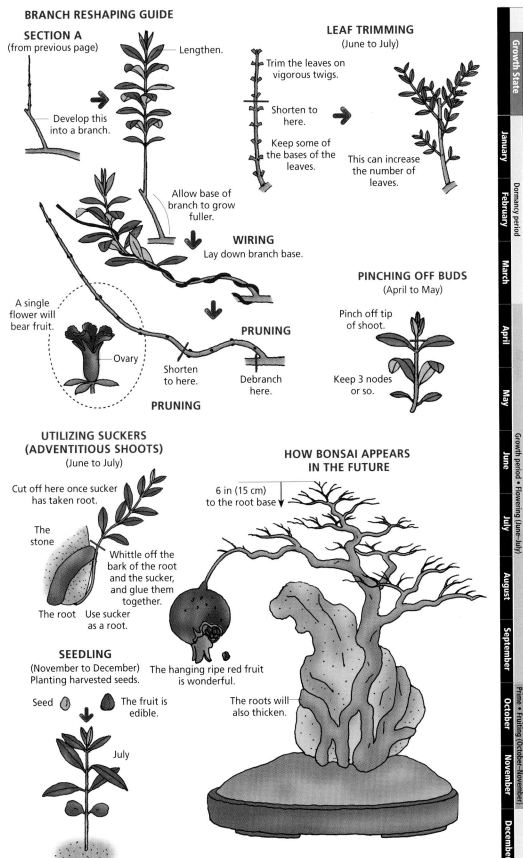

	SCHEDULE		
Growth State	Transplanting	Sterilization	Shaping	Protection	Fertilizing	Watering	Propagating

Month	Transplanting	Sterilization	Shaping	Protection	Fertilizing	Watering	Propagating
January	Dormancy period					1–2 times / week	Seedling •Cutting
February	Dormancy period	Winter	Pruning	Protection room		1–2 times / week	Seedling •Cutting
March							Seedling •Cutting
April					Add fertilizer	2–3 times / day	
May	Growth period		Growth period		Add fertilizer	2–3 times / day	
June	Growth period • Flowering (June–July)			Wiring		2–3 times / day	Cutting
July	Growth period • Flowering (June–July)				Water & fertilizer	3–4 times / day	Cutting
August	Growth period • Flowering (June–July)			Shading		3–4 times / day	Cutting
September	Prime • Fruiting (October–November)				Add fertilizer	2–3 times / day	
October	Prime • Fruiting (October–November)				Add fertilizer	2–3 times / day	Seedling
November	Prime • Fruiting (October–November)			Winter		2–3 times / day	Seedling
December		Winter					

83

Crepe-Myrtle

JAPANESE NAME
Hyakujikou

ALTERNATIVE NAMES
n/a

SCIENTIFIC NAME
Lagerstroemia indica

CLASSIFICATION
**Loosestrife family
(deciduous broad-leaved
tree / *kotakagi*)**

SYMBOLIC OF
Charm

FLOWERING
July to September

Between summer and
autumn, the six fan-
shaped purple petals of
this red 1⅛-in (3-cm)
flower open and bloom
for long periods. It
gets its name from the
smooth bark that even
monkeys, those dexter-
ous tree climbers, seem
to slide right off. Prop-
agating with cuttings is
recommended.

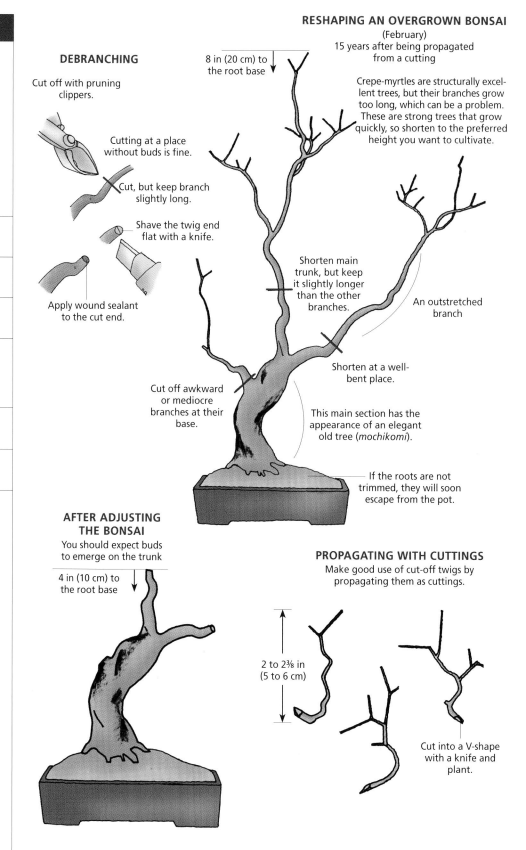

DEBRANCHING

Cut off with pruning
clippers.

Cutting at a place
without buds is fine.

Cut, but keep branch
slightly long.

Shave the twig end
flat with a knife.

Apply wound sealant
to the cut end.

Cut off awkward
or mediocre
branches at their
base.

RESHAPING AN OVERGROWN BONSAI
(February)
15 years after being propagated
from a cutting

8 in (20 cm) to
the root base

Crepe-myrtles are structurally excellent trees, but their branches grow
too long, which can be a problem.
These are strong trees that grow
quickly, so shorten to the preferred
height you want to cultivate.

Shorten main
trunk, but keep
it slightly longer
than the other
branches.

An outstretched
branch

Shorten at a well-
bent place.

This main section has the
appearance of an elegant
old tree (*mochikomi*).

If the roots are not
trimmed, they will soon
escape from the pot.

AFTER ADJUSTING
THE BONSAI
You should expect buds
to emerge on the trunk

4 in (10 cm) to
the root base

PROPAGATING WITH CUTTINGS
Make good use of cut-off twigs by
propagating them as cuttings.

2 to 2⅜ in
(5 to 6 cm)

Cut into a V-shape
with a knife and
plant.

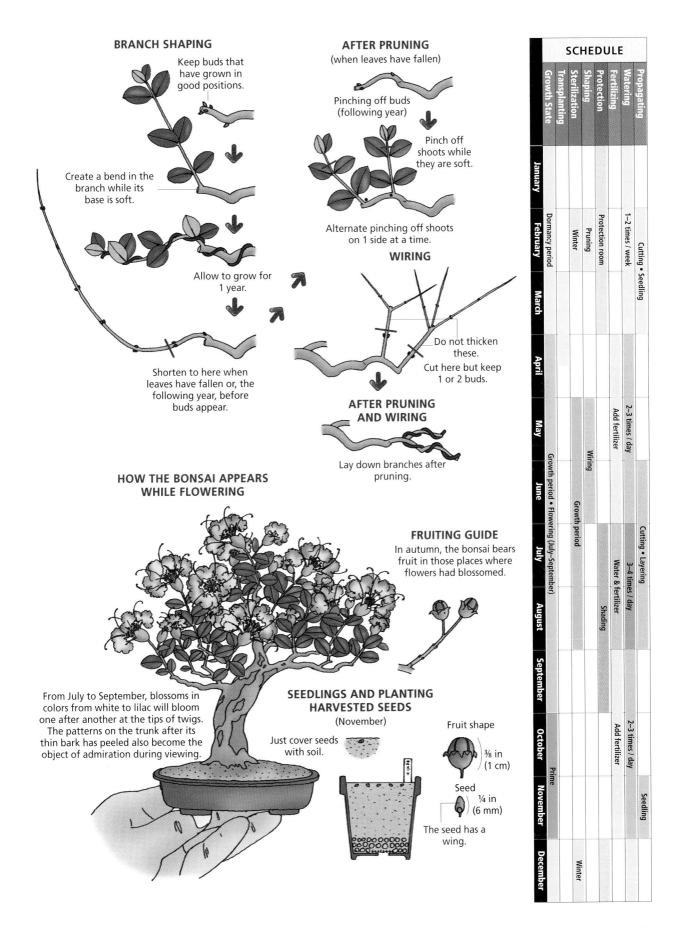

BRANCH SHAPING

Keep buds that have grown in good positions.

Create a bend in the branch while its base is soft.

Allow to grow for 1 year.

Shorten to here when leaves have fallen or, the following year, before buds appear.

AFTER PRUNING
(when leaves have fallen)

Pinching off buds (following year)

Pinch off shoots while they are soft.

Alternate pinching off shoots on 1 side at a time.

WIRING

Do not thicken these.

Cut here but keep 1 or 2 buds.

AFTER PRUNING AND WIRING

Lay down branches after pruning.

HOW THE BONSAI APPEARS WHILE FLOWERING

From July to September, blossoms in colors from white to lilac will bloom one after another at the tips of twigs. The patterns on the trunk after its thin bark has peeled also become the object of admiration during viewing.

FRUITING GUIDE

In autumn, the bonsai bears fruit in those places where flowers had blossomed.

SEEDLINGS AND PLANTING HARVESTED SEEDS
(November)

Just cover seeds with soil.

Fruit shape

⅜ in (1 cm)

Seed

¼ in (6 mm)

The seed has a wing.

SCHEDULE

Growth State	Transplanting	Sterilization	Shaping	Protection	Fertilizing	Watering	Propagating
January						1–2 times / week	Cutting • Seedling
February	Dormancy period	Winter	Pruning	Protection room			
March							
April					Add fertilizer	2–3 times / day	
May			Wiring				
June	Growth period • Flowering (July–September)		Growth period				Cutting • Layering
July					Water & fertilizer	3–4 times / day	
August					Shading		
September							
October					Add fertilizer	2–3 times / day	
November			Prime				Seedling
December		Winter					

Star Magnolia

JAPANESE NAME
Shidekobushi

ALTERNATIVE NAMES
Star magnolia

SCIENTIFIC NAME
Magnolia stellata

CLASSIFICATION
Magnoliaceae
(deciduous broad-leaved tree / shrub)

SYMBOLIC OF
Welcome, Friendship

FLOWERING
March to April

Fragrant flowers, of either white or a pale red, bloom before the leaves have opened. Characterized by large buds that open to reveal flowers of 12 or more 1½-in (4-cm) petals, these are worth viewing, even if just one flower blooms. Propagating with cuttings or from seed-grown seedlings is recommended. Air-layering is recommended if causing flowers to bloom quickly is desired.

PROPAGATING WITH CUTTINGS
(Dormant period)

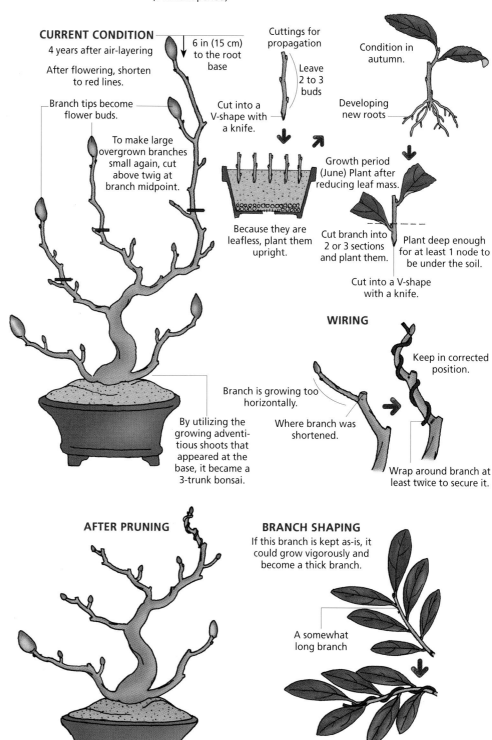

CURRENT CONDITION
4 years after air-layering

6 in (15 cm) to the root base

After flowering, shorten to red lines.

Branch tips become flower buds.

To make large overgrown branches small again, cut above twig at branch midpoint.

By utilizing the growing adventitious shoots that appeared at the base, it became a 3-trunk bonsai.

Cuttings for propagation

Leave 2 to 3 buds

Cut into a V-shape with a knife.

Because they are leafless, plant them upright.

Condition in autumn.

Developing new roots

Growth period (June) Plant after reducing leaf mass.

Cut branch into 2 or 3 sections and plant them.

Plant deep enough for at least 1 node to be under the soil.

Cut into a V-shape with a knife.

WIRING

Keep in corrected position.

Branch is growing too horizontally.

Where branch was shortened.

Wrap around branch at least twice to secure it.

AFTER PRUNING

To improve the tree by tightening its shape, shorten long overgrown branches to cause more twigs to appear near the bases of branches.

BRANCH SHAPING
If this branch is kept as-is, it could grow vigorously and become a thick branch.

A somewhat long branch

Wire and lay it down.

Cut off twig, keeping 2 or so buds.

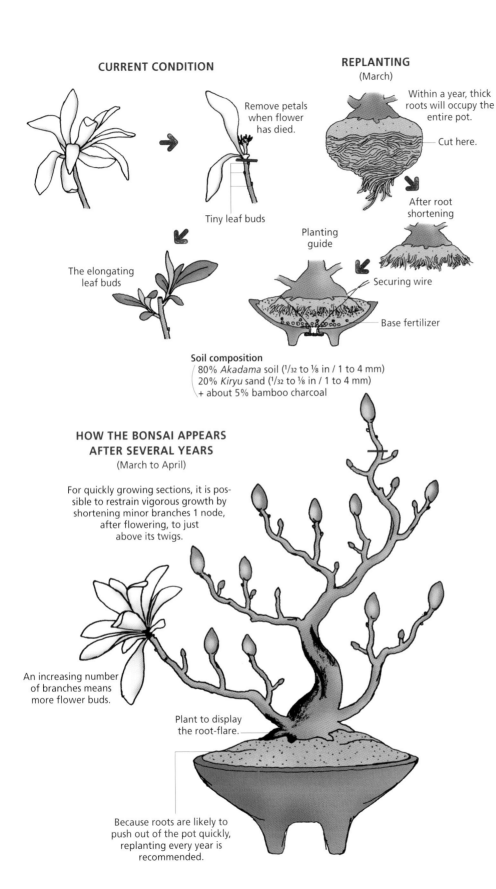

CURRENT CONDITION

Remove petals when flower has died.

Tiny leaf buds

The elongating leaf buds

REPLANTING
(March)

Within a year, thick roots will occupy the entire pot.

Cut here.

After root shortening

Planting guide

Securing wire

Base fertilizer

Soil composition
80% *Akadama* soil ($^1/_{32}$ to $^1/_8$ in / 1 to 4 mm)
20% *Kiryu* sand ($^1/_{32}$ to $^1/_8$ in / 1 to 4 mm)
+ about 5% bamboo charcoal

HOW THE BONSAI APPEARS
AFTER SEVERAL YEARS
(March to April)

For quickly growing sections, it is possible to restrain vigorous growth by shortening minor branches 1 node, after flowering, to just above its twigs.

An increasing number of branches means more flower buds.

Plant to display the root-flare.

Because roots are likely to push out of the pot quickly, replanting every year is recommended.

SCHEDULE									
Growth State	Transplanting	Sterilization	Protection	Shaping	Fertilizing	Watering	Propagating		
January	Dormancy period	Winter	Protection room	Pruning		1–2 times / week	Grafting	Seedling	
February									
March						Seedling			
April									
May	Growth period • Flowering (March–April) • Sprout separating (July–August)			Wiring	Add fertilizer	2–3 times / day	Cutting • Layering		
June				Growth period					
July					Water & fertilizer	3–4 times / day			
August				Shading					
September									
October					Add fertilizer	2–3 times / day			
November			Prime					Seedling	
December			Winter						

87

Lilac

JAPANESE NAME
Murasakihashidoi

ALTERNATIVE NAMES
Hanahashidoi, Rira

ACADEMIC NAME
Syringa vulgaris

CATEGORY
Oleaceae (deciduous hardwood / shrub)

SYMBOLIC OF
New love

BLOOM
April to May

Spike-shaped flowers of purple and white are attached in large numbers to the tips of branches. Lilacs have a strong fragrance, so they are also used as raw material for perfumes. May flower for long periods due to their high tolerance to cold. Propagating is done with cuttings. Cutting off two to three nodes from shoots during rainy seasons is important to reduce leaf volumes.

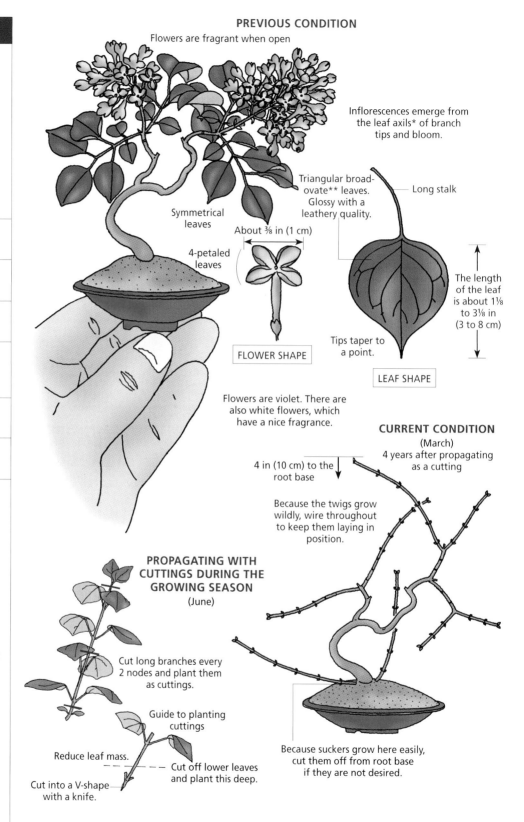

PREVIOUS CONDITION

Flowers are fragrant when open

Inflorescences emerge from the leaf axils* of branch tips and bloom.

Triangular broad-ovate** leaves. Glossy with a leathery quality.

Long stalk

Symmetrical leaves

About ⅜ in (1 cm)

4-petaled leaves

The length of the leaf is about 1⅛ to 3⅛ in (3 to 8 cm)

FLOWER SHAPE

Tips taper to a point.

LEAF SHAPE

Flowers are violet. There are also white flowers, which have a nice fragrance.

CURRENT CONDITION
(March)
4 years after propagating as a cutting

4 in (10 cm) to the root base

Because the twigs grow wildly, wire throughout to keep them laying in position.

PROPAGATING WITH CUTTINGS DURING THE GROWING SEASON
(June)

Cut long branches every 2 nodes and plant them as cuttings.

Guide to planting cuttings

Reduce leaf mass.

Cut into a V-shape with a knife.

Cut off lower leaves and plant this deep.

Because suckers grow here easily, cut them off from root base if they are not desired.

*Leaf axil: The base area where a leaf stalk is attached to a branch. The part of this junction where leaves grew that is attached to the stalk, with buds that form here being called axillary buds.
**Triangular broad-ovate: Refer to page 191, "Names of Leaf Parts and How They are Attached."

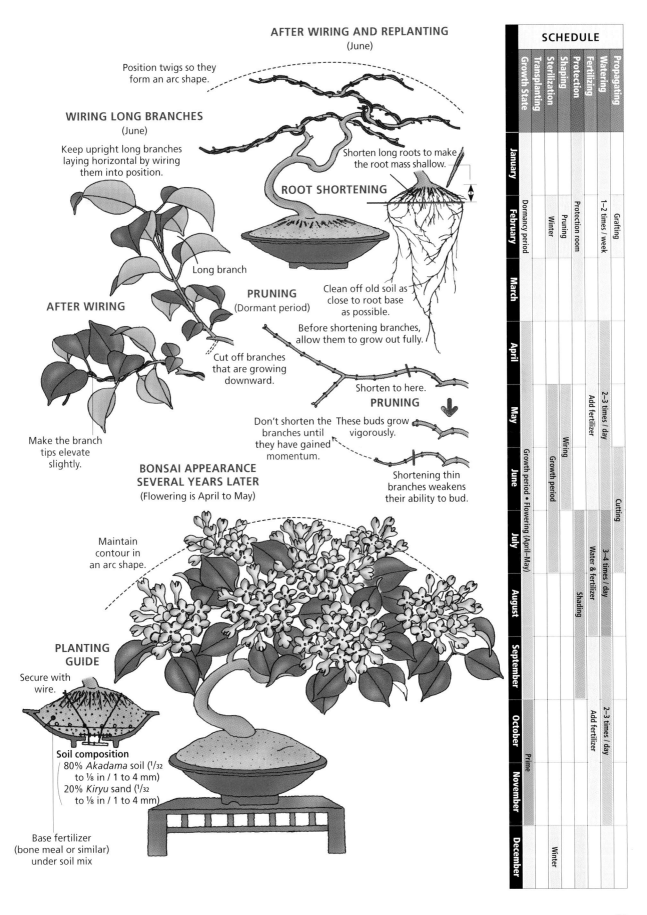

Cape Jasmine

JAPANESE NAME
Kuchinashi

ALTERNATIVE NAMES
n/a

SCIENTIFIC NAME
Gardenia jasminoides

CLASSIFICATION
Rubiaceae (evergreen broad–leaved tree / shrub)

SYMBOLIC OF
Elegance

BEARING FRUIT
November to December

In June and July, white flowers bloom and release a sweet fragrance. The flowers have a velvety texture and soon turn a pale yellow. The leaves are glossy. They were probably named *kuchinashi* ("no mouth") in Japanese due to the way their fruit do not open, even when they are ripe. Their tolerance of the cold is poor, and propagating using cuttings, seed-grown seedlings, or through air-layering is possible.

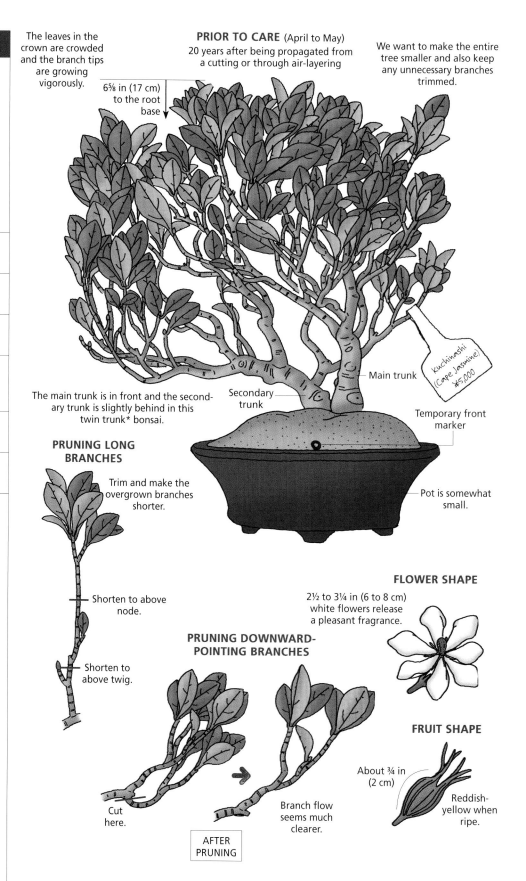

The leaves in the crown are crowded and the branch tips are growing vigorously.

PRIOR TO CARE (April to May)
20 years after being propagated from a cutting or through air-layering

We want to make the entire tree smaller and also keep any unnecessary branches trimmed.

6⅝ in (17 cm) to the root base

The main trunk is in front and the secondary trunk is slightly behind in this twin trunk* bonsai.

Main trunk

Secondary trunk

Kuchinashi (Cape Jasmine) ¥5,000

Temporary front marker

Pot is somewhat small.

PRUNING LONG BRANCHES

Trim and make the overgrown branches shorter.

Shorten to above node.

Shorten to above twig.

PRUNING DOWNWARD-POINTING BRANCHES

Cut here.

Branch flow seems much clearer.

AFTER PRUNING

FLOWER SHAPE

2½ to 3¼ in (6 to 8 cm) white flowers release a pleasant fragrance.

FRUIT SHAPE

About ¾ in (2 cm)

Reddish-yellow when ripe.

*Twin trunk: Refer to page 12, "Basic Tree Forms."

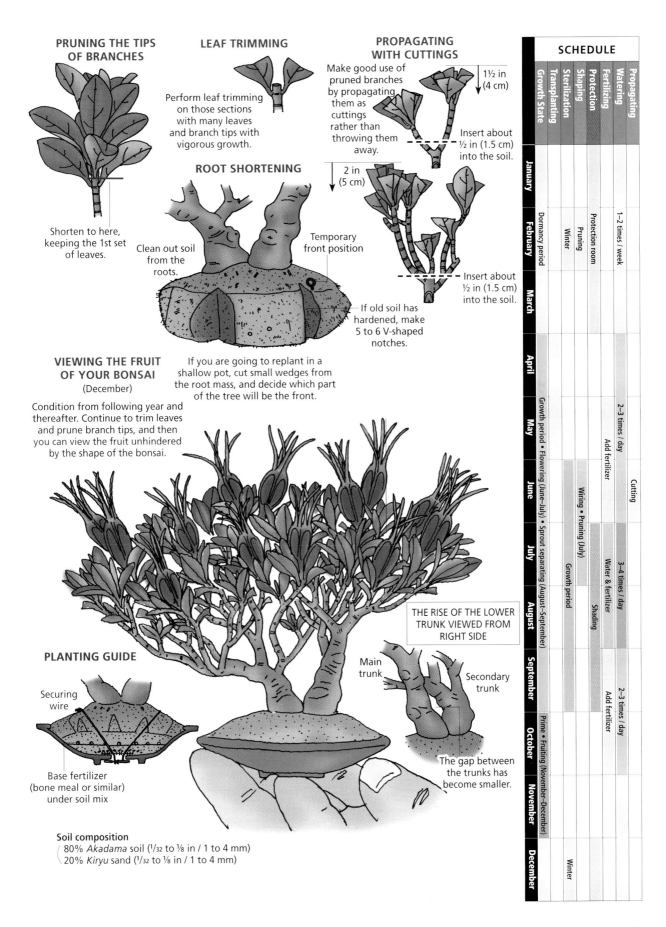

PRUNING THE TIPS OF BRANCHES

Shorten to here, keeping the 1st set of leaves.

LEAF TRIMMING

Perform leaf trimming on those sections with many leaves and branch tips with vigorous growth.

PROPAGATING WITH CUTTINGS

Make good use of pruned branches by propagating them as cuttings rather than throwing them away.

1½ in (4 cm)

Insert about ½ in (1.5 cm) into the soil.

2 in (5 cm)

Insert about ½ in (1.5 cm) into the soil.

ROOT SHORTENING

Clean out soil from the roots.

Temporary front position

If old soil has hardened, make 5 to 6 V-shaped notches.

If you are going to replant in a shallow pot, cut small wedges from the root mass, and decide which part of the tree will be the front.

VIEWING THE FRUIT OF YOUR BONSAI
(December)

Condition from following year and thereafter. Continue to trim leaves and prune branch tips, and then you can view the fruit unhindered by the shape of the bonsai.

PLANTING GUIDE

Securing wire

Base fertilizer (bone meal or similar) under soil mix

Soil composition
80% Akadama soil (¹/₃₂ to ⅛ in / 1 to 4 mm)
20% Kiryu sand (¹/₃₂ to ⅛ in / 1 to 4 mm)

THE RISE OF THE LOWER TRUNK VIEWED FROM RIGHT SIDE

Main trunk

Secondary trunk

The gap between the trunks has become smaller.

SCHEDULE

Growth State	Transplanting	Sterilization	Shaping	Protection	Fertilizing	Watering	Propagating
January	Dormancy period	Winter	Pruning	Protection room		1–2 times / week	
February							
March							
April	Growth period • Flowering (June–July) • Sprout separating (August–September)		Wiring • Pruning (July)		Add fertilizer	2–3 times / day	Cutting
May							
June							
July			Growth period	Shading	Water & fertilizer	3–4 times / day	
August							
September					Add fertilizer	2–3 times / day	
October	Prime • Fruiting (November–December)						
November							
December						Winter	

93

Linden Arrowwood

JAPANESE NAME
Kyomei, gamazumi

ALTERNATIVE NAMES
Linden viburnum

SCIENTIFIC NAME
Viburnum dilatatum

CLASSIFICATION
Scaffol daceae (deciduous broad-leaved tree / shrub)

SYMBOLIC OF
Union

BEARING FRUIT
October to November

Flower buds grow on lateral shoots* and the tips of new shoots. The following spring, the buds sprout**, new branches grow and at their tips, the buds flower and bear fruit. Their white flowers bloom through May and June. Most noteworthy is when it bears clusters of ruby-colored fruit. The fruit are flat ovals, with a lustrous appearance.
  Propagating with cuttings or through air-layering is recommended.

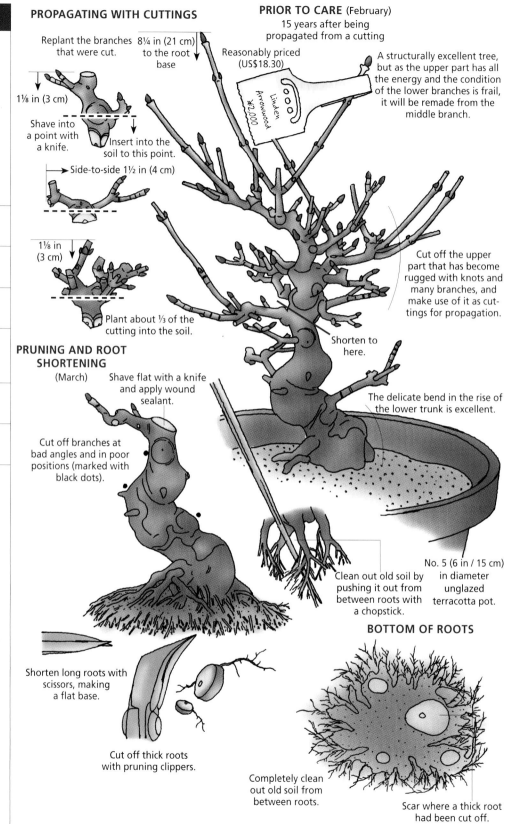

PROPAGATING WITH CUTTINGS

Replant the branches that were cut. 8¼ in (21 cm) to the root base

1⅛ in (3 cm)

Shave into a point with a knife.

Insert into the soil to this point.

Side-to-side 1½ in (4 cm)

1⅛ in (3 cm)

Plant about ⅓ of the cutting into the soil.

PRIOR TO CARE (February)
15 years after being propagated from a cutting

Reasonably priced (US$18.30)

Linden Arrowwood ¥2,000

A structurally excellent tree, but as the upper part has all the energy and the condition of the lower branches is frail, it will be remade from the middle branch.

Cut off the upper part that has become rugged with knots and many branches, and make use of it as cuttings for propagation.

Shorten to here.

The delicate bend in the rise of the lower trunk is excellent.

Clean out old soil by pushing it out from between roots with a chopstick.

No. 5 (6 in / 15 cm) in diameter unglazed terracotta pot.

PRUNING AND ROOT SHORTENING
(March)

Shave flat with a knife and apply wound sealant.

Cut off branches at bad angles and in poor positions (marked with black dots).

Shorten long roots with scissors, making a flat base.

Cut off thick roots with pruning clippers.

BOTTOM OF ROOTS

Completely clean out old soil from between roots.

Scar where a thick root had been cut off.

*Lateral shoots: When there is a bud at the base of a leaf ("lateral" meaning "to / at the side").
 Also known as an axillary bud. Buds at the tip of a branch are known as apical buds.
**Sprouting: When newly grown buds first open their leaves. Also known as germination.

PLANTING GUIDE

Position tree roots on the mound of soil mix.

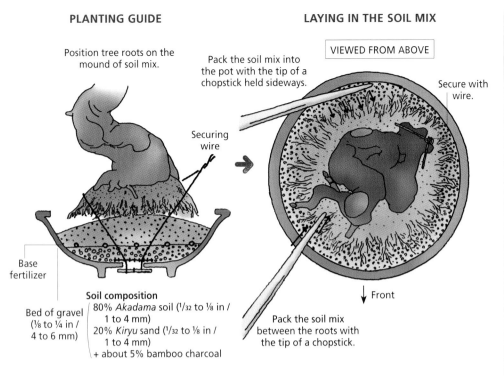

Securing wire

Base fertilizer

Bed of gravel (⅛ to ¼ in / 4 to 6 mm)

Soil composition
80% *Akadama* soil (¹/₃₂ to ⅛ in / 1 to 4 mm)
20% *Kiryu* sand (¹/₃₂ to ⅛ in / 1 to 4 mm)
+ about 5% bamboo charcoal

LAYING IN THE SOIL MIX

Pack the soil mix into the pot with the tip of a chopstick held sideways.

VIEWED FROM ABOVE

Secure with wire.

↓ Front

Pack the soil mix between the roots with the tip of a chopstick.

FLOWERING
(Flowers May to June)

White florets cluster and bloom on branch tips.

AFTER REPLANTING

(AS VIEWED FROM FRONT)

2⅜ in (6 cm) to the root base

Tamp and make the soil mix surface uniformly level using the handle of a pair of tweezers.

Tamping down the soil mix with the tip of your thumb is also fine.

FRUIT
(September to November)

Autumn leaves will turn red.

Accompanied by red ripened fruit

With its bent trunk and good taper*, you can create an excellent sloping trunk.

Another view of the handle of a pair of tweezers.

No. 3 (3½-in / 9-cm diameter) glazed pot

Taper: A main trunk is said to have "good taper" when it gradually narrows from the base upward. Because a bonsai with good taper gives the impression of a large tree, it is not off-base to say that creating a bonsai with excellent taper is the foundation of bonsai.

SCHEDULE

Growth State	Month	Propagating	Watering	Fertilizing	Protection	Shaping	Sterilization	Transplanting	Growth State
	January		1–2 times / week		Protection room				
Dormancy period	February	Seedling • Cutting				Pruning / Winter	Winter		
	March								
	April		2–3 times / day	Add fertilizer					
Growth period • Flowering (June–July) • Sprout separating (July–August)	May	Layering • Cutting				Wiring			Growth period
	June								
	July		3–4 times / day	Water & fertilizer	Shading				
	August								
	September								
Prime • Fruiting (October–November)	October		2–3 times / day	Add fertilizer					
	November								
	December						Winter		

Oriental Bittersweet

JAPANESE NAME
Shiruumemodoki

ALTERNATIVE NAMES
n/a

SCIENTIFIC NAME
Celastrus orbiculatus

CLASSIFICATION
Euphoridae (deciduous hardwood / shrub)

SYMBOLIC OF
Great talent

BEARING FRUIT
September to November

In May and June, inconspicuous flowers bloom (during cross-pollination season). From November to December, the yellow fruit split to reveal bright red seeds. Because they reproduce dioeciously, in order to bear fruit, you will need to grow both male and female trees.

This bonsai has a robust ability to root, so propagating by grafting or by planting cuttings are easy methods.

PRIOR TO CARE (October)
5 years after air-layering

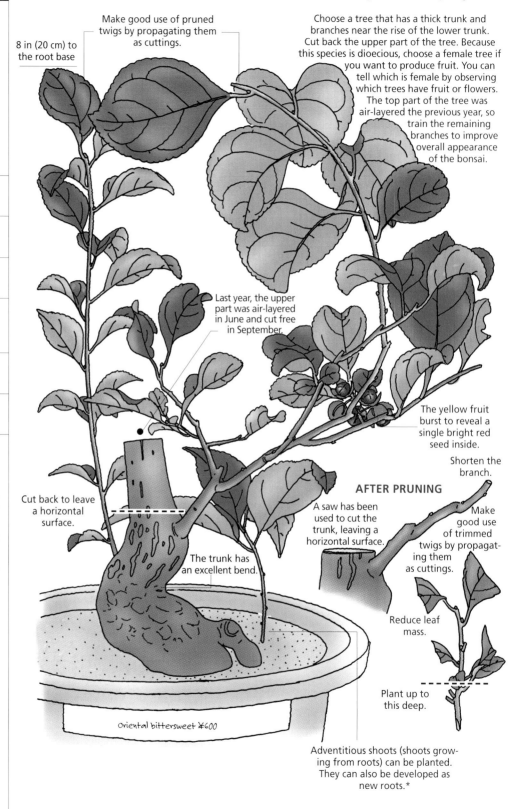

Make good use of pruned twigs by propagating them as cuttings.

8 in (20 cm) to the root base

Choose a tree that has a thick trunk and branches near the rise of the lower trunk. Cut back the upper part of the tree. Because this species is dioecious, choose a female tree if you want to produce fruit. You can tell which is female by observing which trees have fruit or flowers. The top part of the tree was air-layered the previous year, so train the remaining branches to improve overall appearance of the bonsai.

Last year, the upper part was air-layered in June and cut free in September.

The yellow fruit burst to reveal a single bright red seed inside.

Shorten the branch.

AFTER PRUNING

A saw has been used to cut the trunk, leaving a horizontal surface.

Make good use of trimmed twigs by propagating them as cuttings.

Cut back to leave a horizontal surface.

The trunk has an excellent bend.

Reduce leaf mass.

Plant up to this deep.

Oriental bittersweet ¥600

Adventitious shoots (shoots growing from roots) can be planted. They can also be developed as new roots.*

*To develop adventitious shoots as new roots, refer to page 18.

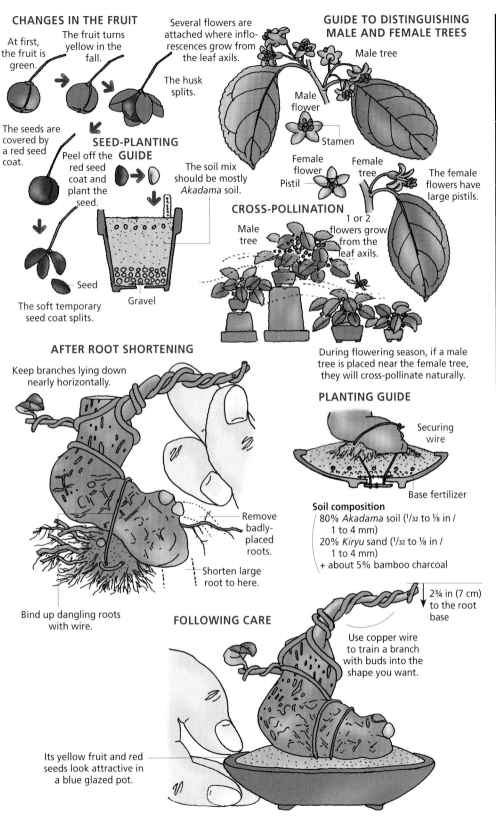

CHANGES IN THE FRUIT

At first, the fruit is green.

The fruit turns yellow in the fall.

The husk splits.

Several flowers are attached where inflorescences grow from the leaf axils.

The seeds are covered by a red seed coat.

SEED-PLANTING GUIDE

Peel off the red seed coat and plant the seed.

The soil mix should be mostly *Akadama* soil.

Seed

Gravel

The soft temporary seed coat splits.

GUIDE TO DISTINGUISHING MALE AND FEMALE TREES

Male tree

Male flower

Stamen

Female flower

Pistil

Female tree

The female flowers have large pistils.

CROSS-POLLINATION

Male tree

1 or 2 flowers grow from the leaf axils.

During flowering season, if a male tree is placed near the female tree, they will cross-pollinate naturally.

AFTER ROOT SHORTENING

Keep branches lying down nearly horizontally.

Remove badly-placed roots.

Shorten large root to here.

Bind up dangling roots with wire.

PLANTING GUIDE

Securing wire

Base fertilizer

Soil composition
80% *Akadama* soil (1/32 to 1/8 in / 1 to 4 mm)
20% *Kiryu* sand (1/32 to 1/8 in / 1 to 4 mm)
+ about 5% bamboo charcoal

FOLLOWING CARE

2¾ in (7 cm) to the root base

Use copper wire to train a branch with buds into the shape you want.

Its yellow fruit and red seeds look attractive in a blue glazed pot.

SCHEDULE

	Growth State	Transplanting	Sterilization	Shaping	Protection	Fertilizing	Watering	Propagating
January	Dormancy period						1–2 times / week	Seedling • Roots insertion • Cutting
February			Winter	Pruning	Protection room			
March								
April	Growth period • Flowering (May–June)							Layering • Cutting
May						Add fertilizer	2–3 times / day	
June				Wiring				
July	Growth period					Water & fertilizer	3–4 times / day	
August				Shading				
September	Prime • Fruiting (October–November)							
October						Add fertilizer	2–3 times / day	
November								
December			Winter					

Crabapple

JAPANESE NAME
Himeringo

ALTERNATIVE NAMES
n/a

SCIENTIFIC NAME
Malus prunifolia

CLASSIFICATION
Rosaceae (deciduous broadleaf tree / macrophanerophyte)

SYMBOLIC OF
Temptation

BEARING FRUIT
October to November

With white flowers blooming in spring, and ¾ to 1⅛-in (2 to 3-cm) fruit ripening and slowly turning a deep red in autumn, this bonsai can be viewed for a long period of time. Because it is dioecious*, furnish bonsai with pollen from another crabapple tree or another apple variety during flowering season to enable it to bear fruit. Grafting or seed-grown seedlings are recommended for propagation.

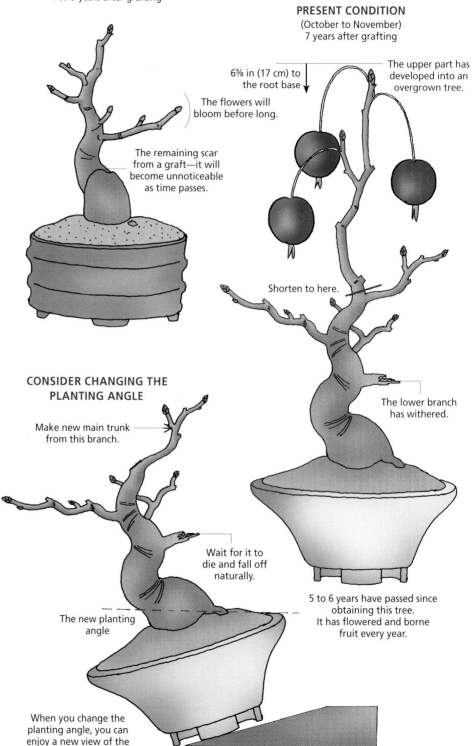

CONDITION WHEN THE BONSAI WAS FIRST ACQUIRED
(April)
4 to 5 years after grafting

The flowers will bloom before long.

The remaining scar from a graft—it will become unnoticeable as time passes.

PRESENT CONDITION
(October to November)
7 years after grafting

6⅝ in (17 cm) to the root base

The upper part has developed into an overgrown tree.

Shorten to here.

The lower branch has withered.

CONSIDER CHANGING THE PLANTING ANGLE

Make new main trunk from this branch.

Wait for it to die and fall off naturally.

The new planting angle

5 to 6 years have passed since obtaining this tree. It has flowered and borne fruit every year.

When you change the planting angle, you can enjoy a new view of the bonsai.

*Dioecious: When a tree cannot bear fruit through self-pollination. Even if self-pollination occurs, it does not result in fertilization, and successfully bearing fruit is difficult. Fertilization with the pollen from another tree or a different variety of tree is required.

CROSS-POLLINATING
(April to May)

Furnish with pollen from a *Malus halliana* flower to cross-pollinate.

Place on pistil.

Flower buds opening on short branches.

ROOT SHORTENING
(Autumn or spring)

Shorten long, over-grown roots.

PRUNING
(Dormant period)

Because the long branches have no flower buds, shorten to here.

Long branch

Flow

Flower buds grow on short branches.

Cut off out-stretched branches to transform the flow of your bonsai.

PLANTING GUIDE

Display a tugging root* by revealing root-flare.

Securing wire

Plant the tree set on its side.

Planing angle up until now.

HOW THE BONSAI APPEARS AFTER SEVERAL YEARS

5⅛ in (13 cm) to the root base

Turned to the left, the flow has been altered.

These will be flower buds next year.

It becomes a tugging root.

Just be sure to display the root base.**

AFTER PLANTING

It has a solid rise of the lower trunk and its display of stability has improved.

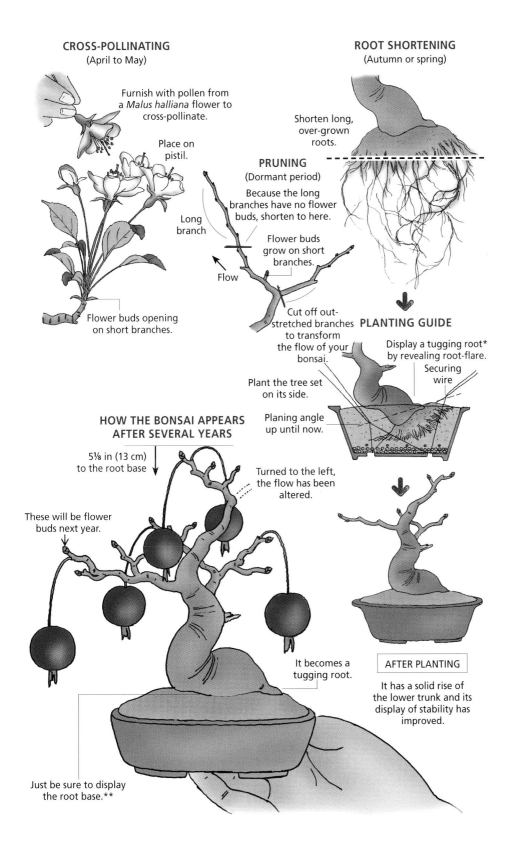

*Tugging root: Root-flare that appears to slope away from the main trunk. Having root-flare to support a powerful trunk is excellent.

**Root base: One type of presentation of the surface-visible roots of trees. The situation where roots that have formed as one root mass, or are about to form into one root mass.

SCHEDULE

Month	Propagating	Watering	Fertilizing	Protection	Shaping	Sterilization	Transplanting	Growth State
January	Grafting	1–2 times / week		Protection room				Dormancy period
February	Seedling	1–2 times / week		Protection room	Winter / Pruning			Dormancy period
March	Seedling				Pruning			
April		2–3 times / day	Add fertilizer				Growth period	Growth period • Flowering (April–May) • Sprout separating (July–August)
May	Layering	2–3 times / day	Add fertilizer				Growth period	Growth period • Flowering (April–May) • Sprout separating (July–August)
June	Layering	2–3 times / day			Wiring			Growth period • Flowering (April–May) • Sprout separating (July–August)
July	Layering	3–4 times / day	Water & fertilizer		Wiring			Growth period • Flowering (April–May) • Sprout separating (July–August)
August		3–4 times / day	Water & fertilizer		Shading			Growth period • Flowering (April–May) • Sprout separating (July–August)
September								Prime • Fruits form (October–November)
October		2–3 times / day	Add fertilizer					Prime • Fruits form (October–November)
November	Seedling	2–3 times / day	Add fertilizer					Prime • Fruits form (October–November)
December							Winter	

Hamilton's Spindle-tree

JAPANESE NAME
Mayumi

ALTERNATIVE NAME
Himalayan spindle

SCIENTIFIC NAME
Euonymus hamiltonianus

CLASSIFICATION
Celastraceae family
(deciduous broadleaf tree /
macrophanerophyte)

SYMBOLIC OF
Charm

BEARING FRUIT
October to November

The origin of the Japanese name refers to the way that this tree was once used to construct bows for archers. Blooming through April and May, this tree bears fruit in the autumn, which ripen to a pale crimson color and split into four quadrants, allowing red seeds to peek out.

Being dioecious, a male tree is required for cross-pollination. As this is a robust variety, propagating with cuttings is recommended.

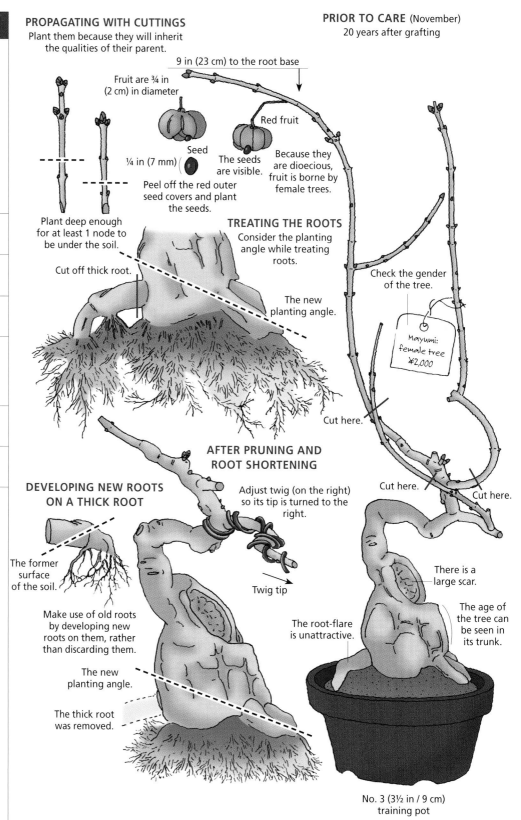

PROPAGATING WITH CUTTINGS
Plant them because they will inherit the qualities of their parent.

Fruit are ¾ in (2 cm) in diameter

9 in (23 cm) to the root base

Red fruit

Seed

¼ in (7 mm)

The seeds are visible.

Because they are dioecious, fruit is borne by female trees.

Peel off the red outer seed covers and plant the seeds.

Plant deep enough for at least 1 node to be under the soil.

Cut off thick root.

PRIOR TO CARE (November)
20 years after grafting

TREATING THE ROOTS
Consider the planting angle while treating roots.

The new planting angle.

Check the gender of the tree.

Mayumi: female tree ¥2,000

Cut here.

AFTER PRUNING AND ROOT SHORTENING

Adjust twig (on the right) so its tip is turned to the right.

Twig tip

Cut here.

Cut here.

DEVELOPING NEW ROOTS ON A THICK ROOT

The former surface of the soil.

Make use of old roots by developing new roots on them, rather than discarding them.

The new planting angle.

The thick root was removed.

There is a large scar.

The root-flare is unattractive.

The age of the tree can be seen in its trunk.

No. 3 (3½ in / 9 cm) training pot

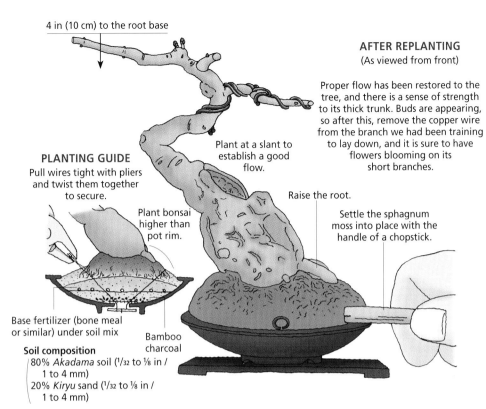

4 in (10 cm) to the root base

PLANTING GUIDE
Pull wires tight with pliers and twist them together to secure.

Plant bonsai higher than pot rim.

Base fertilizer (bone meal or similar) under soil mix

Bamboo charcoal

Soil composition
80% *Akadama* soil ($\frac{1}{32}$ to $\frac{1}{8}$ in / 1 to 4 mm)
20% *Kiryu* sand ($\frac{1}{32}$ to $\frac{1}{8}$ in / 1 to 4 mm)

Plant at a slant to establish a good flow.

Raise the root.

Settle the sphagnum moss into place with the handle of a chopstick.

AFTER REPLANTING
(As viewed from front)

Proper flow has been restored to the tree, and there is a sense of strength to its thick trunk. Buds are appearing, so after this, remove the copper wire from the branch we had been training to lay down, and it is sure to have flowers blooming on its short branches.

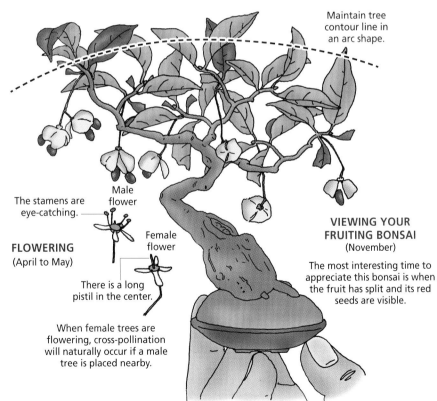

Maintain tree contour line in an arc shape.

The stamens are eye-catching.

Male flower

Female flower

FLOWERING
(April to May)

There is a long pistil in the center.

When female trees are flowering, cross-pollination will naturally occur if a male tree is placed nearby.

VIEWING YOUR FRUITING BONSAI
(November)

The most interesting time to appreciate this bonsai is when the fruit has split and its red seeds are visible.

SCHEDULE								
	Propagating	Watering	Fertilizing	Protection	Shaping	Sterilization	Transplanting	Growth State
January								
February	Cutting	1–2 times / week		Protection room	Pruning	Winter	Dormancy period	
March	Seedling							
April								
May		2–3 times / day	Add fertilizer				Growth period • Flowering (April–May) • Sprout separating (July–August)	
June	Layering • Cutting				Wiring		Growth period	
July		3–4 times / day	Water & fertilizer					
August				Shading				
September								
October		2–3 times / day	Add fertilizer				Prime • Fruits form (October–November)	
November								
December						Winter		

Diamond Leaf Persimmon

JAPANESE NAME
Miyakobeni

ALTERNATIVE NAME
Red-fruited Chinese persimmon

SCIENTIFIC NAME
Diospyros rhombifolia

CLASSIFICATION
Persimmon (deciduous broadleaf tree / shrub)

SYMBOLIC OF
Longevity

BEARING FRUIT
October to November

Just five to six years after developing from seedlings, flowers will bloom in April and May. There is a charm in the color and varying shapes of its fruit and its green leaves. As the fruit remain even after the leaves have fallen, viewing can continue for a long time. Because it is dioecious, a male tree is needed for cross-pollination. Propagating with cuttings or laying root cuttings down to develop new roots is recommended.

PRIOR TO CARE (March)
3 years after developing new roots

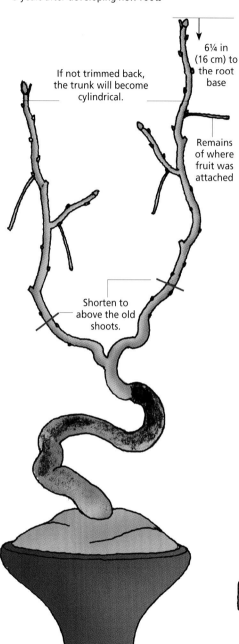

If not trimmed back, the trunk will become cylindrical.

6¼ in (16 cm) to the root base

Remains of where fruit was attached

Shorten to above the old shoots.

DEVELOPING NEW ROOTS (March)
Use the unneeded roots from replanting.

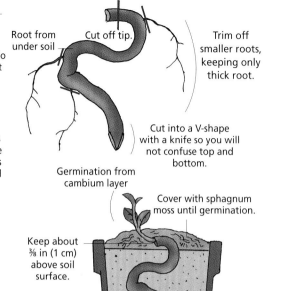

Root from under soil

Cut off tip.

Trim off smaller roots, keeping only thick root.

Cut into a V-shape with a knife so you will not confuse top and bottom.

Germination from cambium layer

Cover with sphagnum moss until germination.

Keep about ⅜ in (1 cm) above soil surface.

As of now, the root has become a trunk.

New roots are emerging.

PROPAGATING WITH CUTTINGS
Replant the cut branches.

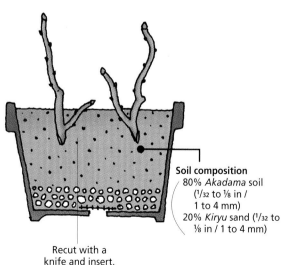

Soil composition
80% *Akadama* soil (¹/₃₂ to ⅛ in / 1 to 4 mm)
20% *Kiryu* sand (¹/₃₂ to ⅛ in / 1 to 4 mm)

Recut with a knife and insert.

PRUNING
(March)

Keep 1 to 3 nodes of this thickened branch base and cut off the rest.

AFTER PRUNING
Cut here, keeping 2 or 3 buds on each twig.

If a dark trunk surface is unappealing, clean it off with a scrubbing brush and water.

BRANCH SHAPING
(June)

Lay the branch down and set a bend in it.

Secure the wire firmly by wrapping it twice around the branch before beginning wiring.

For new shoots, growing upright and straight comes naturally.

HOW BONSAI APPEARS AFTER SEVERAL YEARS
Do not allow the tree to become tall—lay down the branches to the left and right, and front and back.

REPLANTING
Because its roots grow well, replant every year.

Keep the buds on the shoot growing from the trunk in a good position.

FLOWERING AND CROSS-POLLINATION
(April)

Male Flower

Female flower

There are no sepals*

There is a long peduncle.

There are 4 branch sepals.

Remove the petals.

Tweezers

Male Flower

Apply male flower while the pistil is still yellow.

Soil composition
80% *Akadama* soil ($1/32$ to $1/8$ in / 1 to 4 mm)
20% *Kiryu* sand ($1/32$ to $1/8$ in / 1 to 4 mm)

Mix about 10% bamboo charcoal with the soil mix.

*Sepal: The separate parts of the calyx are the sepals. Calyx is a botanical term meaning the exterior parts of the corolla (either individual flower petals or a set of petals).

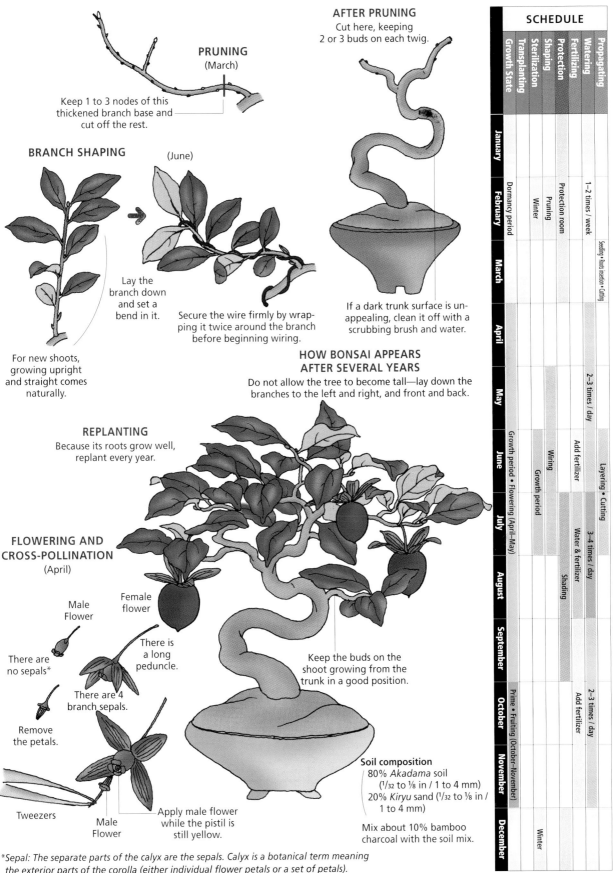

SCHEDULE

Month	Growth State	Transplanting	Sterilization	Shaping	Protection	Fertilizing	Watering	Propagating
January	Dormancy period				Protection room		1-2 times / week	Seedling • Roots insertion • Cutting
February	Dormancy period		Winter	Pruning	Protection room		1-2 times / week	
March					Protection room		1-2 times / week	
April	Growth period • Flowering (April-May)						1-2 times / week	Layering • Cutting
May							2-3 times / day	
June	Growth period	Growth period		Wiring		Add fertilizer	2-3 times / day	
July						Water & fertilizer	3-4 times / day	
August					Shading	Water & fertilizer	3-4 times / day	
September							3-4 times / day	
October	Prime • Fruiting (October-November)					Add fertilizer	2-3 times / day	
November							2-3 times / day	
December			Winter				2-3 times / day	

Thorny Olive

JAPANESE NAME
Nawashirogumi

ALTERNATIVE NAME
Oleaster

SCIENTIFIC NAME
Elaeagnus pungens

CLASSIFICATION
Elaeagnaceae (evergreen hardwood / shrub)

SYMBOLIC OF
n/a

BEARING FRUIT
April to May

From October to November, pale yellow and white flowers bloom from leaf axils, and their fruit ripen, turning red over the winter and into the following spring. The Japanese name *nawashirogumi* derives from the way that the fruit ripen when rice seedlings are being cultivated for spring (*nawashiro* are rice seedling nursery beds). For propagation, cultivating the seedlings grown from sowing the red seeds from ripe fruit is recommended. Otherwise, propagating with cuttings is easy.

Make good use of its bends by adjusting this tree into a half-hanging cliff* bonsai

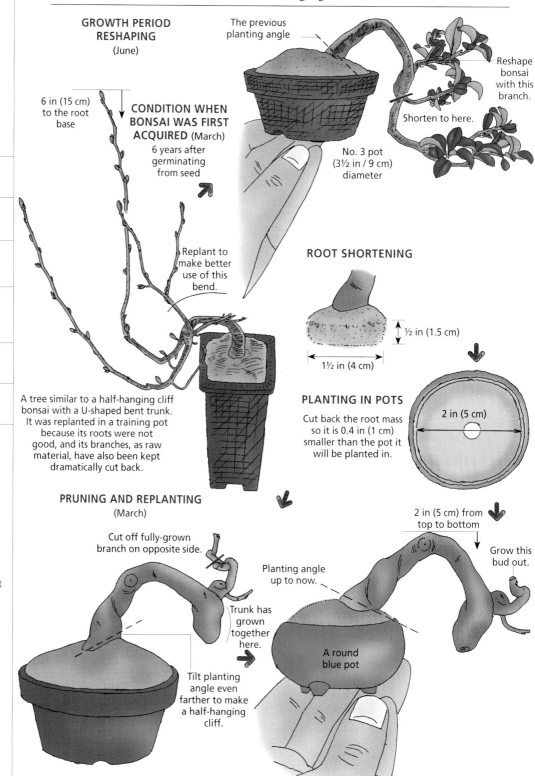

GROWTH PERIOD RESHAPING
(June)

The previous planting angle

Reshape bonsai with this branch.

Shorten to here.

No. 3 pot (3½ in / 9 cm) diameter

6 in (15 cm) to the root base

CONDITION WHEN BONSAI WAS FIRST ACQUIRED (March)
6 years after germinating from seed

Replant to make better use of this bend.

ROOT SHORTENING

½ in (1.5 cm)

1½ in (4 cm)

A tree similar to a half-hanging cliff bonsai with a U-shaped bent trunk. It was replanted in a training pot because its roots were not good, and its branches, as raw material, have also been kept dramatically cut back.

PLANTING IN POTS

Cut back the root mass so it is 0.4 in (1 cm) smaller than the pot it will be planted in.

2 in (5 cm)

PRUNING AND REPLANTING
(March)

Cut off fully-grown branch on opposite side.

Trunk has grown together here.

Planting angle up to now.

A round blue pot

Tilt planting angle even farther to make a half-hanging cliff.

2 in (5 cm) from top to bottom

Grow this bud out.

*Half-hanging cliff: A standard style of tree shape where the trunk and branches do not hang down as far as with a hanging-cliff-style bonsai and the branch tip is at or above the base of the pot. Refer to page 13.

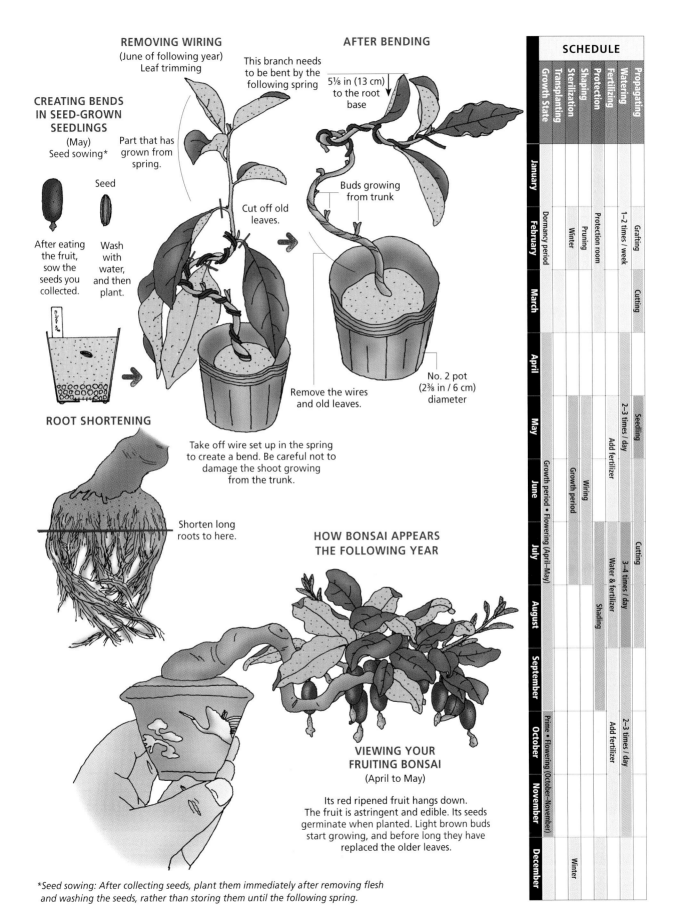

CREATING BENDS IN SEED-GROWN SEEDLINGS
(May)
Seed sowing*

Seed

After eating the fruit, sow the seeds you collected.

Wash with water, and then plant.

REMOVING WIRING
(June of following year)
Leaf trimming

Part that has grown from spring.

Cut off old leaves.

Remove the wires and old leaves.

ROOT SHORTENING

Shorten long roots to here.

Take off wire set up in the spring to create a bend. Be careful not to damage the shoot growing from the trunk.

AFTER BENDING

This branch needs to be bent by the following spring

5⅛ in (13 cm) to the root base

Buds growing from trunk

No. 2 pot (2⅜ in / 6 cm) diameter

HOW BONSAI APPEARS THE FOLLOWING YEAR

VIEWING YOUR FRUITING BONSAI
(April to May)

Its red ripened fruit hangs down. The fruit is astringent and edible. Its seeds germinate when planted. Light brown buds start growing, and before long they have replaced the older leaves.

*Seed sowing: After collecting seeds, plant them immediately after removing flesh and washing the seeds, rather than storing them until the following spring.

	SCHEDULE		
Growth State	Propagating	Watering	Protection	Fertilizing	Sterilization	Shaping	Transplanting
January	Dormancy period	1–2 times / week	Protection room		Winter		
February						Pruning	
March		Cutting					
April							
May	Growth period • Flowering (April–May)	Seedling	2–3 times / day	Add fertilizer			
June						Wiring / Growth period	
July		Cutting	3–4 times / day	Water & fertilizer			
August				Shading			
September							
October	Prime • Flowering (October–November)		2–3 times / day	Add fertilizer			
November							
December					Winter		

105

Jolcham Oak

JAPANESE NAME
Konara

ALTERNATIVE NAME
Houso

SCIENTIFIC NAME
Quercus serrata

CLASSIFICATION
Beech family (deciduous broadleaf tree / macrophanerophyte)

SYMBOLIC OF
Courage, Independence

BEARING FRUIT
October to November

Flowering is from April to May. This tree is a hermaphrodite*, so it has both long male flowers and short inconspicuous female flowers, which open for self-pollination. Their fruit (acorns) ripen in the autumn. Because oak produces durable lumber, it has been used for making sturdy tools for hundreds of years. Japanese forests are composed of this typical species of tree. Propagation is through air-layering or with cuttings.

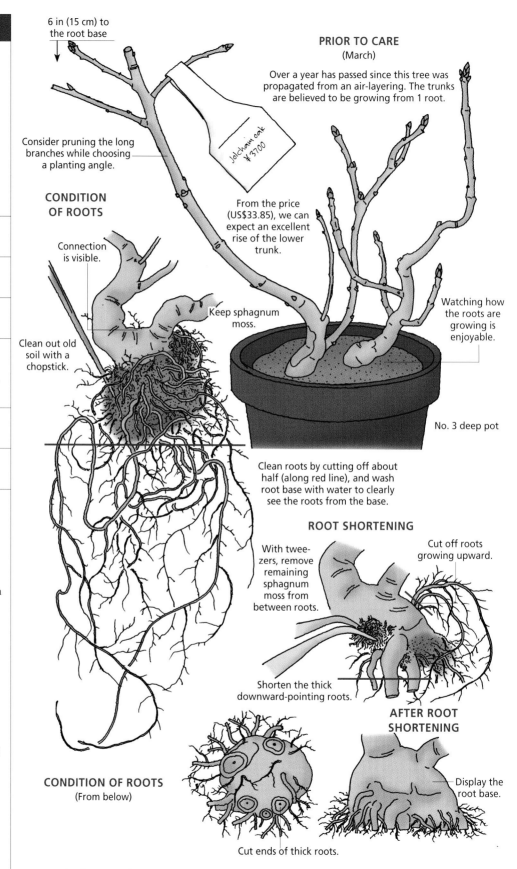

6 in (15 cm) to the root base

PRIOR TO CARE
(March)

Over a year has passed since this tree was propagated from an air-layering. The trunks are believed to be growing from 1 root.

Consider pruning the long branches while choosing a planting angle.

Jolcham oak ¥3700

From the price (US$33.85), we can expect an excellent rise of the lower trunk.

CONDITION OF ROOTS

Connection is visible.

Keep sphagnum moss.

Watching how the roots are growing is enjoyable.

Clean out old soil with a chopstick.

No. 3 deep pot

Clean roots by cutting off about half (along red line), and wash root base with water to clearly see the roots from the base.

ROOT SHORTENING

Cut off roots growing upward.

With tweezers, remove remaining sphagnum moss from between roots.

Shorten the thick downward-pointing roots.

AFTER ROOT SHORTENING

Display the root base.

CONDITION OF ROOTS
(From below)

Cut ends of thick roots.

*Hermaphrodite: A tree (or other plant) that is furnished with both male and female flowers.

SEED SOWING
(October)

June of the following year

Former soil surface

Put sphagnum moss on top in winter.

Plant up to about half in soil.

Root will sprout from pointed part.

The root is thick.

FLOWERS AND FRUIT
Flowers (April to May)

It bears several flowers.

Female flower

Downy hairs

Oblong

Acorn cupule

Female flowers are attached to the twig tip.

The male flowers hang down, attached to a lower part on long stems.

Pollen attaches to female flowers, causing cross-pollination to occur.

Male flower

Outstretched filaments*

When opened

Yellow pollen is energetically released.

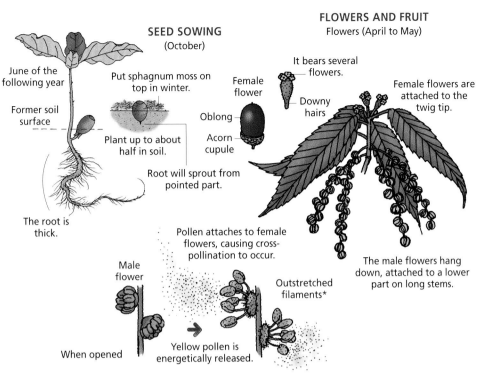

AFTER REPLANTING
(Front view)

Wire slightly upright branches to lay down.

4⅜ in (11 cm) from side to side

2¾ in (7 cm) to the root base

Bud

Once the planting angle is decided, shorten to above the middle bud.

Soil composition
80% *Akadama* soil
(¹/₃₂ to ⅛ in / 1 to 4 mm)
20% *Kiryu* sand
(¹/₃₂ to ⅛ in / 1 to 4 mm)
+ some bamboo charcoal

PLANTING GUIDE

Make sure there are no gaps between roots.

Twist wire with pliers to secure tree.

Plant bonsai on a slight mound.

Gravel bed (⅛ to ¼ in / 6 to 8 mm)

Base fertilizer (bone meal or similar) under soil mix

Filaments: Thread-like stalks that support the anthers of stamens.

SCHEDULE

Growth State	Transplanting	Sterilization	Shaping	Protection	Fertilizing	Watering	Propagating
January						1–2 times / week	Seedling
February — Dormancy period		Winter	Pruning	Protection room		1–2 times / week	Seedling
March							
April					Add fertilizer	2–3 times / day	Layering • Cutting
May — Growth period • Flowering (April–May) • Sprout separating (July–August)					Add fertilizer	2–3 times / day	Layering • Cutting
June — Growth period			Wiring				Layering • Cutting
July					Water & fertilizer	3–4 times / day	
August				Shading	Water & fertilizer	3–4 times / day	
September							
October — Prime • Fruiting (October–November)					Add fertilizer	2–3 times / day	Seedling
November					Add fertilizer	2–3 times / day	Seedling
December		Winter					

Autumn Olive

JAPANESE NAME
Akigumi

ALTERNATIVE NAME
Japanese silverberry

SCIENTIFIC NAME
Elaeagnus umbellata

CLASSIFICATION
Oleaster family (deciduous hardwood / shrub)

SYMBOLIC OF
Watchfulness

BEARING FRUIT
October to November

Blooming in April and May, its flowers, which are hermaphroditic, change from white to yellow. There are thorns on the branches, and several flowers dangle from each leaf axil. These have no petals, but the sepals are petal-shaped. Its name derives from the ¼ in (6 to 8 mm) red spherical fruit that ripens in autumn. Propagation is with seed-grown seedlings, cuttings and so on.

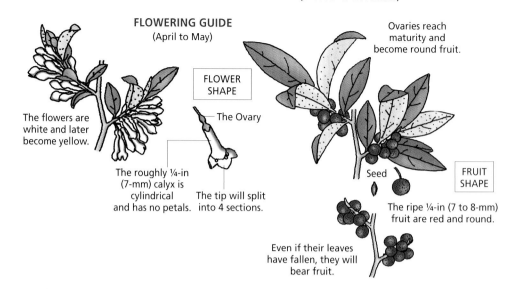

FRUIT-BEARING GUIDE
(October to November)

FLOWERING GUIDE
(April to May)

The flowers are white and later become yellow.

FLOWER SHAPE

The Ovary

The roughly ¼-in (7-mm) calyx is cylindrical and has no petals.

The tip will split into 4 sections.

Ovaries reach maturity and become round fruit.

Seed

FRUIT SHAPE

The ripe ¼-in (7 to 8-mm) fruit are red and round.

Even if their leaves have fallen, they will bear fruit.

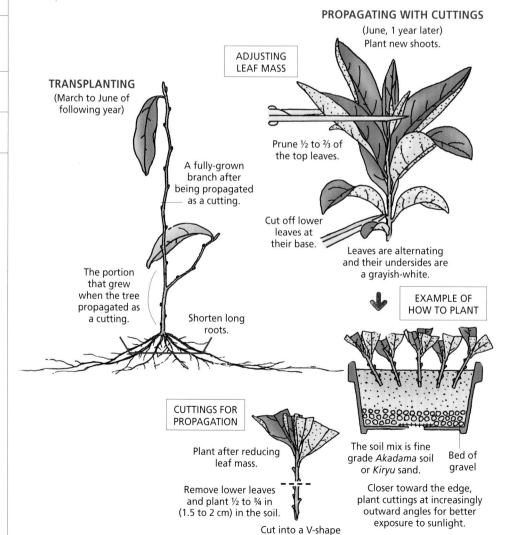

PROPAGATING WITH CUTTINGS
(June, 1 year later)
Plant new shoots.

ADJUSTING LEAF MASS

TRANSPLANTING
(March to June of following year)

A fully-grown branch after being propagated as a cutting.

Prune ½ to ⅔ of the top leaves.

The portion that grew when the tree propagated as a cutting.

Shorten long roots.

Cut off lower leaves at their base.

Leaves are alternating and their undersides are a grayish-white.

EXAMPLE OF HOW TO PLANT

CUTTINGS FOR PROPAGATION

Plant after reducing leaf mass.

Remove lower leaves and plant ½ to ¾ in (1.5 to 2 cm) in the soil.

Cut into a V-shape and plant.

The soil mix is fine grade *Akadama* soil or *Kiryu* sand.

Bed of gravel

Closer toward the edge, plant cuttings at increasingly outward angles for better exposure to sunlight.

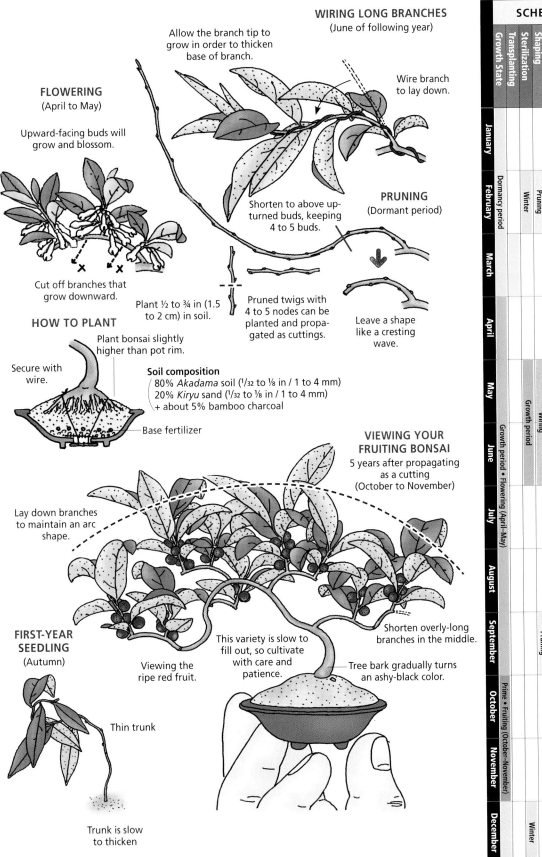

FLOWERING
(April to May)

Upward-facing buds will grow and blossom.

Cut off branches that grow downward.

Allow the branch tip to grow in order to thicken base of branch.

WIRING LONG BRANCHES
(June of following year)

Wire branch to lay down.

Shorten to above up-turned buds, keeping 4 to 5 buds.

PRUNING
(Dormant period)

Plant ½ to ¾ in (1.5 to 2 cm) in soil.

Pruned twigs with 4 to 5 nodes can be planted and propagated as cuttings.

Leave a shape like a cresting wave.

HOW TO PLANT

Plant bonsai slightly higher than pot rim.

Secure with wire.

Soil composition
80% *Akadama* soil (¹/₃₂ to ⅛ in / 1 to 4 mm)
20% *Kiryu* sand (¹/₃₂ to ⅛ in / 1 to 4 mm)
+ about 5% bamboo charcoal

Base fertilizer

VIEWING YOUR FRUITING BONSAI

5 years after propagating as a cutting
(October to November)

Lay down branches to maintain an arc shape.

Shorten overly-long branches in the middle.

This variety is slow to fill out, so cultivate with care and patience.

Tree bark gradually turns an ashy-black color.

FIRST-YEAR SEEDLING
(Autumn)

Viewing the ripe red fruit.

Thin trunk

Trunk is slow to thicken

SCHEDULE

Category	January	February	March	April	May	June	July	August	September	October	November	December
Propagating		Seedling			Layering • Cutting					Seedling		
Watering	1–2 times / week				2–3 times / day		3–4 times / day			2–3 times / day		
Fertilizing					Add fertilizer		Water & fertilizer			Add fertilizer		
Protection		Protection room						Shading				
Shaping		Pruning			Wiring				Pruning			
Sterilization		Winter										
Transplanting					Growth period							Winter
Growth State		Dormancy period				Growth period • Flowering (April–May)				Prime • Fruiting (October–November)		

109

Japanese Barberry

JAPANESE NAME
Megi

ALTERNATIVE NAME
Thunberg's barberry

SCIENTIFIC NAME
Berberis thunbergii

CLASSIFICATION
Barberry (deciduous broadleaf tree / shrub)

SYMBOLIC OF
Irritability

BEARING FRUIT
October to November

Pale yellow flowers open in April and May. The fruit will ripen and turn red from autumn into winter. The changes in color of the leaves are lovely as well. Its Japanese name (*megi*, literally "eye-tree") originated from the past use of its boiled leaves and bark for washing the eyes. Also known in Japan as *kotori tomarazu*, which refers to the way that its many twigs and thorns prevent even small birds from landing on it. Propagating is with cuttings, seed-grown seedlings, or laying down roots to develop new roots.

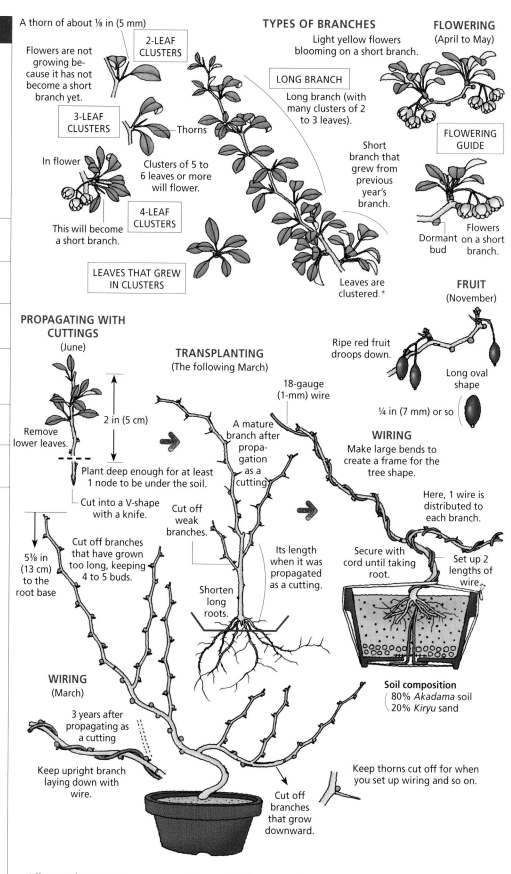

A thorn of about ⅛ in (5 mm)

2-LEAF CLUSTERS

Flowers are not growing because it has not become a short branch yet.

3-LEAF CLUSTERS

In flower

Thorns

Clusters of 5 to 6 leaves or more will flower.

4-LEAF CLUSTERS

This will become a short branch.

LEAVES THAT GREW IN CLUSTERS

TYPES OF BRANCHES

Light yellow flowers blooming on a short branch.

LONG BRANCH

Long branch (with many clusters of 2 to 3 leaves).

Short branch that grew from previous year's branch.

Leaves are clustered.*

FLOWERING
(April to May)

FLOWERING GUIDE

Dormant bud

Flowers on a short branch.

FRUIT
(November)

Ripe red fruit droops down.

Long oval shape

¼ in (7 mm) or so

PROPAGATING WITH CUTTINGS
(June)

Remove lower leaves.

2 in (5 cm)

Plant deep enough for at least 1 node to be under the soil.

Cut into a V-shape with a knife.

5⅛ in (13 cm) to the root base

Cut off branches that have grown too long, keeping 4 to 5 buds.

TRANSPLANTING
(The following March)

Cut off weak branches.

18-gauge (1-mm) wire

A mature branch after propagation as a cutting

Its length when it was propagated as a cutting.

Shorten long roots.

WIRING

Make large bends to create a frame for the tree shape.

Here, 1 wire is distributed to each branch.

Secure with cord until taking root.

Set up 2 lengths of wire.

Soil composition
80% *Akadama* soil
20% *Kiryu* sand

WIRING
(March)

3 years after propagating as a cutting

Keep upright branch laying down with wire.

Cut off branches that grow downward.

Keep thorns cut off for when you set up wiring and so on.

*Cluster: When several leaves appear to be growing from one point.

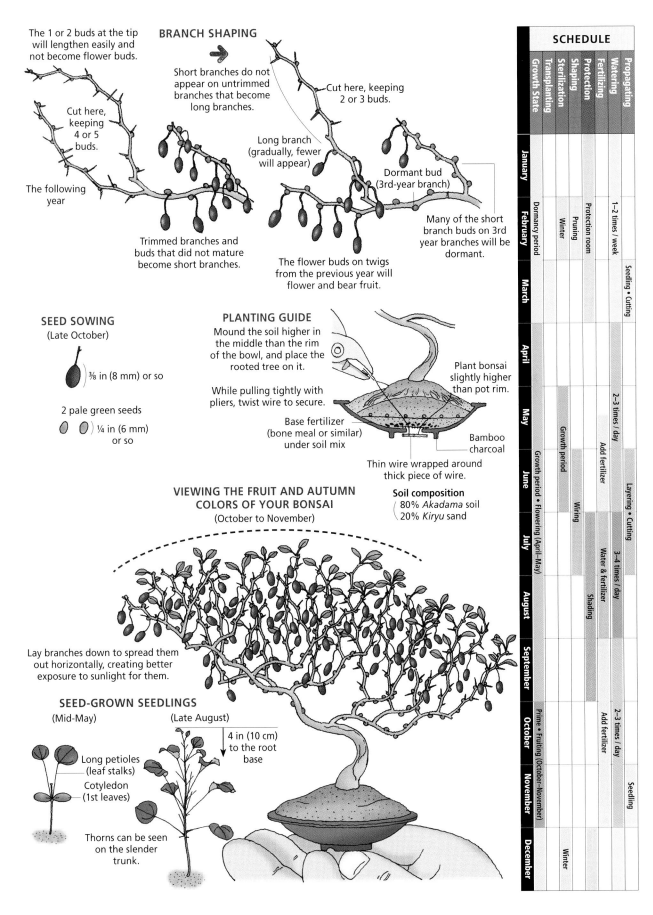

The 1 or 2 buds at the tip will lengthen easily and not become flower buds.

BRANCH SHAPING

Short branches do not appear on untrimmed branches that become long branches.

Cut here, keeping 2 or 3 buds.

Cut here, keeping 4 or 5 buds.

Long branch (gradually, fewer will appear)

Dormant bud (3rd-year branch)

The following year

Many of the short branch buds on 3rd year branches will be dormant.

Trimmed branches and buds that did not mature become short branches.

The flower buds on twigs from the previous year will flower and bear fruit.

SEED SOWING
(Late October)

⅜ in (8 mm) or so

2 pale green seeds

¼ in (6 mm) or so

PLANTING GUIDE

Mound the soil higher in the middle than the rim of the bowl, and place the rooted tree on it.

While pulling tightly with pliers, twist wire to secure.

Base fertilizer (bone meal or similar) under soil mix

Plant bonsai slightly higher than pot rim.

Bamboo charcoal

Thin wire wrapped around thick piece of wire.

Soil composition
80% *Akadama* soil
20% *Kiryu* sand

VIEWING THE FRUIT AND AUTUMN COLORS OF YOUR BONSAI
(October to November)

Lay branches down to spread them out horizontally, creating better exposure to sunlight for them.

SEED-GROWN SEEDLINGS
(Mid-May)   (Late August)

4 in (10 cm) to the root base

Long petioles (leaf stalks)

Cotyledon (1st leaves)

Thorns can be seen on the slender trunk.

SCHEDULE

Month	Growth State	Transplanting	Sterilization	Shaping	Protection	Fertilizing	Watering	Propagating
January							1–2 times / week	
February	Dormancy period		Winter	Pruning	Protection room			Seedling • Cutting
March								
April							2–3 times / day	
May						Add fertilizer		Layering • Cutting
June	Growth period			Wiring				
July	Growth period • Flowering (April–May)					Water & fertilizer	3–4 times / day	
August					Shading			
September								
October	Prime • Fruiting (October–November)					Add fertilizer	2–3 times / day	
November								Seedling
December			Winter					

Queen Coralbead

JAPANESE NAME
Aoshijirafuji

ALTERNATIVE NAME
Kamiebi

SCIENTIFIC NAME
Cocculus orbiculatus

CLASSIFICATION
Menispermaceae
(deciduous vine)

SYMBOLIC OF
n/a

BEARING FRUIT
September to November

Conical inflorescences of yellow and white florets grow from leaf axils and open during July and August. It is a dioecious plant. The spherical fruit, ¼ in (6 to 7 mm) are indigo-black, and ripen in the autumn. Propagating with cuttings or seed-grown seedlings is recommended. If the fruit is harvested and sown in autumn, it will germinate the following spring.

Ordinarily, the plants are difficult to recognize, but they're easily discovered in the autumn when their fruit ripens and changes color. It is often found entwined around trees, fences and so on. One way to obtain seeds is to get a landowner's permission to pick some of their fruit. Because propagating can also be done by laying down root cuttings to develop new roots, besides using branch cuttings and seed-grown seedlings, you can make good use of pruned roots rather than discarding them—even bent roots.

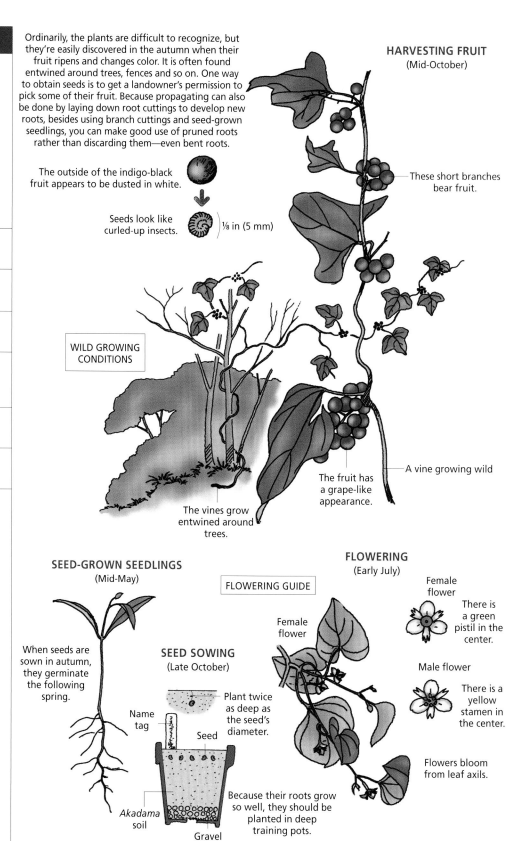

The outside of the indigo-black fruit appears to be dusted in white.

Seeds look like curled-up insects. ⅛ in (5 mm)

HARVESTING FRUIT
(Mid-October)

These short branches bear fruit.

WILD GROWING CONDITIONS

A vine growing wild

The fruit has a grape-like appearance.

The vines grow entwined around trees.

SEED-GROWN SEEDLINGS
(Mid-May)

When seeds are sown in autumn, they germinate the following spring.

SEED SOWING
(Late October)

Name tag

Seed

Plant twice as deep as the seed's diameter.

Akadama soil

Gravel

Because their roots grow so well, they should be planted in deep training pots.

FLOWERING
(Early July)

FLOWERING GUIDE

Female flower

Female flower

Female flower
There is a green pistil in the center.

Male flower
There is a yellow stamen in the center.

Flowers bloom from leaf axils.

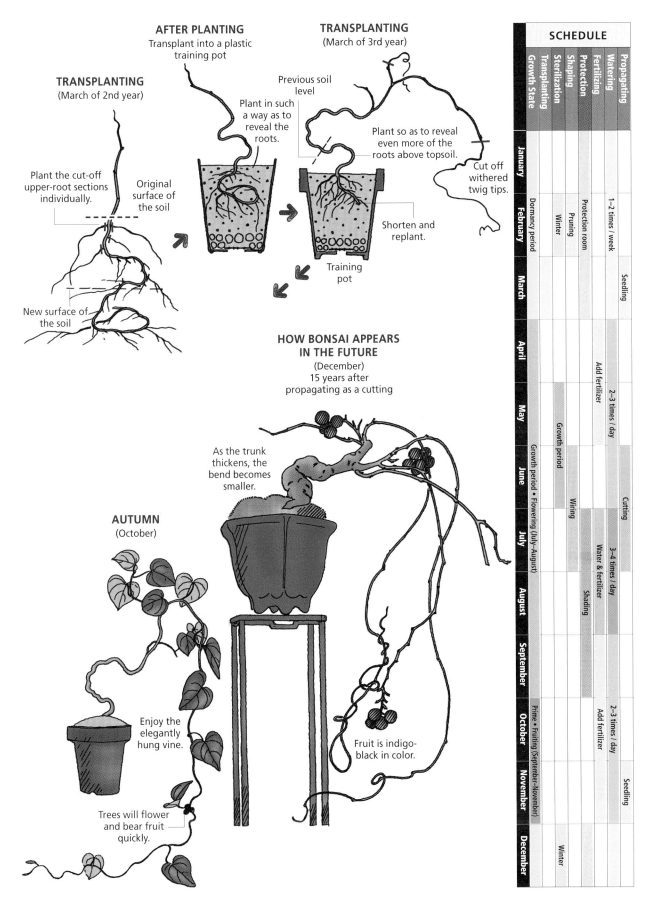

TRANSPLANTING
(March of 2nd year)

Plant the cut-off upper-root sections individually.

Original surface of the soil

New surface of the soil

AFTER PLANTING
Transplant into a plastic training pot

Plant in such a way as to reveal the roots.

Training pot

TRANSPLANTING
(March of 3rd year)

Previous soil level

Plant so as to reveal even more of the roots above topsoil.

Cut off withered twig tips.

Shorten and replant.

HOW BONSAI APPEARS IN THE FUTURE
(December)
15 years after propagating as a cutting

As the trunk thickens, the bend becomes smaller.

AUTUMN
(October)

Enjoy the elegantly hung vine.

Fruit is indigo-black in color.

Trees will flower and bear fruit quickly.

SCHEDULE

Growth State		Propagating	Watering	Fertilizing	Protection	Shaping	Sterilization	Transplanting
January	Dormancy period	Seedling	1–2 times / week		Protection room	Pruning	Winter	
February								
March								
April	Growth period • Flowering (July–August)	Cutting	2–3 times / day	Add fertilizer				
May					Growth period			
June						Wiring		
July			3–4 times / day	Water & fertilizer				
August					Shading			
September								
October	Prime • Fruiting (September–November)	Seedling	2–3 times / day	Add fertilizer				
November								
December							Winter	

113

Ginkgo

JAPANESE NAME
Ichou

ALTERNATIVE NAME
Maidenhair tree

SCIENTIFIC NAME
Ginkgo biloba

CLASSIFICATION
Ginkgo (deciduous /
macrophanerophyte)

SYMBOLIC OF
Longevity

BEARING FRUIT
October to November

Its pale yellow flowers bloom in April. It is dioecious, and fruit is borne on the female trees. That such large trees, both male and female, can be the source of small bonsai itself deserves admiration. If you desire a female tree, you should choose from seeds, buy a fruit-bearing tree, or graft a female branch onto a male tree.

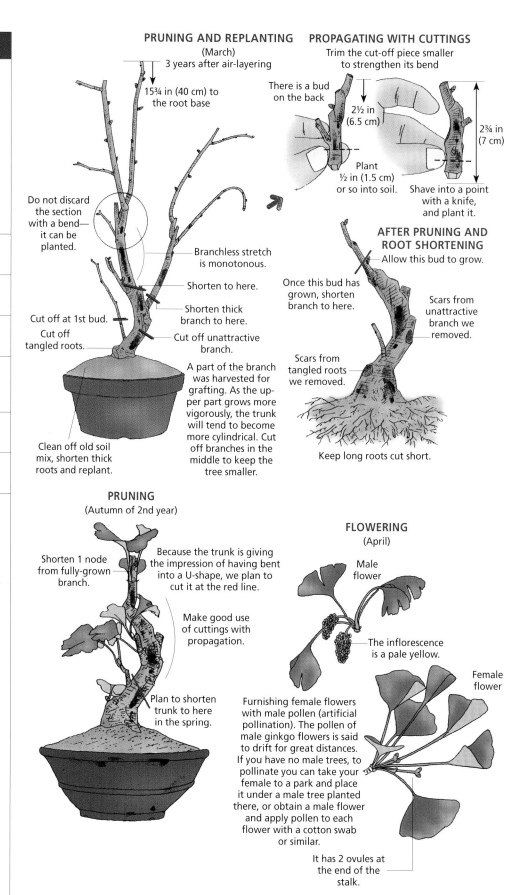

PRUNING AND REPLANTING
(March)
3 years after air-layering

15¾ in (40 cm) to the root base

Do not discard the section with a bend—it can be planted.

Branchless stretch is monotonous.

Shorten to here.

Shorten thick branch to here.

Cut off at 1st bud.
Cut off tangled roots.

Cut off unattractive branch.

A part of the branch was harvested for grafting. As the upper part grows more vigorously, the trunk will tend to become more cylindrical. Cut off branches in the middle to keep the tree smaller.

Clean off old soil mix, shorten thick roots and replant.

PROPAGATING WITH CUTTINGS
Trim the cut-off piece smaller to strengthen its bend

There is a bud on the back

2½ in (6.5 cm)

2¾ in (7 cm)

Plant ½ in (1.5 cm) or so into soil.

Shave into a point with a knife, and plant it.

AFTER PRUNING AND ROOT SHORTENING
Allow this bud to grow.

Once this bud has grown, shorten branch to here.

Scars from unattractive branch we removed.

Scars from tangled roots we removed.

Keep long roots cut short.

PRUNING
(Autumn of 2nd year)

Shorten 1 node from fully-grown branch.

Because the trunk is giving the impression of having bent into a U-shape, we plan to cut it at the red line.

Make good use of cuttings with propagation.

Plan to shorten trunk to here in the spring.

FLOWERING
(April)

Male flower

The inflorescence is a pale yellow.

Female flower

Furnishing female flowers with male pollen (artificial pollination). The pollen of male ginkgo flowers is said to drift for great distances. If you have no male trees, to pollinate you can take your female to a park and place it under a male tree planted there, or obtain a male flower and apply pollen to each flower with a cotton swab or similar.

It has 2 ovules at the end of the stalk.

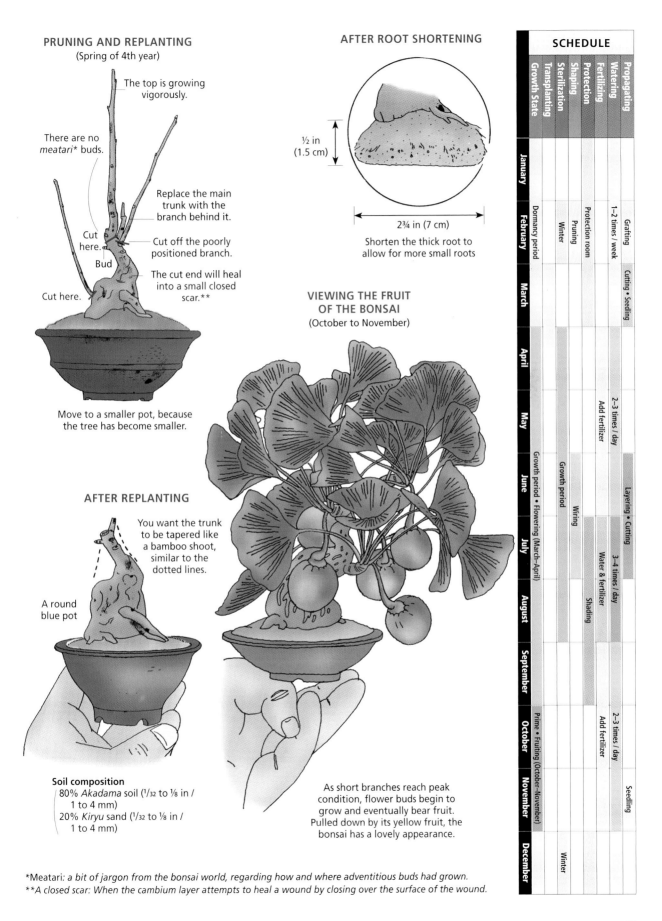

PRUNING AND REPLANTING
(Spring of 4th year)

The top is growing vigorously.

There are no *meatari** buds.

Replace the main trunk with the branch behind it.

Cut here.

Cut off the poorly positioned branch.

Bud

The cut end will heal into a small closed scar.**

Cut here.

Move to a smaller pot, because the tree has become smaller.

AFTER REPLANTING

You want the trunk to be tapered like a bamboo shoot, similar to the dotted lines.

A round blue pot

Soil composition
80% *Akadama* soil (¹⁄₃₂ to ⅛ in / 1 to 4 mm)
20% *Kiryu* sand (¹⁄₃₂ to ⅛ in / 1 to 4 mm)

AFTER ROOT SHORTENING

½ in (1.5 cm)

2¾ in (7 cm)

Shorten the thick root to allow for more small roots

VIEWING THE FRUIT OF THE BONSAI
(October to November)

As short branches reach peak condition, flower buds begin to grow and eventually bear fruit. Pulled down by its yellow fruit, the bonsai has a lovely appearance.

*Meatari: *a bit of jargon from the bonsai world, regarding how and where adventitious buds had grown.*
**A closed scar: *When the cambium layer attempts to heal a wound by closing over the surface of the wound.*

SCHEDULE

	Growth State	Transplanting	Sterilization	Shaping	Protection	Fertilizing	Watering	Propagating
January					Protection room		1–2 times / week	Grafting
February	Dormancy period		Winter	Pruning				Cutting • Seedling
March								
April						Add fertilizer	2–3 times / day	
May								Layering • Cutting
June	Growth period	Growth period						
July				Wiring		Water & fertilizer	3–4 times / day	
August						Shading		
September								
October	Prime • Fruiting (October–November)					Add fertilizer	2–3 times / day	Seedling
November								
December			Winter					

(Growth period • Flowering (March–April))

Chinese Quince

JAPANESE NAME
Karin

ALTERNATIVE NAME
Karanashi

SCIENTIFIC NAME
Pseudocydonia sinensis

CLASSIFICATION
Rosaceae (deciduous evergreen tree, macrophanerophyte)

SYMBOLIC OF
Possibility

BEARING FRUIT
October to November

Flowers in March and April. A small bonsai, it bears fruit that are 1⅛ to 1¾ in (3 to 4.5 cm) in diameter. Be sure to provide plenty of additional fertilizer rich in phosphoric acid. If tree becomes too dry while it is bearing fruit, this may cause the fruit to fall. If propagation was through grafting, the tree will bloom and bear fruit in about four to five years. Use seed-grown seedlings for grafting rootstock.

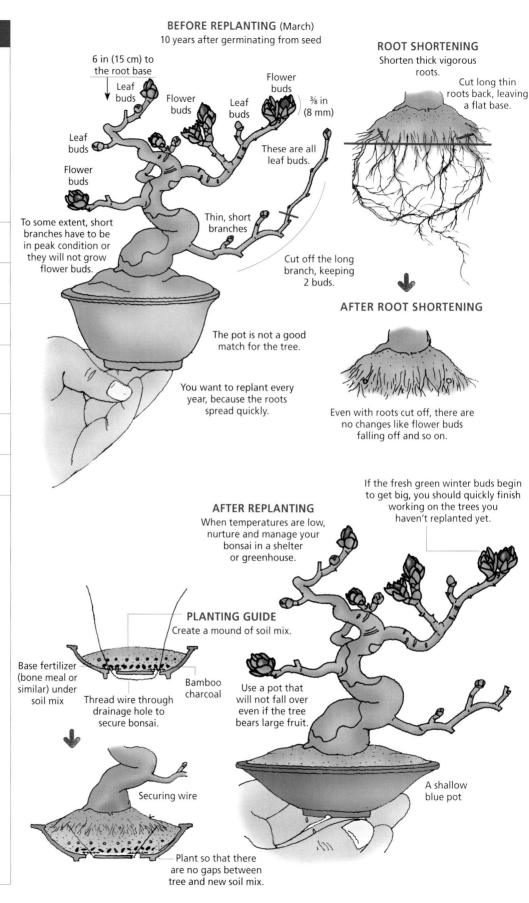

BEFORE REPLANTING (March)
10 years after germinating from seed

6 in (15 cm) to the root base

Leaf buds

Flower buds

Flower buds

Leaf buds

Leaf buds

⅜ in (8 mm)

Leaf buds

These are all leaf buds.

Flower buds

Thin, short branches

To some extent, short branches have to be in peak condition or they will not grow flower buds.

Cut off the long branch, keeping 2 buds.

The pot is not a good match for the tree.

You want to replant every year, because the roots spread quickly.

ROOT SHORTENING
Shorten thick vigorous roots.

Cut long thin roots back, leaving a flat base.

AFTER ROOT SHORTENING

Even with roots cut off, there are no changes like flower buds falling off and so on.

If the fresh green winter buds begin to get big, you should quickly finish working on the trees you haven't replanted yet.

AFTER REPLANTING
When temperatures are low, nurture and manage your bonsai in a shelter or greenhouse.

PLANTING GUIDE
Create a mound of soil mix.

Base fertilizer (bone meal or similar) under soil mix

Bamboo charcoal

Thread wire through drainage hole to secure bonsai.

Use a pot that will not fall over even if the tree bears large fruit.

Securing wire

A shallow blue pot

Plant so that there are no gaps between tree and new soil mix.

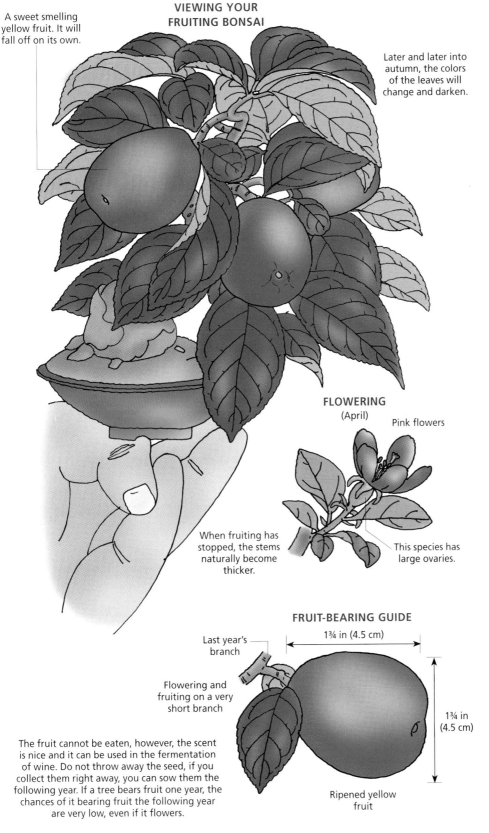

A sweet smelling yellow fruit. It will fall off on its own.

VIEWING YOUR FRUITING BONSAI

Later and later into autumn, the colors of the leaves will change and darken.

FLOWERING
(April)

Pink flowers

When fruiting has stopped, the stems naturally become thicker.

This species has large ovaries.

FRUIT-BEARING GUIDE

Last year's branch

Flowering and fruiting on a very short branch

1¾ in (4.5 cm)

1¾ in (4.5 cm)

Ripened yellow fruit

The fruit cannot be eaten, however, the scent is nice and it can be used in the fermentation of wine. Do not throw away the seed, if you collect them right away, you can sow them the following year. If a tree bears fruit one year, the chances of it bearing fruit the following year are very low, even if it flowers.

	SCHEDULE			
Growth State	**Propagating**	**Watering**	**Fertilizing**	**Protection** **Shaping** **Sterilization** **Transplanting**
January		1–2 times / week		Protection room / Pruning / Winter
February	Dormancy period			
March	Seedling • Cutting			
April		2–3 times / day		
May	Growth period • Flowering (March–April) • Sprout separating (July–August)		Add fertilizer	Layering • Cutting
June				Growth period / Wiring
July		3–4 times / day	Water & fertilizer	
August			Shading	
September				
October	Prime • Fruiting (October–December)	2–3 times / day	Add fertilizer	
November				
December				Winter

Japanese Hawthorn

JAPANESE NAME
Sanzashi

ALTERNATIVE NAMES
n/a

SCIENTIFIC NAME
Crataegus cuneata

CLASSIFICATION
Rosaceae (deciduous evergreen tree / shrub)

SYMBOLIC OF
Hope, Only love

BEARING FRUIT
October to November

The white flower and red flower hawthorns of Japan are varieties* of Western hawthorn. Both single-layer and double-blossomed flowers bloom around May. Fruit are ⅜ to ¾ in (1 or 2 cm) or so. Its sharp thorns are actually specialized twigs. Grafting is recommended for propagation, but may take a number of years to bloom.

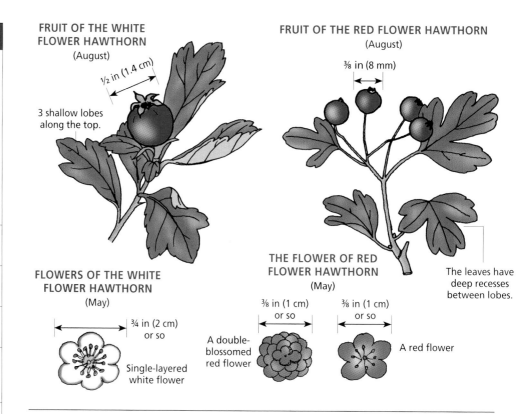

FRUIT OF THE WHITE FLOWER HAWTHORN (August)

½ in (1.4 cm)

3 shallow lobes along the top.

FRUIT OF THE RED FLOWER HAWTHORN (August)

⅜ in (8 mm)

The leaves have deep recesses between lobes.

FLOWERS OF THE WHITE FLOWER HAWTHORN (May)

¾ in (2 cm) or so

Single-layered white flower

THE FLOWER OF RED FLOWER HAWTHORN (May)

⅜ in (1 cm) or so

A double-blossomed red flower

⅜ in (1 cm) or so

A red flower

The current shape of the tree

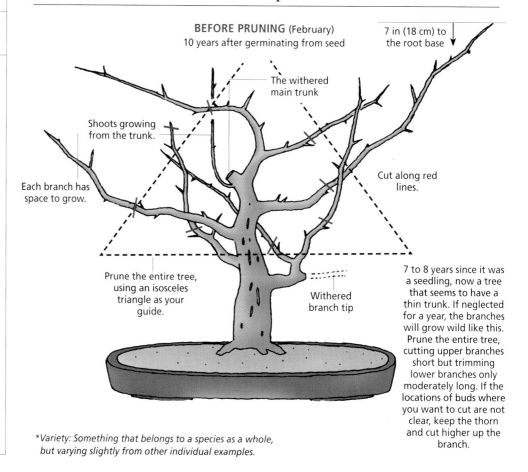

BEFORE PRUNING (February)
10 years after germinating from seed

7 in (18 cm) to the root base

The withered main trunk

Shoots growing from the trunk.

Cut along red lines.

Each branch has space to grow.

Prune the entire tree, using an isosceles triangle as your guide.

Withered branch tip

7 to 8 years since it was a seedling, now a tree that seems to have a thin trunk. If neglected for a year, the branches will grow wild like this. Prune the entire tree, cutting upper branches short but trimming lower branches only moderately long. If the locations of buds where you want to cut are not clear, keep the thorn and cut higher up the branch.

Variety: Something that belongs to a species as a whole, but varying slightly from other individual examples.

AFTER PRUNING (March)

Shorten every branch midway, following down to old buds, so tree is nicely balanced throughout.

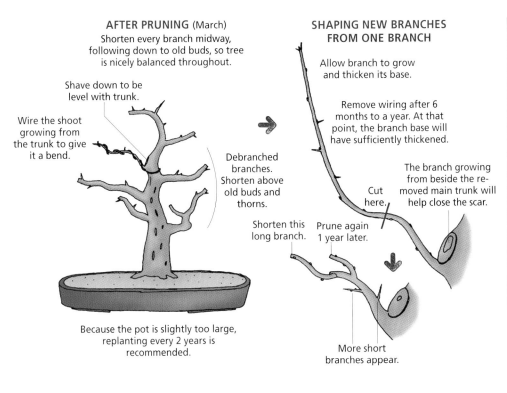

Shave down to be level with trunk.

Wire the shoot growing from the trunk to give it a bend.

Debranched branches. Shorten above old buds and thorns.

Because the pot is slightly too large, replanting every 2 years is recommended.

SHAPING NEW BRANCHES FROM ONE BRANCH

Allow branch to grow and thicken its base.

Remove wiring after 6 months to a year. At that point, the branch base will have sufficiently thickened.

Cut here.

The branch growing from beside the re-moved main trunk will help close the scar.

Shorten this long branch.

Prune again 1 year later.

More short branches appear.

SHAPING BRANCHES THAT WERE DEBRANCHED

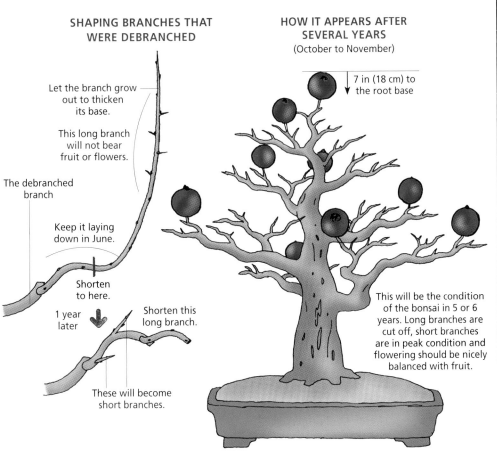

Let the branch grow out to thicken its base.

This long branch will not bear fruit or flowers.

The debranched branch

Keep it laying down in June.

Shorten to here.

1 year later

Shorten this long branch.

These will become short branches.

HOW IT APPEARS AFTER SEVERAL YEARS
(October to November)

7 in (18 cm) to the root base

This will be the condition of the bonsai in 5 or 6 years. Long branches are cut off, short branches are in peak condition and flowering should be nicely balanced with fruit.

SCHEDULE

Growth State	Transplanting	Sterilization	Shaping	Protection	Fertilizing	Watering	Propagating
January — Dormancy period	Winter			Protection room		1–2 times / week	Grafting
February — Dormancy period	Winter		Pruning	Protection room		1–2 times / week	Roots insertion
March — Dormancy period							Roots insertion
April — Growth period					Add fertilizer	2–3 times / day	
May — Growth period • Flowering (May–June)					Add fertilizer	2–3 times / day	Layering • Cutting
June — Growth period • Flowering			Wiring		Add fertilizer	2–3 times / day	Layering • Cutting
July			Wiring		Water & fertilizer	3–4 times / day	Layering • Cutting
August		Shading				3–4 times / day	
September						2–3 times / day	
October — Prime • Fruiting (October–November)					Add fertilizer	2–3 times / day	Seedling
November — Prime • Fruiting							Seedling
December — Winter	Winter						

Firethorn

JAPANESE NAME
Pirakansa

ALTERNATIVE NAMES
Tokiwasanzashi,
tachibanamodoki

SCIENTIFIC NAMES
Pyracantha coccinea,
Pyracantha angustifolium

CLASSIFICATION
Rosaceae (evergreen
broadleaf tree / under 33
feet /10 m)

SYMBOLIC OF
Mercy

BEARING FRUIT
October to November

Flowering is in May and
June. Small florets like
hydrangeas flower in
groups around the top
of the tree. Firethorn is a
general term that covers
both *Pyracantha coccinea*
M.Roem (with red fruit)
and *Pyracantha angusti-*
folia (with orange fruit).
There is little reason to
fret about fruiting, as
most flowers become
fruit. Propagation is with
cuttings, seed-grown
seedlings, and air-layering.

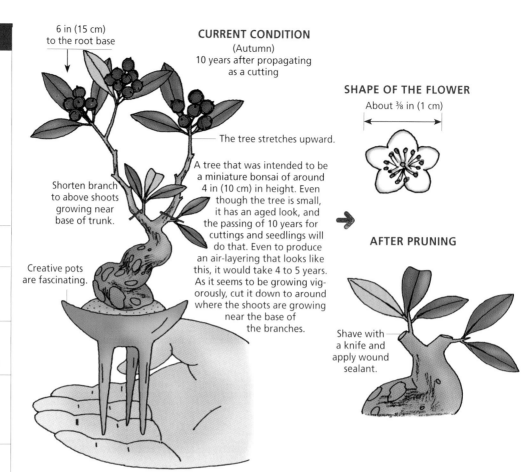

6 in (15 cm)
to the root base

CURRENT CONDITION
(Autumn)
10 years after propagating
as a cutting

The tree stretches upward.

Shorten branch
to above shoots
growing near
base of trunk.

Creative pots
are fascinating.

A tree that was intended to be
a miniature bonsai of around
4 in (10 cm) in height. Even
though the tree is small,
it has an aged look, and
the passing of 10 years for
cuttings and seedlings will
do that. Even to produce
an air-layering that looks like
this, it would take 4 to 5 years.
As it seems to be growing vigorously, cut it down to around
where the shoots are growing
near the base of
the branches.

SHAPE OF THE FLOWER
About ⅜ in (1 cm)

AFTER PRUNING

Shave with
a knife and
apply wound
sealant.

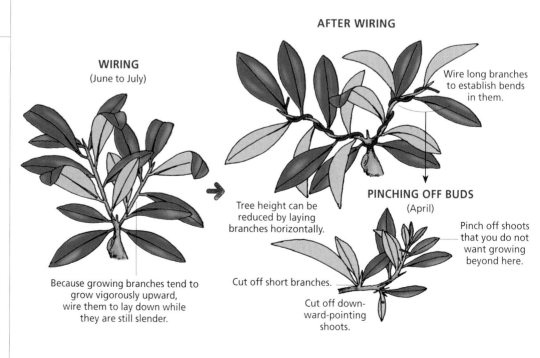

AFTER WIRING

WIRING
(June to July)

Wire long branches
to establish bends
in them.

Tree height can be
reduced by laying
branches horizontally.

PINCHING OFF BUDS
(April)

Pinch off shoots
that you do not
want growing
beyond here.

Cut off short branches.

Cut off down-
ward-pointing
shoots.

Because growing branches tend to
grow vigorously upward,
wire them to lay down while
they are still slender.

Pyracantha will frequently spontaneously cross-pollinate, and even the shapes of the leaves have become similar. *Pyracantha angustifolium* should be kept separate before the flowering season.

FLOWERING
(May to end of June)

Some flowering on a fully-grown twig tip.

FRUIT
(Autumn)

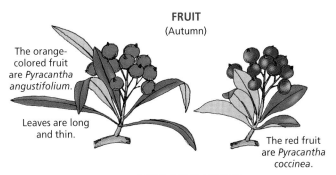

The orange-colored fruit are *Pyracantha angustifolium*.

Leaves are long and thin.

The red fruit are *Pyracantha coccinea*.

LEAF COMPARISON

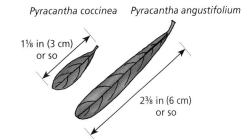

Pyracantha coccinea

Pyracantha angustifolium

1⅛ in (3 cm) or so

2⅜ in (6 cm) or so

AFTER TWO YEARS
(Autumn)

2¾ in (7 cm) to the root base

Try to grow fruit on short branches by restraining the long branches.

If you cultivate a small tree, it will flower and even bear fruit well. The longer it is cultivated, the more the trunk gradually becomes tinged with an antique look and the greater the prestige of the tree.

Even the roughness of its tree bark is a delight.

Branch bent by wiring

A solid fertilizer containing mainly phosphoric acid and water-soluble potassium.

September is the best time to replant every year, but replanting can even be done in late March, around the Vernal Equinox.

Soil composition
80% *Akadama* soil
20% *Kiryu* sand
+ about 10% bamboo charcoal

PRUNING
(Dormant period)

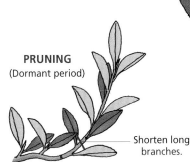

Shorten long branches.

Keep the short branches.

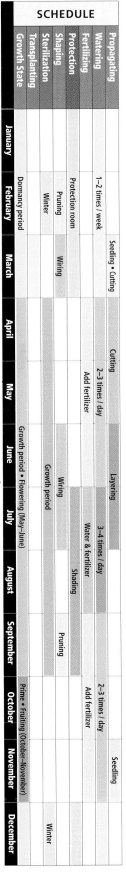

	SCHEDULE							
Growth State	Transplanting	Sterilization	Shaping	Protection	Fertilizing	Watering	Propagating	
January					Protection room		1–2 times / week	Seedling • Cutting
February	Dormancy period	Winter		Pruning	Protection room		1–2 times / week	Seedling • Cutting
March				Wiring				
April						Add fertilizer		Cutting
May	Growth period • Flowering (May-June)					Add fertilizer	2–3 times / day	Cutting
June	Growth period • Flowering (May-June)	Growth period					2–3 times / day	Layering
July				Wiring		Water & fertilizer	3–4 times / day	
August					Shading	Water & fertilizer	3–4 times / day	
September				Pruning				
October	Prime • Fruiting (October-November)					Add fertilizer	2–3 times / day	Seedling
November	Prime • Fruiting (October-November)					Add fertilizer		Seedling
December		Winter						

121

Kadsura Vine

JAPANESE NAME
Binangazura

ALTERNATIVE NAME
Kadsura

SCIENTIFIC NAME
Kadsura japonica

CLASSIFICATION
**Pine family
(deciduous broadleaf tree /
shrub)**

SYMBOLIC OF
Reunion

BEARING FRUIT
October to November

In August, pale yellow flowers bloom. Looking much like Japanese sweets, its red fruit can be viewed for some time, until the following February or so. Although a hermaphroditic plant, using male flowers from the same plant for cross-pollination makes bearing fruit difficult, so furnishing pollen from the flowers of other trees is best. Propagating with cuttings or seed-grown seedlings is recommended.

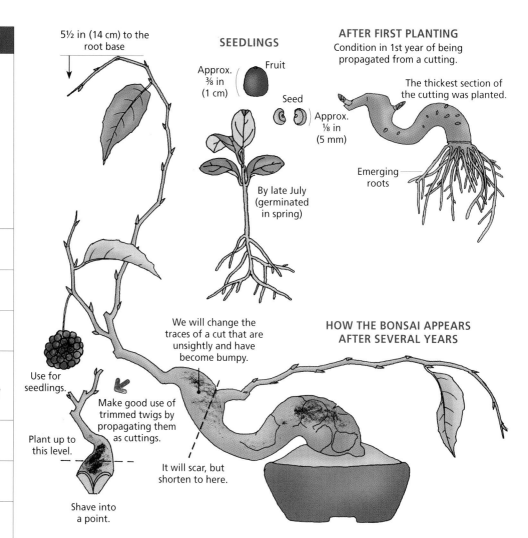

5½ in (14 cm) to the root base

SEEDLINGS

Approx. ⅜ in (1 cm) — Fruit

Seed

Approx. ⅛ in (5 mm)

By late July (germinated in spring)

AFTER FIRST PLANTING
Condition in 1st year of being propagated from a cutting.

The thickest section of the cutting was planted.

Emerging roots

We will change the traces of a cut that are unsightly and have become bumpy.

HOW THE BONSAI APPEARS AFTER SEVERAL YEARS

Use for seedlings.

Make good use of trimmed twigs by propagating them as cuttings.

Plant up to this level.

It will scar, but shorten to here.

Shave into a point.

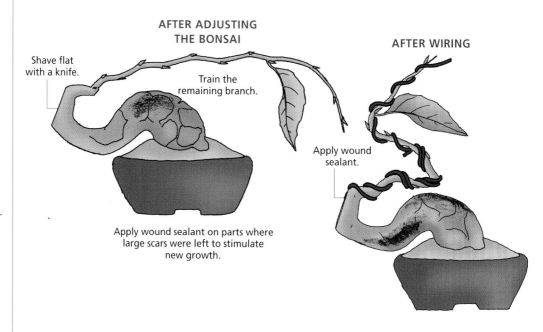

AFTER ADJUSTING THE BONSAI

Shave flat with a knife.

Train the remaining branch.

AFTER WIRING

Apply wound sealant.

Apply wound sealant on parts where large scars were left to stimulate new growth.

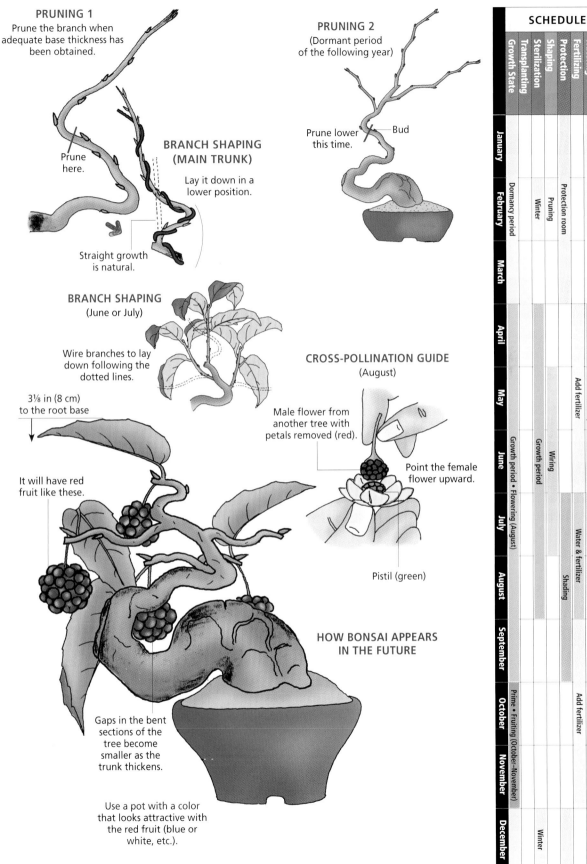

PRUNING 1

Prune the branch when adequate base thickness has been obtained.

Prune here.

PRUNING 2

(Dormant period of the following year)

Prune lower this time.

Bud

BRANCH SHAPING (MAIN TRUNK)

Lay it down in a lower position.

Straight growth is natural.

BRANCH SHAPING

(June or July)

Wire branches to lay down following the dotted lines.

3⅛ in (8 cm) to the root base

It will have red fruit like these.

CROSS-POLLINATION GUIDE

(August)

Male flower from another tree with petals removed (red).

Point the female flower upward.

Pistil (green)

HOW BONSAI APPEARS IN THE FUTURE

Gaps in the bent sections of the tree become smaller as the trunk thickens.

Use a pot with a color that looks attractive with the red fruit (blue or white, etc.).

SCHEDULE

Growth State	Transplanting	Sterilization	Shaping	Protection	Fertilizing	Watering	Propagating
January		Winter	Pruning	Protection room		1–2 times / week	
February	Dormancy period	Winter	Pruning	Protection room		1–2 times / week	Seedling • Cutting
March						1–2 times / week	Seedling • Cutting
April	Growth period				Add fertilizer	2–3 times / day	Layering • Cutting
May	Growth period				Add fertilizer	2–3 times / day	Layering • Cutting
June	Growth period • Flowering (August)		Wiring			3–4 times / day	Layering • Cutting
July	Growth period • Flowering (August)		Wiring		Water & fertilizer	3–4 times / day	Layering • Cutting
August	Growth period • Flowering (August)			Shading	Water & fertilizer	3–4 times / day	Layering • Cutting
September	Growth period • Flowering (August)			Shading	Water & fertilizer	3–4 times / day	
October	Prime • Fruiting (October–November)				Add fertilizer	2–3 times / day	Seedling
November	Prime • Fruiting (October–November)				Add fertilizer	2–3 times / day	Seedling
December		Winter				2–3 times / day	

Japanese Winterberry

JAPANESE NAME
Ume-modoki

ALTERNATIVE NAMES
n/a

SCIENTIFIC NAME
Ilex serrata

CLASSIFICATION
Aquifoliaceae (deciduous broadleaf tree / shrub)

SYMBOLIC OF
Clarity

BEARING FRUIT
October to November

The source of this tree's Japanese name (meaning "false plum") is that the leaves look similar to plum leaves. Expect flowers from May to June. There are several varieties, with the ¼ to ⅜-in (6 to 8-mm) diameter fruit of the "Dainagon" variety being well known in Japan. It is a species of tree with thin mesophyll (leaf tissue) and demands a great deal of water. As it is dioecious, any difference between male and female seed-grown seedlings cannot be perceived until after the tree has flowered.

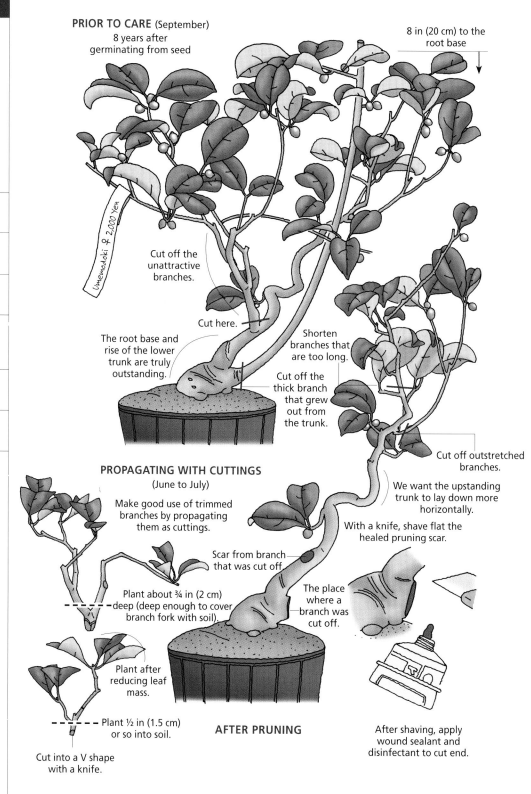

PRIOR TO CARE (September)
8 years after germinating from seed

8 in (20 cm) to the root base

Cut off the unattractive branches.

Umemodoki ￥ 2,000 Yen

Cut here.

Shorten branches that are too long.

The root base and rise of the lower trunk are truly outstanding.

Cut off the thick branch that grew out from the trunk.

Cut off outstretched branches.

We want the upstanding trunk to lay down more horizontally.

PROPAGATING WITH CUTTINGS
(June to July)

Make good use of trimmed branches by propagating them as cuttings.

With a knife, shave flat the healed pruning scar.

Scar from branch that was cut off

Plant about ¾ in (2 cm) deep (deep enough to cover branch fork with soil).

The place where a branch was cut off.

Plant after reducing leaf mass.

Plant ½ in (1.5 cm) or so into soil.

AFTER PRUNING

After shaving, apply wound sealant and disinfectant to cut end.

Cut into a V shape with a knife.

ROOT SHORTENING
AFTER PRUNING (February)

With a chopstick, check locations of root-flare.

Cut off "shoulder" (top edge) of the hard-packed soil, all the way around.

ROOT SHORTENING

Cut off roots wrapped around soil mass.

Where the shoulder of the packed soil was cut off.

GUIDE TO CLEANING SOIL FROM SMALL ROOTS

Thin roots have spread throughout root mass and become closely-packed.

Where roots wrapped around soil mass were cut off.

Cut back with small scissors to leave a horizontal surface.

AFTER PLANTING

Reposition the upright trunk by wiring from near its tip down through the edge of the root base and pulling the trunk tightly into position.

Tighten the guy-wire.

PREPARING A MOUND OF SOIL

Use a chopstick to dig at the roots and scrape old soil out toward edge.

Base fertilizer (bone meal or similar) under the soil mix

Soil composition
80% *Akadama* soil
20% *Kiryu* sand

Bamboo charcoal

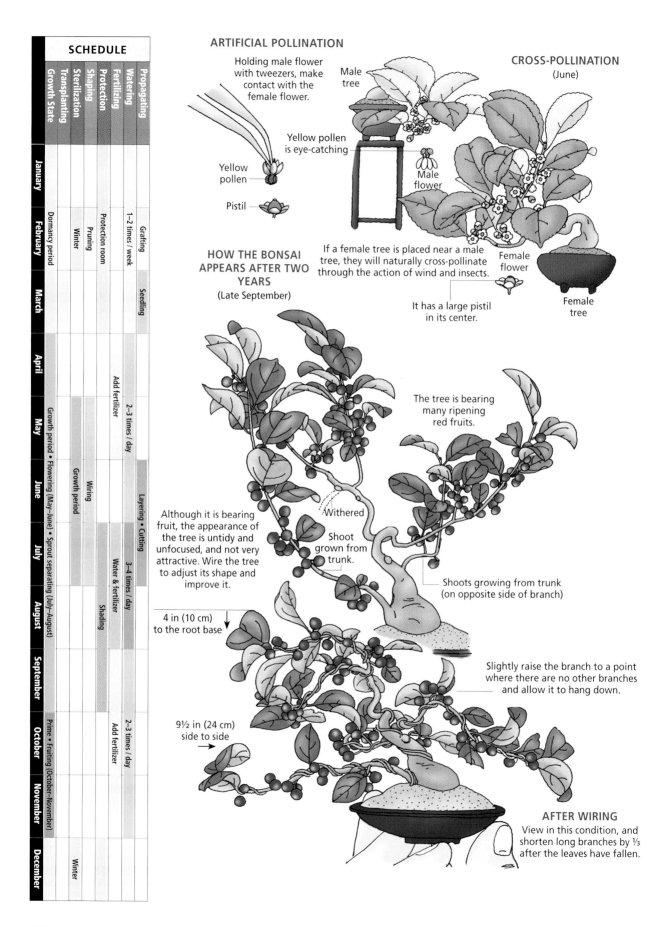

SCHEDULE

Growth State	Transplanting	Sterilization	Shaping	Protection	Fertilizing	Watering	Propagating	
							Grafting	January
Dormancy period		Winter	Pruning	Protection room		1-2 times / week		February
							Seedling	March
					Add fertilizer			April
Growth period • Flowering (May–June) • Sprout separating (July–August)						2-3 times / day	Layering • Cutting	May
			Wiring					June
						3-4 times / day		July
		Shading			Water & fertilizer			August
								September
Prime • Fruiting (October–November)					Add fertilizer	2-3 times / day		October
								November
		Winter						December

ARTIFICIAL POLLINATION

Holding male flower with tweezers, make contact with the female flower.

Yellow pollen is eye-catching

Yellow pollen

Pistil

CROSS-POLLINATION
(June)

Male tree

Male flower

Female flower

Female tree

If a female tree is placed near a male tree, they will naturally cross-pollinate through the action of wind and insects.

It has a large pistil in its center.

HOW THE BONSAI APPEARS AFTER TWO YEARS
(Late September)

The tree is bearing many ripening red fruits.

Although it is bearing fruit, the appearance of the tree is untidy and unfocused, and not very attractive. Wire the tree to adjust its shape and improve it.

Withered

Shoot grown from trunk.

Shoots growing from trunk (on opposite side of branch)

4 in (10 cm) to the root base

Slightly raise the branch to a point where there are no other branches and allow it to hang down.

9½ in (24 cm) side to side

AFTER WIRING
View in this condition, and shorten long branches by ⅓ after the leaves have fallen.

126

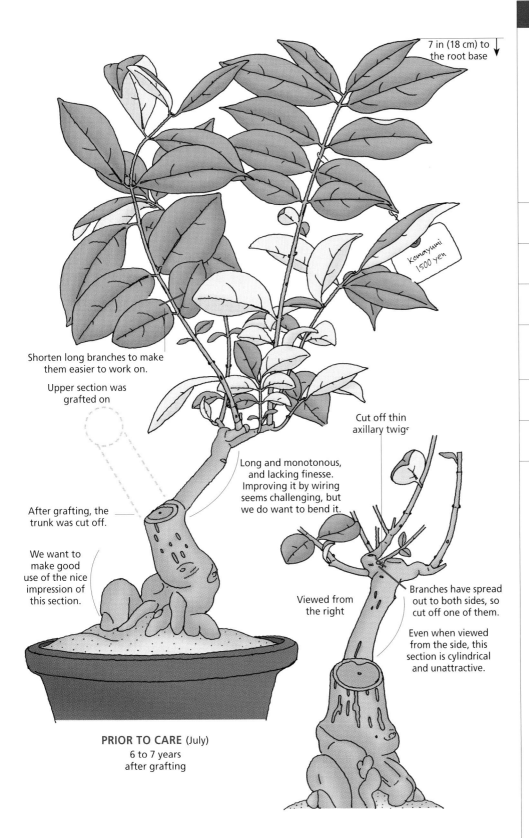

7 in (18 cm) to the root base

Komayumi 1500 yen

Shorten long branches to make them easier to work on.

Upper section was grafted on

After grafting, the trunk was cut off.

We want to make good use of the nice impression of this section.

Long and monotonous, and lacking finesse. Improving it by wiring seems challenging, but we do want to bend it.

Cut off thin axillary twigs

Viewed from the right

Branches have spread out to both sides, so cut off one of them.

Even when viewed from the side, this section is cylindrical and unattractive.

PRIOR TO CARE (July)
6 to 7 years
after grafting

Burning Bush

JAPANESE NAME
Komayumi

ALTERNATIVE NAMES
n/a

SCIENTIFIC NAME
Euonymus alatus

CLASSIFICATION
Euonymus (**deciduous broadleaf tree / shrub**)

SYMBOLIC OF
Reluctance to part

BEARING FRUIT
October to November

Pale yellow and green flowers bloom in May and June. The tops of new apical shoots and the axillary shoots close to them bear flower buds. *Komayumi*, the variety of burning bush found in Japan, is a robust species, and handles aggressive pruning well. Its ripening red fruit are beautiful, as well as the changing autumn colors of its leaves. Propagating with cuttings or through air-layering is recommended.

PRUNING AND WIRING

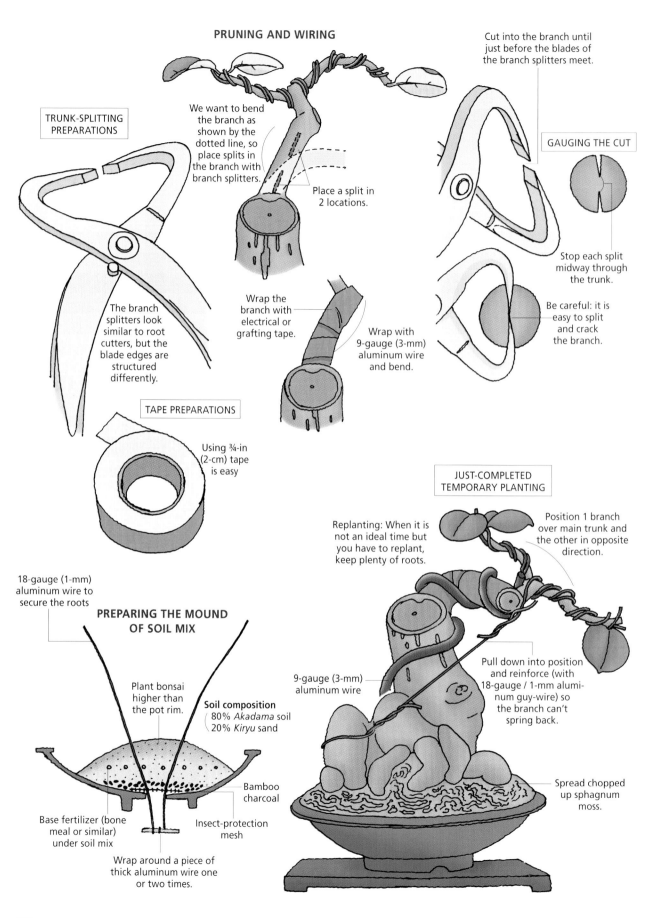

Cut into the branch until just before the blades of the branch splitters meet.

TRUNK-SPLITTING PREPARATIONS

We want to bend the branch as shown by the dotted line, so place splits in the branch with branch splitters.

Place a split in 2 locations.

GAUGING THE CUT

Stop each split midway through the trunk.

The branch splitters look similar to root cutters, but the blade edges are structured differently.

Wrap the branch with electrical or grafting tape.

Wrap with 9-gauge (3-mm) aluminum wire and bend.

Be careful: it is easy to split and crack the branch.

TAPE PREPARATIONS

Using ¾-in (2-cm) tape is easy

JUST-COMPLETED TEMPORARY PLANTING

Replanting: When it is not an ideal time but you have to replant, keep plenty of roots.

Position 1 branch over main trunk and the other in opposite direction.

18-gauge (1-mm) aluminum wire to secure the roots

PREPARING THE MOUND OF SOIL MIX

Plant bonsai higher than the pot rim.

Soil composition
80% *Akadama* soil
20% *Kiryu* sand

9-gauge (3-mm) aluminum wire

Pull down into position and reinforce (with 18-gauge / 1-mm aluminum guy-wire) so the branch can't spring back.

Bamboo charcoal

Base fertilizer (bone meal or similar) under soil mix

Insect-protection mesh

Wrap around a piece of thick aluminum wire one or two times.

Spread chopped up sphagnum moss.

128

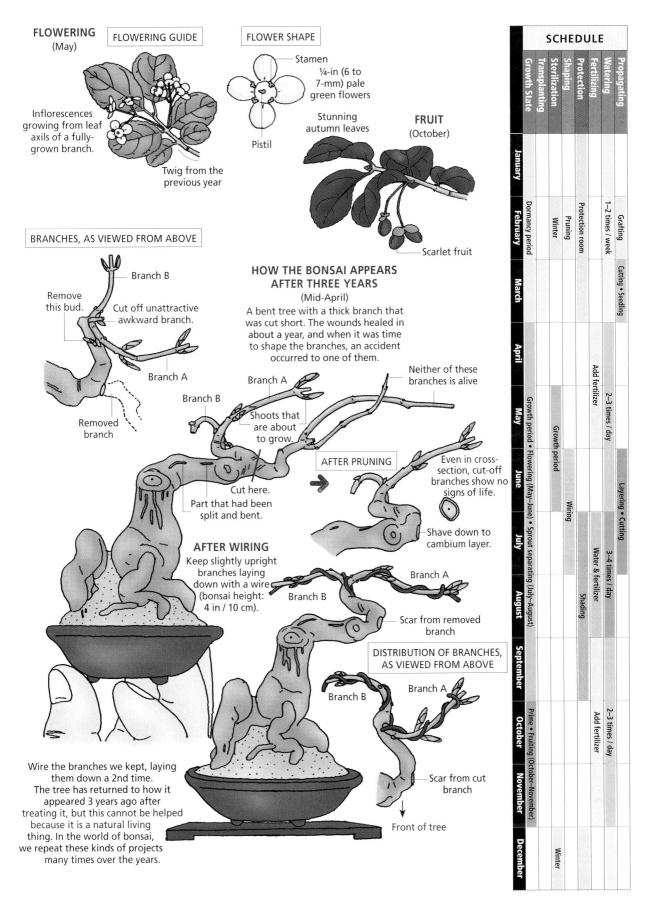

FLOWERING
(May)

FLOWERING GUIDE

Inflorescences growing from leaf axils of a fully-grown branch.

Twig from the previous year

FLOWER SHAPE

Stamen

¼-in (6 to 7-mm) pale green flowers

Pistil

Stunning autumn leaves

FRUIT
(October)

Scarlet fruit

BRANCHES, AS VIEWED FROM ABOVE

Branch B

Remove this bud.

Cut off unattractive awkward branch.

Branch A

Removed branch

HOW THE BONSAI APPEARS AFTER THREE YEARS
(Mid-April)

A bent tree with a thick branch that was cut short. The wounds healed in about a year, and when it was time to shape the branches, an accident occurred to one of them.

Branch A

Branch B

Shoots that are about to grow.

Neither of these branches is alive

Cut here.

Part that had been split and bent.

AFTER PRUNING

Even in cross-section, cut-off branches show no signs of life.

Shave down to cambium layer.

AFTER WIRING

Keep slightly upright branches laying down with a wire (bonsai height: 4 in / 10 cm).

Branch B

Branch A

Scar from removed branch

DISTRIBUTION OF BRANCHES, AS VIEWED FROM ABOVE

Branch B

Branch A

Scar from cut branch

Front of tree

Wire the branches we kept, laying them down a 2nd time. The tree has returned to how it appeared 3 years ago after treating it, but this cannot be helped because it is a natural living thing. In the world of bonsai, we repeat these kinds of projects many times over the years.

SCHEDULE

Month	Growth State	Transplanting	Sterilization	Shaping	Protection	Fertilizing	Watering	Propagating
January	Dormancy period						1–2 times / week	Grafting
February	Dormancy period		Winter	Pruning	Protection room		1–2 times / week	Cutting • Seedling
March								Cutting • Seedling
April	Growth period					Add fertilizer	2–3 times / day	
May	Growth period • Flowering (May–June)					Add fertilizer	2–3 times / day	Layering • Cutting
June	Flowering (May–June) • Growth period			Wiring			2–3 times / day	Layering • Cutting
July	Sprout separating (July–August)			Wiring		Water & fertilizer	3–4 times / day	Layering • Cutting
August	Sprout separating (July–August)		Shading				3–4 times / day	Layering • Cutting
September						Add fertilizer	3–4 times / day	Layering • Cutting
October	Prime • Fruiting (October–November)					Add fertilizer	2–3 times / day	
November	Prime • Fruiting (October–November)							
December			Winter					

129

Toringo Crabapple

JAPANESE NAME
Zumi

ALTERNATIVE NAMES
Mitsubakaido, koringo

SCIENTIFIC NAME
Malus toringo

CLASSIFICATION
Rose family (broadleaf tree / under 33 feet / 10 m)

SYMBOLIC OF
n/a

BEARING FRUIT
October to November

In may and June, white flowers bloom on this tree's branch tips. There are even occasional light pink flowers. Its Japanese name comes from the Japanese word for a dye (*shimi*), owing to the use of its bark for yellow dyes. A strong sturdy tree, it has alternating leaves (not pairs). Its fruit is spherical and red when ripe. The *ki-mizumi* variety has yellow fruit. Propagating with either cuttings or root cuttings is recommended.

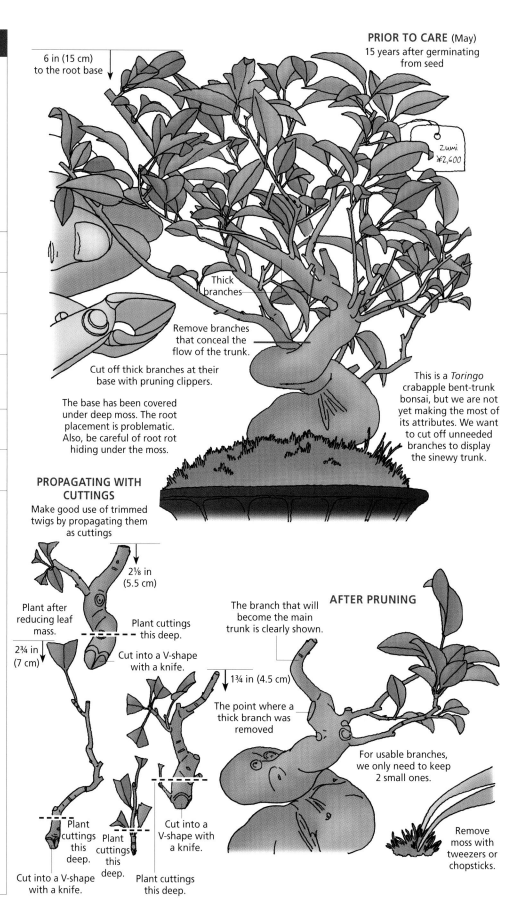

PRIOR TO CARE (May)
15 years after germinating from seed

6 in (15 cm) to the root base

Zumi ¥2,600

Thick branches

Remove branches that conceal the flow of the trunk.

Cut off thick branches at their base with pruning clippers.

The base has been covered under deep moss. The root placement is problematic. Also, be careful of root rot hiding under the moss.

This is a *Toringo* crabapple bent-trunk bonsai, but we are not yet making the most of its attributes. We want to cut off unneeded branches to display the sinewy trunk.

PROPAGATING WITH CUTTINGS
Make good use of trimmed twigs by propagating them as cuttings

2⅛ in (5.5 cm)

Plant after reducing leaf mass.

Plant cuttings this deep.

Cut into a V-shape with a knife.

2¾ in (7 cm)

AFTER PRUNING

The branch that will become the main trunk is clearly shown.

1¾ in (4.5 cm)

The point where a thick branch was removed

For usable branches, we only need to keep 2 small ones.

Plant cuttings this deep.

Plant cuttings this deep.

Cut into a V-shape with a knife.

Cut into a V-shape with a knife.

Plant cuttings this deep.

Remove moss with tweezers or chopsticks.

CHECKING ROOT-FLARE

Uppermost level of moss

Root-flares are somewhat thin roots.

Remove the upper roots that have appeared.

Loosening the old hard-packed soil is challenging—particularly the old soil under the root base of your tree. Clean it all out.

Clean out old soil with a strong spray of water.

Remove old soil stuck between roots with a chopstick or tweezers.

ROOTS VIEWED FROM BOTTOM

The scar left where a thick root had been cut off.

Do not overlook cleaning out all the old soil, even from under the root base.

Wire to secure bonsai

Base fertilizer

Soil composition
80% *Akadama* soil
($1/32$ to $1/8$ in / 1 to 4 mm)
20% *Kiryu* sand
($1/32$ to $1/8$ in / 1 to 4 mm)
+ about 5% bamboo charcoal

4 in (10 cm) to the root base

Make sure the bend in the trunk that flows from the back to the front is visible.

Display the flow of the trunk.

AFTER REPLANTING

Planting angle prior to care.

VIEWED FROM ABOVE

Move fully-grown branch on the right toward the back.

Front

Pull toward the front while positioning wiring.

SCHEDULE

Growth State		January	February	March	April	May	June	July	August	September	October	November	December
Propagating	Grafting			Roots insertion			Layering • Cutting					
Watering	1–2 times / week				2–3 times / day		3–4 times / day			2–3 times / day		
Fertilizing					Add fertilizer		Water & fertilizer			Add fertilizer		
Protection	Protection room											
Shaping						Wiring						
Sterilization	Winter											Winter
	Pruning											
Transplanting		Dormancy period			Growth period • Flowering (May–June) • Sprout separating (July–August)					Prime •Fruiting (October–November)		
					Growth period							
							Growth period					

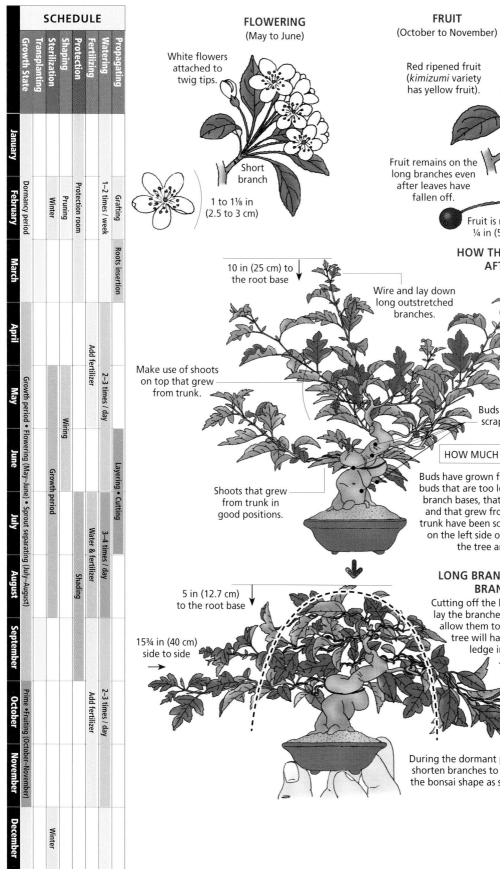

FLOWERING
(May to June)

White flowers attached to twig tips.

Short branch

1 to 1⅛ in (2.5 to 3 cm)

FRUIT
(October to November)

Red ripened fruit (*kimizumi* variety has yellow fruit).

Fruit remains on the long branches even after leaves have fallen off.

Fruit is round, ⅛ to ¼ in (5 to 7 mm)

HOW THE BONSAI APPEARS AFTER ONE YEAR
(June)

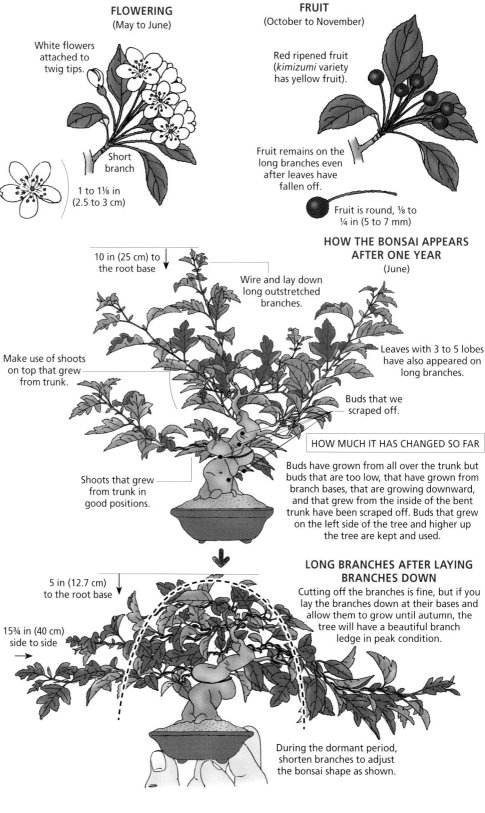

10 in (25 cm) to the root base

Wire and lay down long outstretched branches.

Make use of shoots on top that grew from trunk.

Leaves with 3 to 5 lobes have also appeared on long branches.

Buds that we scraped off.

Shoots that grew from trunk in good positions.

HOW MUCH IT HAS CHANGED SO FAR

Buds have grown from all over the trunk but buds that are too low, that have grown from branch bases, that are growing downward, and that grew from the inside of the bent trunk have been scraped off. Buds that grew on the left side of the tree and higher up the tree are kept and used.

LONG BRANCHES AFTER LAYING BRANCHES DOWN

Cutting off the branches is fine, but if you lay the branches down at their bases and allow them to grow until autumn, the tree will have a beautiful branch ledge in peak condition.

5 in (12.7 cm) to the root base

15¾ in (40 cm) side to side

During the dormant period, shorten branches to adjust the bonsai shape as shown.

132

How to Care for Leafy Bonsai

The highlights of this type are the shapes and colors of leaves, the colors of trunks and the balanced colors of leaves and the pot—all varying depending on species. Not to be forgotten is their most splendid transformation—the changing colors of autumn leaves.

ADMIRE THE FOUR SEASONS THROUGH ITS CHANGING LEAVES

Species of bonsai with leaves that change color and fall in the autumn are known as "leafy bonsai."
The cycle starts with the appearance of spring buds. Before long the season of bright green arrives, followed by the lush rampant growth of summer leaves. In the end, we welcome the season of autumn colors.

And then, after the leaves have fallen, the shape of the winter tree appears—also a highlight—though comprised of only the trunk and branches.

In Japan, bonsai trees that have become bare after all their leaves have fallen are known as "cold trees" (refer to footnote on page 137).

Trees that display their fine branches and trunk patterns clearly are considered to be ideal for viewing. Leafy bonsai that clearly show the changes of the seasons can be said to be traditional Japanese bonsai.

Trident Maple

JAPANESE NAME
Kaede

ALTERNATIVE NAME
Toukaede

SCIENTIFIC NAME
Acer buergeranium

CLASSIFICATION
Maple family (broadleaf tree / under 33 feet / 10 m)

SYMBOLIC OF
Love, Bountiful harvest

PEAK COLOR
November

In the world of bonsai, when one generally refers to maple, more often than not the Trident maple is the tree actually being discussed. This is a dioecious tree native to China. Its leaves and branches grow in opposing pairs, and leaves normally have three lobes toward the top. The tops of the leaves are glossy and both sides are smooth. Three primary veins* emerge from the bottom of the leaf. This is a sturdy species of tree, and propagating with cuttings is easy.

This was the only tree in the bonsai area of my local gardening center that seemed suitable as raw material that I could cut smaller. The others had cylindrical rises of their lower trunks and only branched out toward the top. This tree may become sparse if we were to keep only the branches we needed. Still, the first thing to do is identify parts of this tree that will make for a good structure.

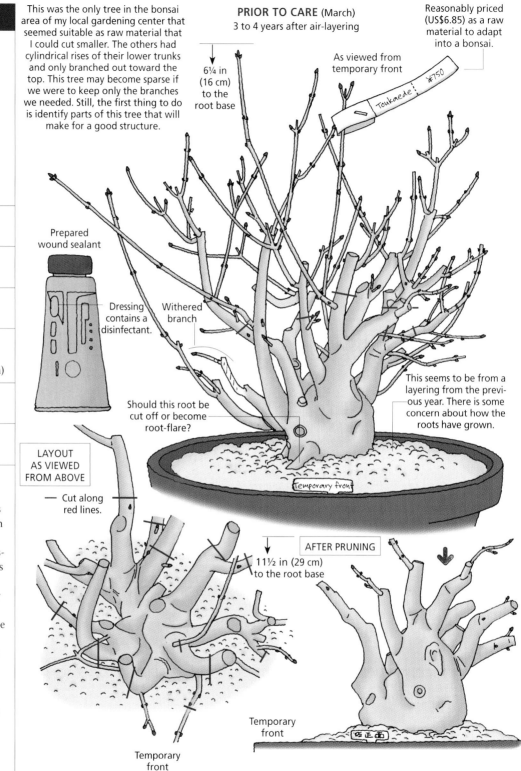

PRIOR TO CARE (March)
3 to 4 years after air-layering

Reasonably priced (US$6.85) as a raw material to adapt into a bonsai.

6¼ in (16 cm) to the root base

As viewed from temporary front

Toukaede ¥750

Prepared wound sealant

Dressing contains a disinfectant.

Withered branch

This seems to be from a layering from the previous year. There is some concern about how the roots have grown.

Should this root be cut off or become root-flare?

LAYOUT AS VIEWED FROM ABOVE

— Cut along red lines.

Temporary front

Temporary front

AFTER PRUNING

11½ in (29 cm) to the root base

Temporary front

*Primary vein: The vascular tissue of the stem connects to the leaves, so nutrients and water pass through this vein, which also plays a role in passing sugars produced through carbon fixation by the leaves back toward the stem. It also serves as the structural framework of the leaf, helping it keep its shape. In coniferous trees, there is only one in the center of each needle, but in broadleaf trees, there are many branching veins. Of these, the large vein in the center is called the "midrib." Refer to page 191.

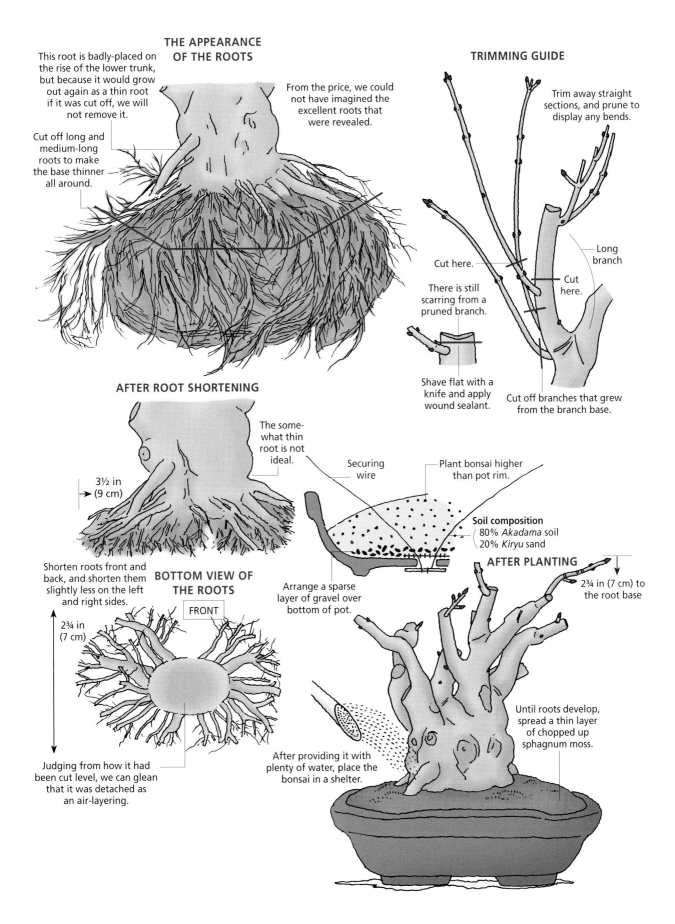

THE APPEARANCE OF THE ROOTS

This root is badly-placed on the rise of the lower trunk, but because it would grow out again as a thin root if it was cut off, we will not remove it.

Cut off long and medium-long roots to make the base thinner all around.

From the price, we could not have imagined the excellent roots that were revealed.

TRIMMING GUIDE

Trim away straight sections, and prune to display any bends.

Cut here.

There is still scarring from a pruned branch.

Shave flat with a knife and apply wound sealant.

Long branch

Cut here.

Cut off branches that grew from the branch base.

AFTER ROOT SHORTENING

3½ in (9 cm)

The somewhat thin root is not ideal.

Securing wire

Plant bonsai higher than pot rim.

Soil composition
80% *Akadama* soil
20% *Kiryu* sand

Arrange a sparse layer of gravel over bottom of pot.

AFTER PLANTING

2¾ in (7 cm) to the root base

BOTTOM VIEW OF THE ROOTS

FRONT

2¾ in (7 cm)

Shorten roots front and back, and shorten them slightly less on the left and right sides.

Judging from how it had been cut level, we can glean that it was detached as an air-layering.

After providing it with plenty of water, place the bonsai in a shelter.

Until roots develop, spread a thin layer of chopped up sphagnum moss.

Pruning and replanting

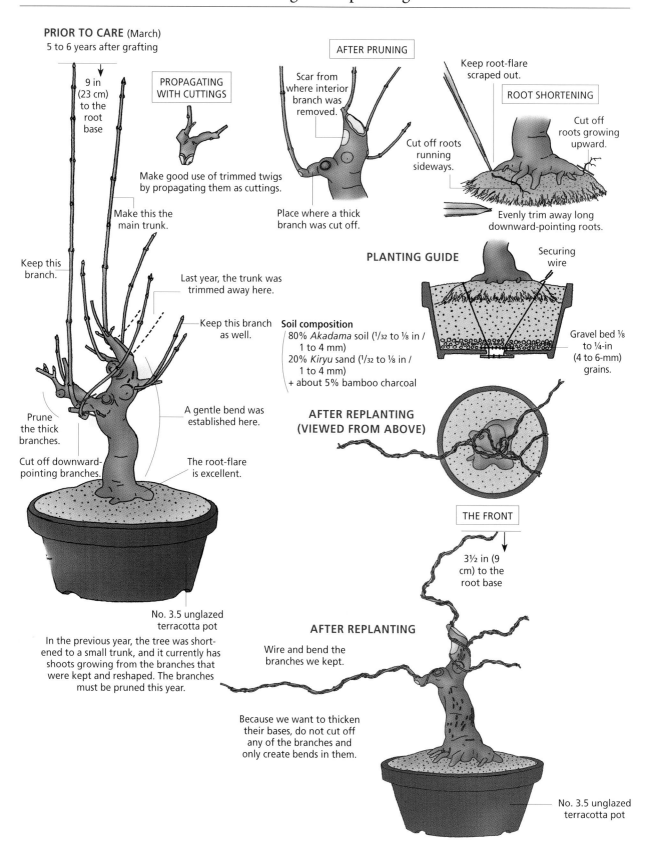

PRIOR TO CARE (March)
5 to 6 years after grafting

9 in (23 cm) to the root base

PROPAGATING WITH CUTTINGS

Make good use of trimmed twigs by propagating them as cuttings.

Make this the main trunk.

Keep this branch.

Last year, the trunk was trimmed away here.

Keep this branch as well.

Prune the thick branches.

Cut off downward-pointing branches.

A gentle bend was established here.

The root-flare is excellent.

No. 3.5 unglazed terracotta pot

In the previous year, the tree was short-ened to a small trunk, and it currently has shoots growing from the branches that were kept and reshaped. The branches must be pruned this year.

AFTER PRUNING

Scar from where interior branch was removed.

Cut off roots running sideways.

Place where a thick branch was cut off.

Soil composition
80% *Akadama* soil ($\frac{1}{32}$ to $\frac{1}{8}$ in / 1 to 4 mm)
20% *Kiryu* sand ($\frac{1}{32}$ to $\frac{1}{8}$ in / 1 to 4 mm)
+ about 5% bamboo charcoal

Keep root-flare scraped out.

ROOT SHORTENING

Cut off roots growing upward.

Evenly trim away long downward-pointing roots.

PLANTING GUIDE

Securing wire

Gravel bed $\frac{1}{8}$ to $\frac{1}{4}$-in (4 to 6-mm) grains.

AFTER REPLANTING (VIEWED FROM ABOVE)

THE FRONT

$3\frac{1}{2}$ in (9 cm) to the root base

AFTER REPLANTING

Wire and bend the branches we kept.

Because we want to thicken their bases, do not cut off any of the branches and only create bends in them.

No. 3.5 unglazed terracotta pot

BRANCH SHAPING AND DEBRANCHING
(Dormant period)

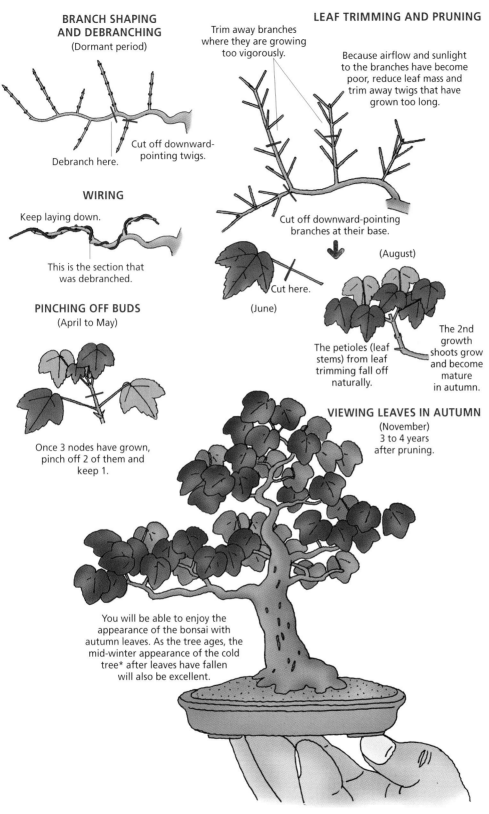

Cut off downward-pointing twigs.

Debranch here.

LEAF TRIMMING AND PRUNING

Trim away branches where they are growing too vigorously.

Because airflow and sunlight to the branches have become poor, reduce leaf mass and trim away twigs that have grown too long.

Cut off downward-pointing branches at their base.

(August)

WIRING

Keep laying down.

This is the section that was debranched.

Cut here.

(June)

The petioles (leaf stems) from leaf trimming fall off naturally.

The 2nd growth shoots grow and become mature in autumn.

PINCHING OFF BUDS
(April to May)

Once 3 nodes have grown, pinch off 2 of them and keep 1.

VIEWING LEAVES IN AUTUMN
(November)
3 to 4 years after pruning.

You will be able to enjoy the appearance of the bonsai with autumn leaves. As the tree ages, the mid-winter appearance of the cold tree* after leaves have fallen will also be excellent.

*Cold tree: Refers to how a deciduous tree appears in winter after its leaves have fallen—a bonsai formed of only branches. Japanese zelkova, trident maple, Japanese maple and so on are good example species. Because they have no leaves in the winter, we can hold the bonsai in our hands and its trunk patterns and fine branch details become clear, and this season is considered to be the most suitable to enjoy the shape of the tree itself.

	SCHEDULE		
Growth State	Transplanting	Sterilization	Shaping	Protection	Fertilizing	Watering	Propagating
January						1–2 times/week	Seedling • Cutting
February	Dormancy period	Winter	Pruning	Protection room			
March							
April			Bud picking		Add fertilizer	2–3 times/day	Layering • Cutting
May							
June	Growth period • Budding (April)		Growth period	Wiring • Leaf cutting (June)		3–4 times/day	
July					Water & fertilizer		
August				Shading			
September							
October	Prime • Autumn leaves (November)				Add fertilizer	2–3 times/day	
November							
December		Winter					

137

Japanese Maple

JAPANESE NAME
Momiji

ALTERNATIVE NAMES
Red emperor maple, Smooth Japanese maple

SCIENTIFIC NAME
Acer palmatum

CLASSIFICATION
Maple (deciduous hardwood / macrophanerophyte)

SYMBOLIC OF
Cautious restraint

PEAK COLOR
November and December

The flowers of the *momiji**
bloom even in the spring.
To truly enjoy the chang-
ing autumn colors of the
Japanese maple, pinching
off buds, trimming leaves,
pruning and wiring must
be done in the appropriate
seasons. *Momiji* prefers
half-days of shade and
some moisture, and in the
summer, being in direct
sunlight can cause leaf
burn, so pay attention to
its needs for water and
shade. Propagation is
by air-layering, or with
seed-grown seedlings or
cuttings.

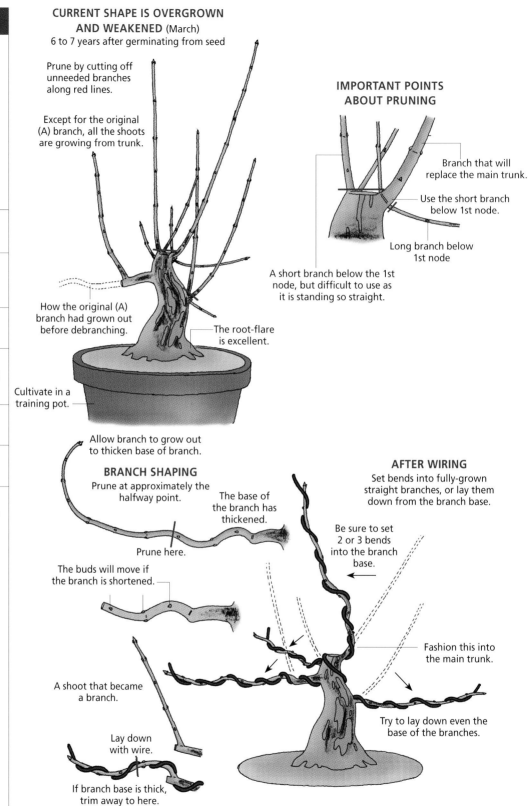

CURRENT SHAPE IS OVERGROWN AND WEAKENED (March)
6 to 7 years after germinating from seed

Prune by cutting off unneeded branches along red lines.

Except for the original (A) branch, all the shoots are growing from trunk.

How the original (A) branch had grown out before debranching.

The root-flare is excellent.

Cultivate in a training pot.

IMPORTANT POINTS ABOUT PRUNING

Branch that will replace the main trunk.

Use the short branch below 1st node.

Long branch below 1st node

A short branch below the 1st node, but difficult to use as it is standing so straight.

Allow branch to grow out to thicken base of branch.

BRANCH SHAPING
Prune at approximately the halfway point.

The base of the branch has thickened.

Prune here.

The buds will move if the branch is shortened.

A shoot that became a branch.

Lay down with wire.

If branch base is thick, trim away to here.

AFTER WIRING
Set bends into fully-grown straight branches, or lay them down from the branch base.

Be sure to set 2 or 3 bends into the branch base.

Fashion this into the main trunk.

Try to lay down even the base of the branches.

*Momiji: *In the horticultural world, among the trees that have been classified into the* Aceraceae *family, mountain maple* (Acer spicatum), *Japanese maple* (Acer palmatum) *and so on have notched leaf shapes, with those that have particularly deep notches being known as* momiji.

REPLACING THE MAIN TRUNK*

Allow main branch to grow so its base becomes thicker, and then shorten it.

After 3 months or so, take off the wiring you installed.

Trim at this point.

Thickened branch base

BRANCH SHAPING, LEAF TRIMMING, & PRUNING
(June)

Leaf trimming (petioles remain)

Twigs alternate

After wiring.

3 to 4 years later.

Steadily create connecting branches.

The base of the main trunk has thickened, and the taper has improved.

Cut off 1 of each set of opposing leaves to make them alternating leaves. Refer to page 191, "Names of Leaf Parts and How They are Attached."

HOW THE BONSAI APPEARS IN THE FUTURE (March)
After 6 years

Using an isosceles triangle as your guide for the entire tree shape, keep lower branches long.

Location of 2nd main trunk replacement.

Location of 1st main trunk replacement.

As trunks grow thicker, their bends decrease.

A pot that complements the colors of autumn leaves

VIEWING LEAVES IN AUTUMN
(December)

Enjoying the beautiful autumn leaves requires managing and nurturing the trees during summer months, as well as mitigating problems such as wildly varying temperatures. Bonsai that has been well-maintained will be most attractive.

*Replacing the main trunk: In situations where the main trunk of a tree has become too big, we shorten the tree by pruning the main trunk and then fashion a branch from the middle of the trunk into a replacement—the new main trunk.

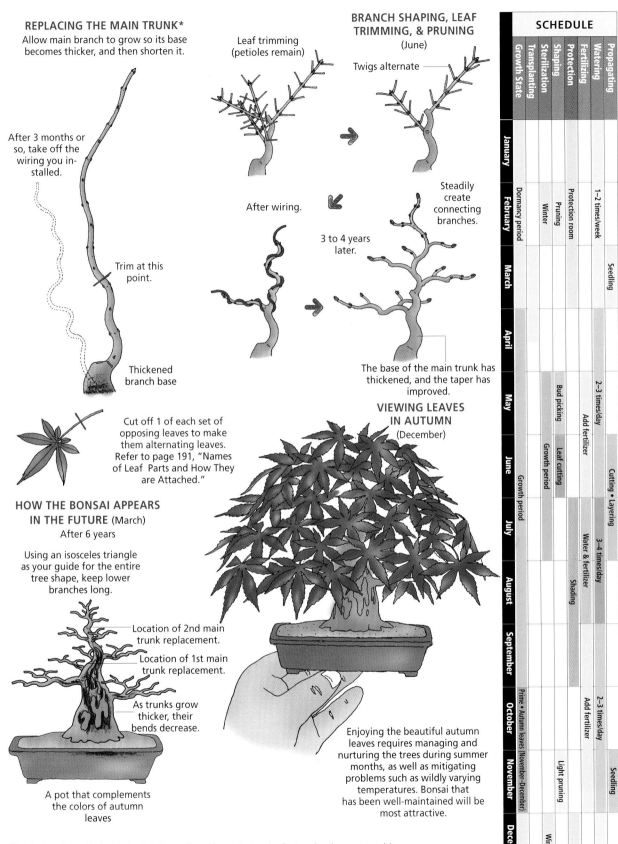

	Growth State	Transplanting	Sterilization	Shaping	Protection	Fertilizing	Watering	Propagating
January							1–2 times/week	Seedling
February	Dormancy period		Winter	Pruning	Protection room			
March								
April								
May				Bud picking		Add fertilizer	2–3 times/day	
June	Growth period			Leaf cutting / Growth period				Cutting • Layering
July							3–4 times/day	
August						Shading	Water & fertilizer	
September								
October	Prime • Autumn leaves (November–December)					Add fertilizer	2–3 times/day	
November				Light pruning				Seedling
December			Winter					

Japanese Zelkova

JAPANESE NAME
Keyaki

ALTERNATIVE NAMES
Tsuki, Tsukinoki

SCIENTIFIC NAME
Zelkova serrata

CLASSIFICATION
Ulmaceae family (deciduous broadleaf tree / macrophanerophyte)

SYMBOLIC OF
Happiness, Longevity

PEAK COLOR
November and December

April to May, tiny light yellow and green male flowers open on new stem tips, and female flowers bloom on the upper leaf veins. Because its delicate twigs become the focus of viewing after bearing fruit, and the autumn leaves change color, do not provide the bonsai with too much fertilizer or water. Pruning, pinching off buds* and leaf trimming should be done at appropriate times. Propagation is with seed-grown seedlings or air-layering.

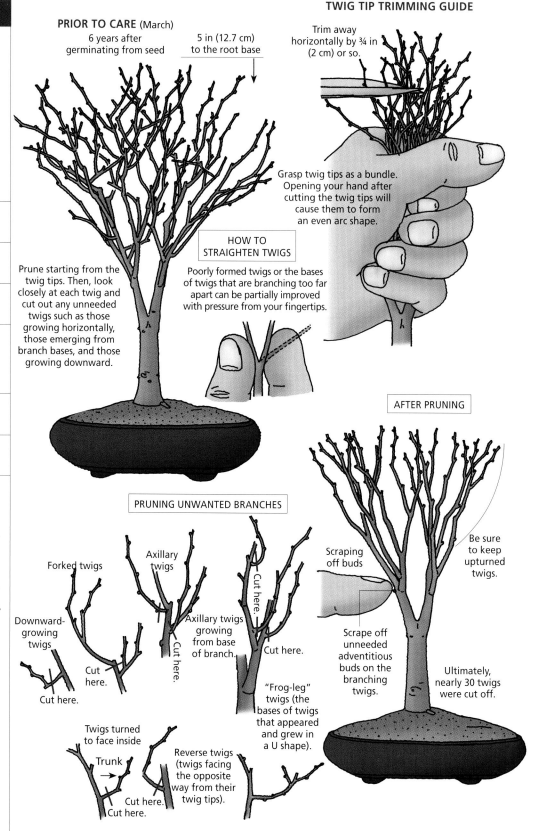

TWIG TIP TRIMMING GUIDE

PRIOR TO CARE (March)
6 years after germinating from seed

5 in (12.7 cm) to the root base

Trim away horizontally by ¾ in (2 cm) or so.

Grasp twig tips as a bundle. Opening your hand after cutting the twig tips will cause them to form an even arc shape.

Prune starting from the twig tips. Then, look closely at each twig and cut out any unneeded twigs such as those growing horizontally, those emerging from branch bases, and those growing downward.

HOW TO STRAIGHTEN TWIGS

Poorly formed twigs or the bases of twigs that are branching too far apart can be partially improved with pressure from your fingertips.

AFTER PRUNING

PRUNING UNWANTED BRANCHES

Forked twigs

Axillary twigs

Downward-growing twigs

Cut here.

Cut here.

Cut here.

Axillary twigs growing from base of branch.

Cut here.

Cut here.

"Frog-leg" twigs (the bases of twigs that appeared and grew in a U shape).

Twigs turned to face inside

Trunk

Cut here.
Cut here.

Reverse twigs (twigs facing the opposite way from their twig tips).

Scraping off buds

Scrape off unneeded adventitious buds on the branching twigs.

Be sure to keep upturned twigs.

Ultimately, nearly 30 twigs were cut off.

Pinching off buds: Because pinching off the first spring buds allows the second buds to grow, many more twigs and smaller leaves are possible.

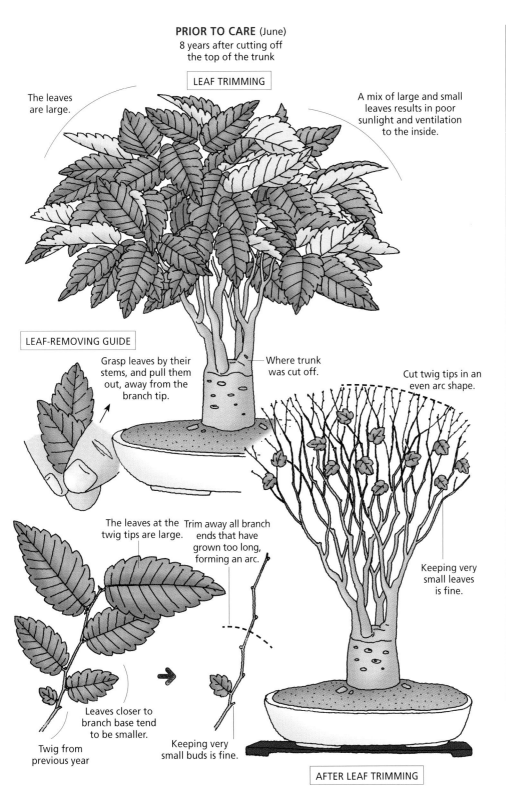

PRIOR TO CARE (June)
8 years after cutting off the top of the trunk

LEAF TRIMMING

The leaves are large.

A mix of large and small leaves results in poor sunlight and ventilation to the inside.

LEAF-REMOVING GUIDE

Grasp leaves by their stems, and pull them out, away from the branch tip.

Where trunk was cut off.

Cut twig tips in an even arc shape.

The leaves at the twig tips are large.

Trim away all branch ends that have grown too long, forming an arc.

Keeping very small leaves is fine.

Leaves closer to branch base tend to be smaller.

Twig from previous year

Keeping very small buds is fine.

AFTER LEAF TRIMMING

SCHEDULE

	Growth State	Transplanting	Sterilization	Shaping	Protection	Fertilizing	Watering	Propagating
January								
February	Dormancy period		Winter	Pruning	Protection room		1–2 times/week	Seedling
March	Dormancy period						1–2 times/week	Seedling
April							1–2 times/week	
May				Bud picking		Add fertilizer	2–3 times/day	Cutting • Layering
June	Growth period			Leaf cutting / Growth period		Add fertilizer	2–3 times/day	Cutting • Layering
July	Growth period					Water & fertilizer	3–4 times/day	Cutting • Layering
August	Growth period				Shading	Water & fertilizer	3–4 times/day	
September	Growth period				Shading			
October	Prime • Autumn leaves (October–November)					Add fertilizer	2–3 times/day	Seedling
November	Prime • Autumn leaves (October–November)			Light pruning			2–3 times/day	Seedling
December			Winter					

Ligistrum Obtusifolius

JAPANESE NAME
Ibotanuki

ALTERNATIVE NAMES
Kowanezumimochi, Ibota

SCIENTIFIC NAME
Ligistrum obtusifolius

CLASSIFICATION
Oleaceae (deciduous broadleaf tree / shrub)

SYMBOLIC OF
Forbiddenness

PEAK COLOR
November and December

In May and June, small white flowers grow densely on the tips of the tree's twigs, which bear purple-black fruit around October. Twigs are a grayish-white color, branching off in many places, with leaves and branches that grow symmetrically, in opposing sets. Do not pinch off buds or prune anything except for new overgrown branch tips. It is resistant to pruning but easy to care for. Propagating is with cuttings, seed-grown seedlings, or air-layering.

PRIOR TO CARE (March)

Air layered from the crown branches of a large potted tree, this tree was cut free 3 years ago. Because only the fully-grown twigs have been trimmed away, the unnecessary twigs are noticeable.

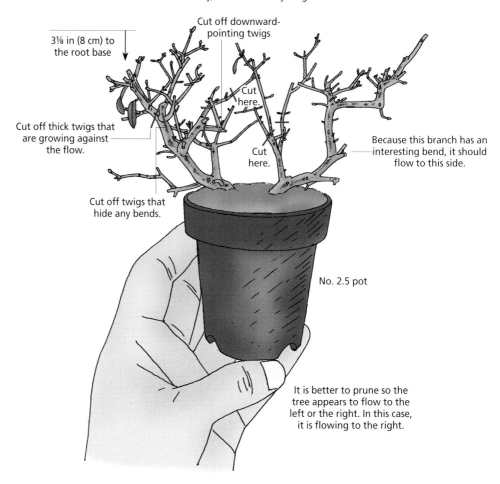

3⅛ in (8 cm) to the root base

Cut off downward-pointing twigs

Cut here.

Cut off thick twigs that are growing against the flow.

Cut here.

Because this branch has an interesting bend, it should flow to this side.

Cut off twigs that hide any bends.

No. 2.5 pot

It is better to prune so the tree appears to flow to the left or the right. In this case, it is flowing to the right.

AFTER ROOT SHORTENING

The tree was buried under soil up to roughly this dotted line.

Scrape out soil until root-flare can be seen.

The few long roots have been trimmed away.

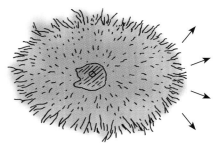

THE ROOTS, VIEWED FROM BELOW

By using a chopstick to scrape old soil out from around the thin roots and turn them facing out, the tree will accept its new soil well.

PLANTING CUTTINGS

Prune so it retains a bend.

3⅛ in (8 cm)

Cut it one more time with a knife, to give it a point like a sharpened pencil.

2⅜ in (6 cm)

Sharpen it with a knife and plant it.

AFTER PLANTING

Plant it so the tree appears to flow.

3⅛ in (8 cm) to the root base

The bonsai appears as though there were a wind blowing through it from this side.

FLOWERING GUIDE
(May to June)

Small white flowers bloom at the end of a fully-grown twig.

FRUIT-BEARING GUIDE
(November to December)

It bears black-purple fruit. They are about ¼ in (7 mm) in diameter.

4¾ in (12 cm) to the root base

VIEWING THE FRUIT
(October to November)

View the fruit attached to the branch tips.

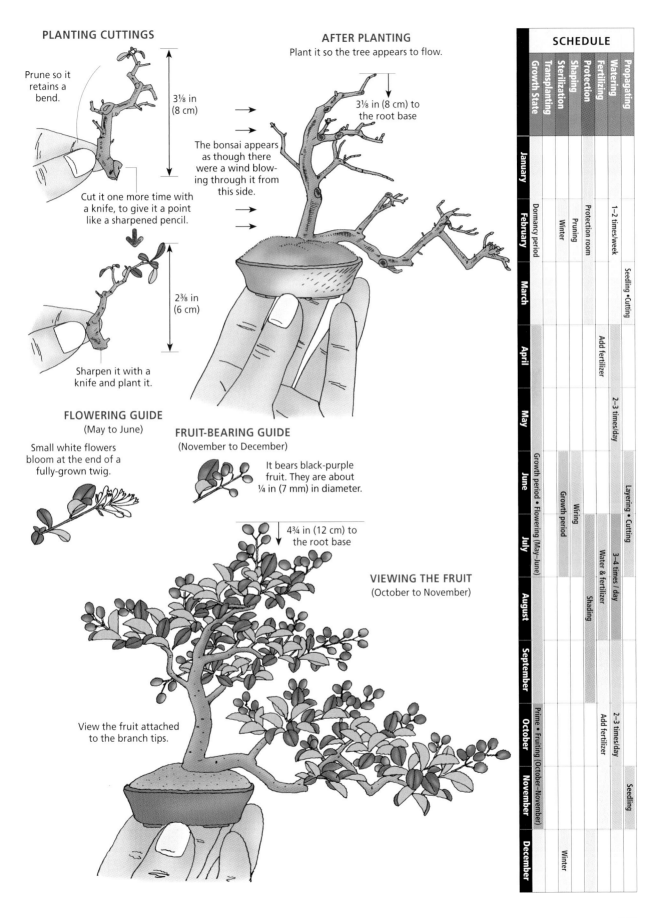

SCHEDULE

Month	Propagating	Watering	Fertilizing	Protection	Shaping	Sterilization	Transplanting	Growth State
January		1–2 times/week						Dormancy period
February	Seedling • Cutting	1–2 times/week		Protection room	Pruning	Winter		Dormancy period
March	Seedling • Cutting	1–2 times/week		Protection room				
April		1–2 times/week	Add fertilizer					
May		2–3 times/day						Growth period • Flowering (May–June)
June	Layering • Cutting	2–3 times/day			Wiring		Growth period	Growth period • Flowering (May–June)
July	Layering • Cutting	3–4 times / day	Water & fertilizer		Wiring			
August				Shading				
September		2–3 times/day						
October		2–3 times/day	Add fertilizer					Prime • Fruiting (October–November)
November	Seedling							Prime • Fruiting (October–November)
December						Winter		

143

Korean Hornbeam

JAPANESE NAME
Iwashide

ALTERNATIVE NAME
*Soro**

SCIENTIFIC NAME
Carpinus turczaninovii

CLASSIFICATION
Betulaceae (deciduous broadleaf plant / macrophanerophyte)

SYMBOLIC OF
n/a

PEAK COLOR
November and December

This tree flowers in April and May. As hornbeams age, shallow tears appear in their milky white bark, resulting in lovely striped patterns. The most vigorous among the hornbeams, the leaves of the Korean hornbeam are small and resilient. New buds will appear successively until August or September, and pinching off buds should be done each time. Propagation is easy with cuttings, seed-grown seedlings, or air-layering.

PRIOR TO CARE (February)
5 years after air-layering

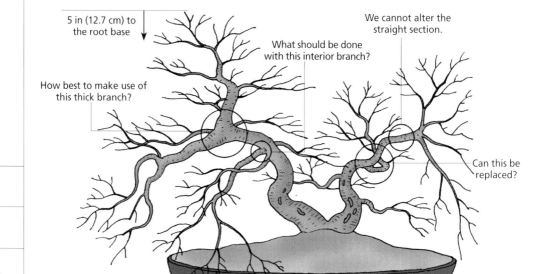

5 in (12.7 cm) to the root base

How best to make use of this thick branch?

What should be done with this interior branch?

We cannot alter the straight section.

Can this be replaced?

MODIFICATION OF THE ENTIRE SHAPE

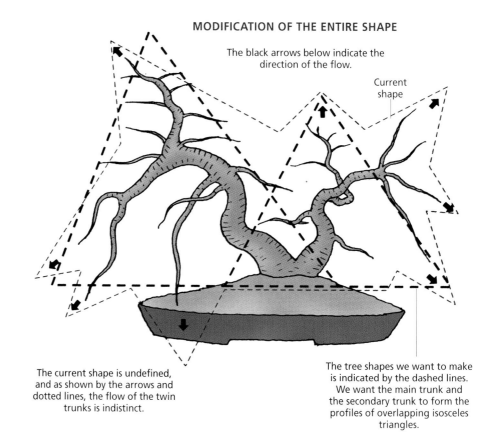

The black arrows below indicate the direction of the flow.

Current shape

The current shape is undefined, and as shown by the arrows and dotted lines, the flow of the twin trunks is indistinct.

The tree shapes we want to make is indicated by the dashed lines. We want the main trunk and the secondary trunk to form the profiles of overlapping isosceles triangles.

*Soro (red-leaved hornbeam): In the bonsai world, there are four subspecies, scalled akashide, inside, iwashide, and kumashide.

RESHAPING BRANCHES

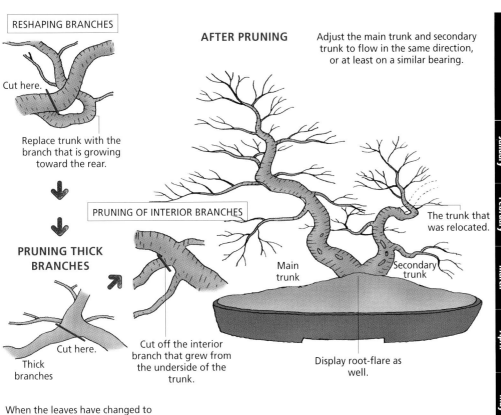

Cut here.

Replace trunk with the branch that is growing toward the rear.

⬇
⬇

PRUNING THICK BRANCHES

Cut here.

Thick branches

PRUNING OF INTERIOR BRANCHES

Cut off the interior branch that grew from the underside of the trunk.

AFTER PRUNING

Adjust the main trunk and secondary trunk to flow in the same direction, or at least on a similar bearing.

The trunk that was relocated.

Main trunk

Secondary trunk

Display root-flare as well.

When the leaves have changed to their autumn colors, the bonsai appears beautiful, and the remaining leaves, becoming a dark brown, pass the winter on the tips of branches.

HOW THE TWIN TRUNK BONSAI APPEARS IN THE AUTUMN

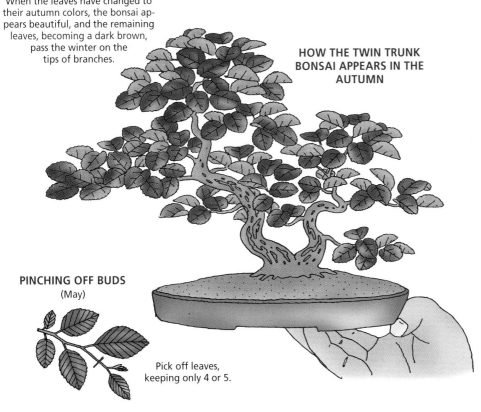

PINCHING OFF BUDS
(May)

Pick off leaves, keeping only 4 or 5.

SCHEDULE

Activity	January	February	March	April	May	June	July	August	September	October	November	December
Propagating	Seedling • Cutting	Seedling • Cutting	Seedling • Cutting			Layering • Cutting	Layering • Cutting				Seedling	
Watering	1–2 times/week	1–2 times/week			2–3 times / day	2–3 times / day	3–4 times/day	3–4 times/day		2–3 times/day		
Fertilizing					Add fertilizer					Add fertilizer		
Protection		Protection room	Protection room					Shading				
Shaping		Pruning	Pruning		Bud picking	Wiring	Wiring					
Sterilization		Winter										Winter
Transplanting												
Growth State		Dormancy period	Dormancy period			Growth period	Growth period			Prime • Autumn leaves (October–November)	Prime • Autumn leaves (October–November)	

Chinese Tamarisk

JAPANESE NAME
Gyoryu

ALTERNATIVE NAMES
Spicewood, Saltcedar

SCIENTIFIC NAME
Tamarix chinensis

CLASSIFICATION
Tamaricaceae **(deciduous broadleaf plant / under 33 feet / 10 m)**

SYMBOLIC OF
Delinquency

PEAK COLOR
November and December

Pale crimson racemose inflorescence (older flowers appear at the bases of the branches, while younger flowers continue to blossom toward the ends) of the tamarisk bloom twice, in May and again in September. Since their thin branches with densely-packed twigs can grow rather long, bend them with wire to appreciate the suppleness of their branches. Leaves are 3/64 to 5/64 in (1 to 2 mm) long and hug the thin twigs. A cold-resistant species, Tamarisk develops new roots vigorously, so propagating with cuttings is easy.

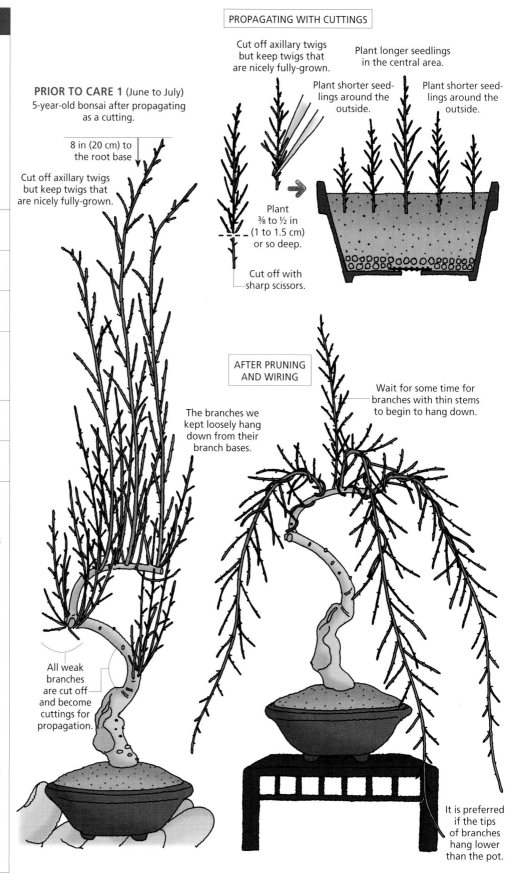

PRIOR TO CARE 1 (June to July)
5-year-old bonsai after propagating as a cutting.

8 in (20 cm) to the root base

Cut off axillary twigs but keep twigs that are nicely fully-grown.

All weak branches are cut off and become cuttings for propagation.

PROPAGATING WITH CUTTINGS

Cut off axillary twigs but keep twigs that are nicely fully-grown.

Plant longer seedlings in the central area.

Plant shorter seed-lings around the outside.

Plant shorter seed-lings around the outside.

Plant 3/8 to 1/2 in (1 to 1.5 cm) or so deep.

Cut off with sharp scissors.

AFTER PRUNING AND WIRING

Wait for some time for branches with thin stems to begin to hang down.

The branches we kept loosely hang down from their branch bases.

It is preferred if the tips of branches hang lower than the pot.

146

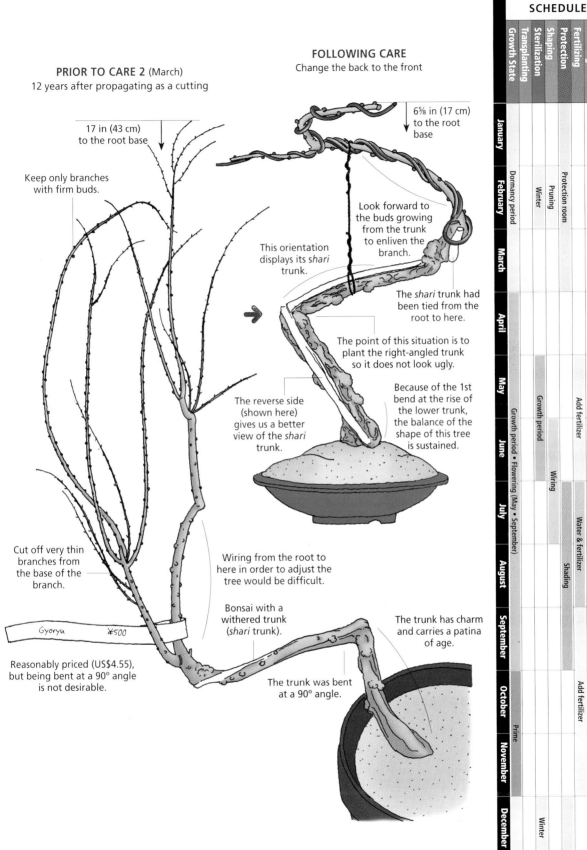

PRIOR TO CARE 2 (March)
12 years after propagating as a cutting

17 in (43 cm) to the root base

Keep only branches with firm buds.

This orientation displays its *shari* trunk.

The reverse side (shown here) gives us a better view of the *shari* trunk.

Cut off very thin branches from the base of the branch.

Wiring from the root to here in order to adjust the tree would be difficult.

Gyoryu   ¥500

Reasonably priced (US$4.55), but being bent at a 90° angle is not desirable.

Bonsai with a withered trunk (*shari* trunk).

The trunk was bent at a 90° angle.

FOLLOWING CARE
Change the back to the front

6⅝ in (17 cm) to the root base

Look forward to the buds growing from the trunk to enliven the branch.

The *shari* trunk had been tied from the root to here.

The point of this situation is to plant the right-angled trunk so it does not look ugly.

Because of the 1st bend at the rise of the lower trunk, the balance of the shape of this tree is sustained.

The trunk has charm and carries a patina of age.

	SCHEDULE		
Growth State	Transplanting	Sterilization	Protection	Fertilizing	Watering	Propagating
January	Dormancy period	Winter	Protection room		1–2 times/week	Cutting
February						
March		Pruning				
April					2–3 times / day	
May	Growth period • Flowering (May • September)	Growth period	Wiring	Add fertilizer		Cutting
June						
July				Water & fertilizer	3–4 times/day	
August			Shading			
September						
October				Add fertilizer	2–3 times/day	
November	Prime					
December		Winter			Winter	

Spicewood

JAPANESE NAME
Yamakobashi

ALTERNATIVE NAMES
Spicebush, Benjamin Bush

SCIENTIFIC NAME
Lindera glauca

CLASSIFICATION
Lauraceae (deciduous broadleaf plant / shrub)

SYMBOLIC OF
n/a

PEAK COLOR
November and December

From April to May, both buds and yellow florets bloom, and black fruit appears on the tree in the autumn. After changing to a tan color, the withered leaves remain on the branches for some time, retaining their elegance. Propagating is with cuttings, air-layering or seed-grown seedlings.

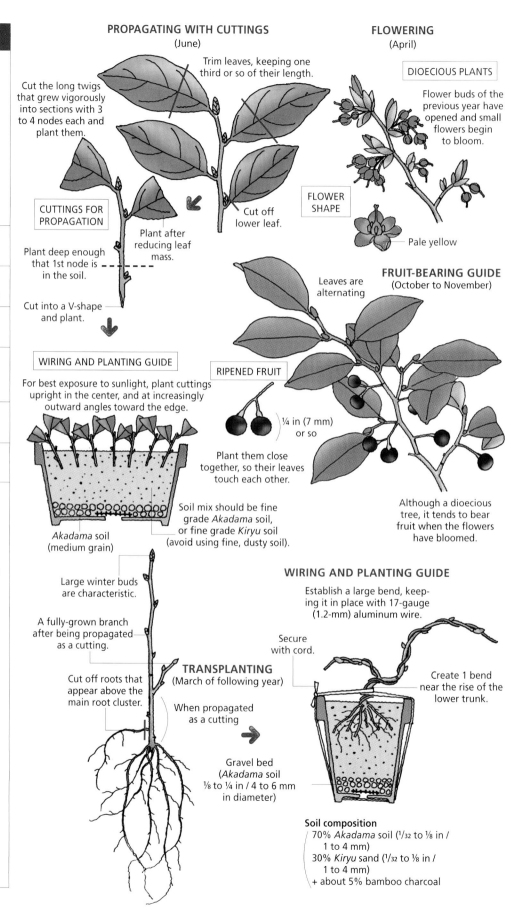

PROPAGATING WITH CUTTINGS
(June)

Cut the long twigs that grew vigorously into sections with 3 to 4 nodes each and plant them.

Trim leaves, keeping one third or so of their length.

CUTTINGS FOR PROPAGATION

Plant after reducing leaf mass.

Plant deep enough that 1st node is in the soil.

Cut off lower leaf.

Cut into a V-shape and plant.

FLOWERING
(April)

DIOECIOUS PLANTS

Flower buds of the previous year have opened and small flowers begin to bloom.

FLOWER SHAPE

Pale yellow

FRUIT-BEARING GUIDE
(October to November)

Leaves are alternating

RIPENED FRUIT

¼ in (7 mm) or so

Plant them close together, so their leaves touch each other.

Although a dioecious tree, it tends to bear fruit when the flowers have bloomed.

WIRING AND PLANTING GUIDE

For best exposure to sunlight, plant cuttings upright in the center, and at increasingly outward angles toward the edge.

Akadama soil (medium grain)

Soil mix should be fine grade *Akadama* soil, or fine grade *Kiryu* soil (avoid using fine, dusty soil).

WIRING AND PLANTING GUIDE

Establish a large bend, keeping it in place with 17-gauge (1.2-mm) aluminum wire.

Secure with cord.

Create 1 bend near the rise of the lower trunk.

Large winter buds are characteristic.

A fully-grown branch after being propagated as a cutting.

Cut off roots that appear above the main root cluster.

TRANSPLANTING
(March of following year)

When propagated as a cutting

Gravel bed (*Akadama* soil ⅛ to ¼ in / 4 to 6 mm in diameter)

Soil composition
70% *Akadama* soil (1/32 to ⅛ in / 1 to 4 mm)
30% *Kiryu* sand (1/32 to ⅛ in / 1 to 4 mm)
+ about 5% bamboo charcoal

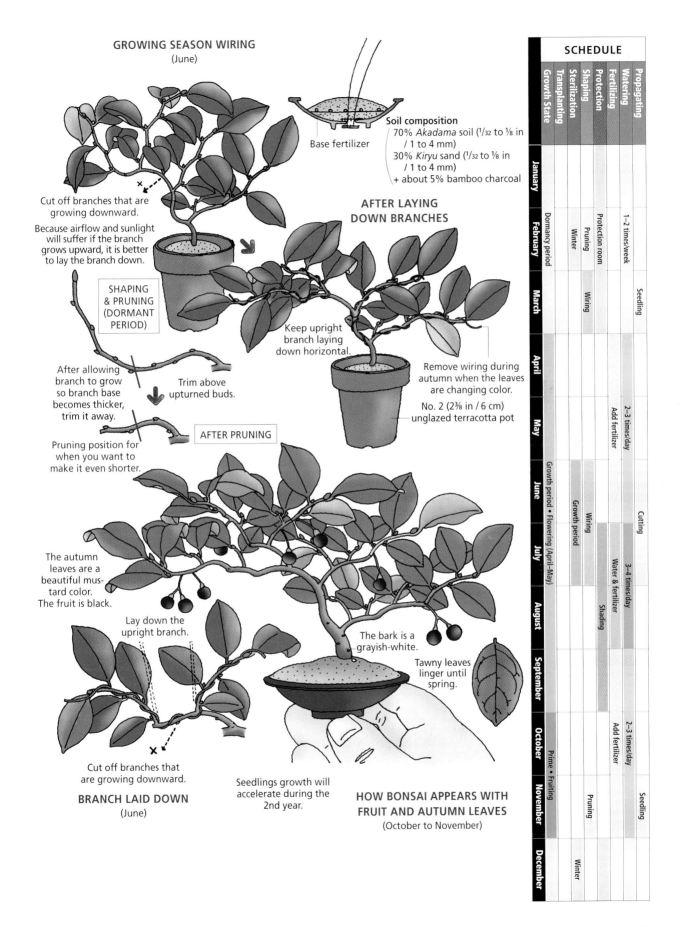

GROWING SEASON WIRING
(June)

Base fertilizer

Soil composition
70% *Akadama* soil ($\frac{1}{32}$ to $\frac{1}{8}$ in / 1 to 4 mm)
30% *Kiryu* sand ($\frac{1}{32}$ to $\frac{1}{8}$ in / 1 to 4 mm)
+ about 5% bamboo charcoal

Cut off branches that are growing downward.

Because airflow and sunlight will suffer if the branch grows upward, it is better to lay the branch down.

AFTER LAYING DOWN BRANCHES

SHAPING & PRUNING (DORMANT PERIOD)

Keep upright branch laying down horizontal.

After allowing branch to grow so branch base becomes thicker, trim it away.

Trim above upturned buds.

Remove wiring during autumn when the leaves are changing color.

No. 2 (2⅜ in / 6 cm) unglazed terracotta pot

AFTER PRUNING

Pruning position for when you want to make it even shorter.

The autumn leaves are a beautiful mustard color. The fruit is black.

Lay down the upright branch.

The bark is a grayish-white.

Tawny leaves linger until spring.

Cut off branches that are growing downward.

BRANCH LAID DOWN
(June)

Seedlings growth will accelerate during the 2nd year.

HOW BONSAI APPEARS WITH FRUIT AND AUTUMN LEAVES
(October to November)

	SCHEDULE							
	Growth State	Transplanting	Sterilization	Shaping	Protection	Fertilizing	Watering	Propagating
January					Protection room		1–2 times/week	
February	Dormancy period		Winter	Pruning				Seedling
March				Wiring				
April							2–3 times/day	
May						Add fertilizer		Cutting
June	Growth period • Flowering (April–May)			Wiring				
July				Growth period		Water & fertilizer	3–4 times/day	
August						Shading		
September								
October	Prime • Fruiting					Add fertilizer	2–3 times/day	Seedling
November				Pruning				
December			Winter					

149

Japanese Beech

JAPANESE NAME
Buna

ALTERNATIVE NAME
Siebold's beech

SCIENTIFIC NAME
Fagus crenata

CLASSIFICATION
Fagaceae (deciduous broadleaf tree)

SYMBOLIC OF
Prosperity

PEAK COLOR
November and December

The bark is a smooth grayish white. Leaves turn brown in autumn, but remain on the branches to pass the winter. In Japanese, this is called yuzuriha (lit. "deferring leaf") because the brown leaves only fall after new leaves have formed in the spring. Its flowers bloom while the new leaf buds open, and its tough, pyramid-shaped seeds ripen in autumn. Propagation is with seed-grown seedlings, planting pinched-off shoots, and air-layering.

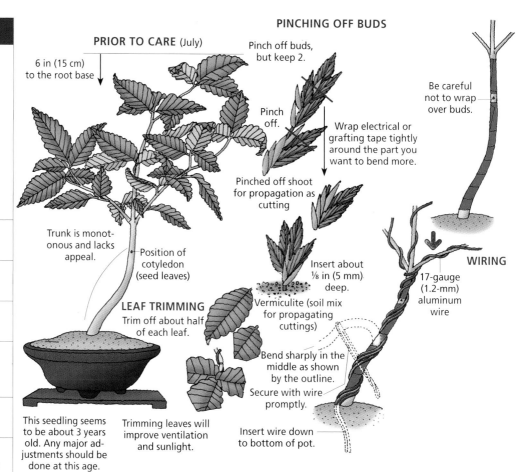

PINCHING OFF BUDS

PRIOR TO CARE (July)

6 in (15 cm) to the root base

Pinch off buds, but keep 2.

Pinch off.

Wrap electrical or grafting tape tightly around the part you want to bend more.

Be careful not to wrap over buds.

Pinched off shoot for propagation as cutting

Trunk is monotonous and lacks appeal.

Position of cotyledon (seed leaves)

LEAF TRIMMING
Trim off about half of each leaf.

Insert about ⅛ in (5 mm) deep.

Vermiculite (soil mix for propagating cuttings)

WIRING

17-gauge (1.2-mm) aluminum wire

Bend sharply in the middle as shown by the outline.
Secure with wire promptly.

This seedling seems to be about 3 years old. Any major adjustments should be done at this age.

Trimming leaves will improve ventilation and sunlight.

Insert wire down to bottom of pot.

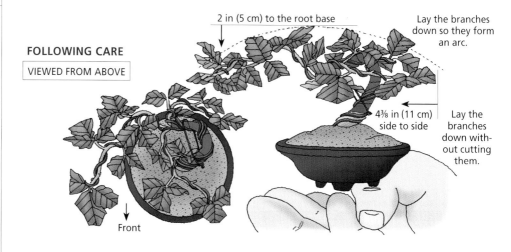

2 in (5 cm) to the root base

Lay the branches down so they form an arc.

FOLLOWING CARE

VIEWED FROM ABOVE

4⅜ in (11 cm) side to side

Lay the branches down without cutting them.

Front

		January	February	March	April	May	June	July	August	September	October	November	December
SCHEDULE	Propagating			Seedling	Cutting		Layering					Seedling	
	Watering	1–2 times / week			2–3 times / day			3–4 times / day		2–3 times / day			
	Fertilizing					Add fertilizer		Water & fertilizer		Add fertilizer			
	Protection	Protection room							Shading				
	Shaping		Pruning			Bud picking		Wiring	Bud cutting				
	Sterilization	Winter			Growth stage							Winter	
	Transplanting												
	Growth State	Dormancy period					Growth period				Prime		

How to Care for Coniferous Bonsai

When we hear the word "bonsai," what naturally comes to mind is a pine or other conifer. Their form possesses both a strength and a patina of maturity that can be said to fully represent the majesty and prestige of bonsai.

OBSERVE THE QUINTESSENCE OF BONSAI IN AN ENDLESS VARIETY OF FORMS

From time immemorial in Japan—due to the way that they maintain their verdure year-round—evergreen conifers such as pine, cedar and cypress have been symbols of unyielding strength and steadfast fidelity in the face of adversity. This is also true for bonsai, generally sharing similar longevity and robust, healthy lives with their counterparts growing in the wild.

Conifers can potentially be trained into any shape of tree (refer to pages 12 and 13). The hanging-cliff tree shape is reminiscent of sheer precipices deep in the mountains, and the windswept tree shape is reminiscent of rock faces in alpine and coastal regions. In addition, the rough, split bark of the trunk and weathered, bleached "bones" of *jin* and *shari* lend great appeal to coniferous bonsai.

The majestic and powerful black pine (*kuromatsu*), the graceful and subdued Japanese white pine (*goyōmatsu*), and the subtle and profound, yet unconventional-looking Japanese emperor oak (*makashiwa*)— these comprise the "big three" of coniferous bonsai.

Japanese Black Pine

JAPANESE NAME
Kuromatsu

ALTERNATIVE NAMES
Japanese Pine, *Omatsu*

SCIENTIFIC NAME
Pinus thunbergii

CLASSIFICATION
Pinaceae (evergreen
conifer / tree)

SYMBOLIC OF
Longevity, Bravery

PEAK SEASON
October to November

As the bark grows older, cracks reminiscent of a turtle's shell will appear and peel off in scales. The winter buds are thick and white and can easily be distinguished from red pine (red pine appears in reddish brown). It is necessary to pluck and cut the buds so that the green buds can grow and divide without causing the branch itself to lengthen much. Breeding can be done through seed-grown seedlings and air-layering.

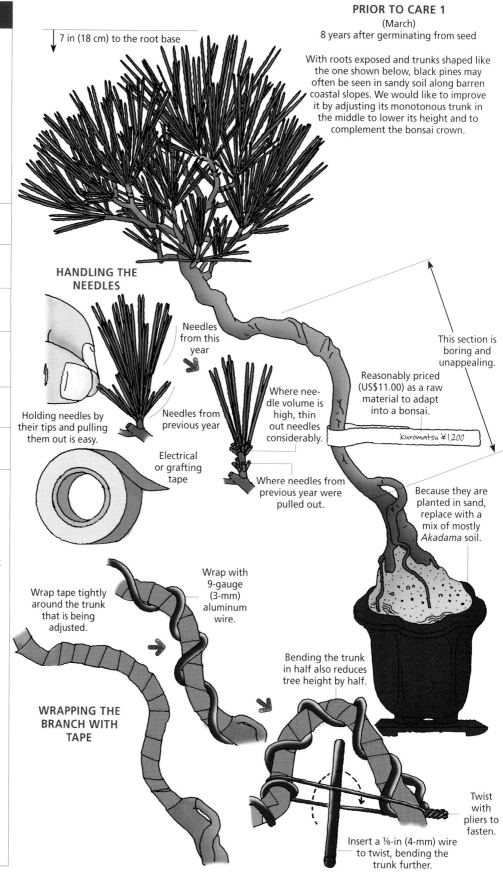

PRIOR TO CARE 1
(March)
8 years after germinating from seed

7 in (18 cm) to the root base

With roots exposed and trunks shaped like the one shown below, black pines may often be seen in sandy soil along barren coastal slopes. We would like to improve it by adjusting its monotonous trunk in the middle to lower its height and to complement the bonsai crown.

HANDLING THE NEEDLES

Needles from this year

Holding needles by their tips and pulling them out is easy.

Needles from previous year

Where needle volume is high, thin out needles considerably.

Electrical or grafting tape

Where needles from previous year were pulled out.

This section is boring and unappealing.

Reasonably priced (US$11.00) as a raw material to adapt into a bonsai.

Kuromatsu ¥1,200

Because they are planted in sand, replace with a mix of mostly *Akadama* soil.

Wrap tape tightly around the trunk that is being adjusted.

Wrap with 9-gauge (3-mm) aluminum wire.

WRAPPING THE BRANCH WITH TAPE

Bending the trunk in half also reduces tree height by half.

Twist with pliers to fasten.

Insert a ⅛-in (4-mm) wire to twist, bending the trunk further.

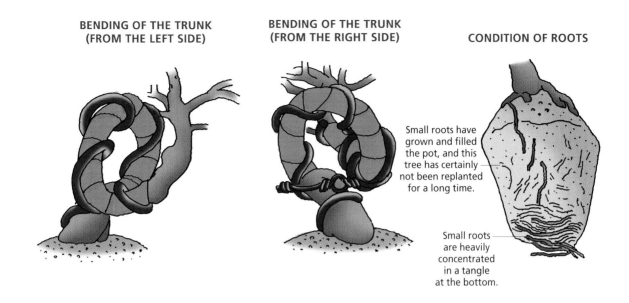

BENDING OF THE TRUNK (FROM THE LEFT SIDE)

BENDING OF THE TRUNK (FROM THE RIGHT SIDE)

CONDITION OF ROOTS

Small roots have grown and filled the pot, and this tree has certainly not been replanted for a long time.

Small roots are heavily concentrated in a tangle at the bottom.

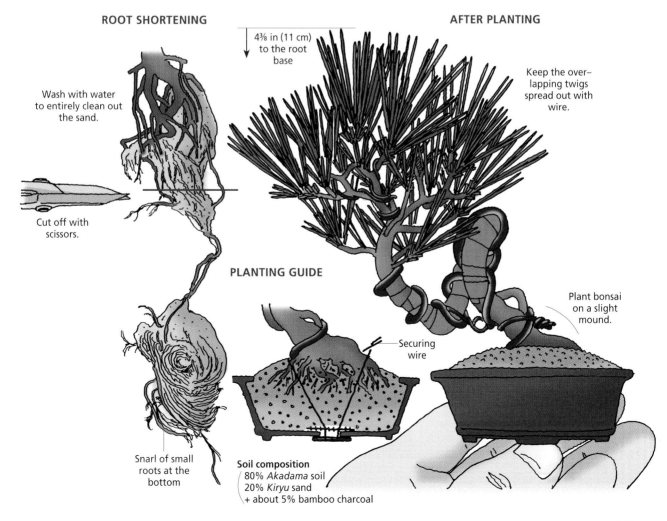

ROOT SHORTENING

Wash with water to entirely clean out the sand.

Cut off with scissors.

Snarl of small roots at the bottom

4⅜ in (11 cm) to the root base

AFTER PLANTING

Keep the over–lapping twigs spread out with wire.

Plant bonsai on a slight mound.

PLANTING GUIDE

Securing wire

Soil composition
80% *Akadama* soil
20% *Kiryu* sand
+ about 5% bamboo charcoal

Replanting

6 in (15 cm) to the root base

Keep the branches that had been upright lying horizontal.

PRIOR TO CARE 2
(April)
30 years after germinating from seed

Thin out branches with many needles.

AFTER ROOT SHORTENING

Cut off withered branch that is obscuring the main branch.

Rotate the thick root to the right.

Temporary front marker

Thick root is visible from the front.

Temporary front marker

Deep pot

Because the shoot is stubborn and has the tendency to grow upward, keeping it lying down is beneficial.

AFTER REPLANTING

4 in (10 cm) to the root base

PLANTING GUIDE

Twist to tighten.

Rotating the thick root displays it as a "tugging root."

Temporary front marker

Mix bamboo charcoal with gravel.

New front marker

Soil composition
80% *Akadama* soil ($^1/_{32}$ to $^1/_8$ in / 1 to 4 mm)
20% *Kiryu* sand ($^1/_{32}$ to $^1/_8$ in / 1 to 4 mm)

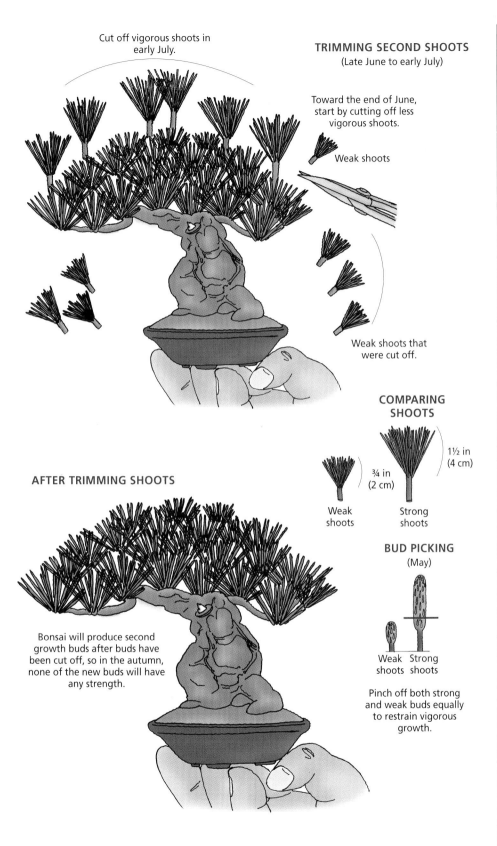

TRIMMING SECOND SHOOTS
(Late June to early July)

Cut off vigorous shoots in early July.

Toward the end of June, start by cutting off less vigorous shoots.

Weak shoots

Weak shoots that were cut off.

COMPARING SHOOTS

¾ in (2 cm)
Weak shoots

1½ in (4 cm)
Strong shoots

AFTER TRIMMING SHOOTS

Bonsai will produce second growth buds after buds have been cut off, so in the autumn, none of the new buds will have any strength.

BUD PICKING
(May)

Weak shoots   Strong shoots

Pinch off both strong and weak buds equally to restrain vigorous growth.

SCHEDULE		
Propagating	Watering	Fertilizing

Growth State · Transplanting · Sterilization · Shaping · Protection · Fertilizing · Watering · Propagating

Month	Growth State	Transplanting	Sterilization	Shaping	Protection	Fertilizing	Watering	Propagating
January	Dormancy period			Winter	Protection room		1–2 times/week	Seedling
February	Dormancy period			Winter	Protection room		1–2 times/week	Seedling
March								Seedling
April	Growth period						2–3 times/day	
May	Growth period		Bud picking			Add fertilizer	2–3 times/day	
June	Growth period		Wiring			Water & fertilizer	3–4 times/day	Layering
July	Growth period		Wiring			Water & fertilizer	3–4 times/day	Layering
August	Growth period				Shading	Water & fertilizer	3–4 times/day	
September	Growth period						3–4 times/day	
October	Prime					Add fertilizer	2–3 times/day	
November				Winter	Needle removal	Add fertilizer	2–3 times/day	
December				Winter	Needle removal			

Japanese White Pine

JAPANESE NAME
Goyomatsu

ALTERNATE NAME
Five-needle pine

SCIENTIFIC NAME
Pinus parviflora

CLASSIFICATION
Pinaceae (evergreen conifer / tree)

SYMBOLIC OF
Longevity, Bravery

PEAK SEASON
October to November

This tree's bark is a dark gray and, with age, peels off in thin layers. Branches will divide frequently, and the tendency of short branches to germinate is strong. The tips of the winter buds are rounded and the needles turn gray. The fresh green buds of black pine are not so vigorous, and are thwarted simply by pinching them off. Propagation is with seed-grown seedlings, grafting, or air-layering.

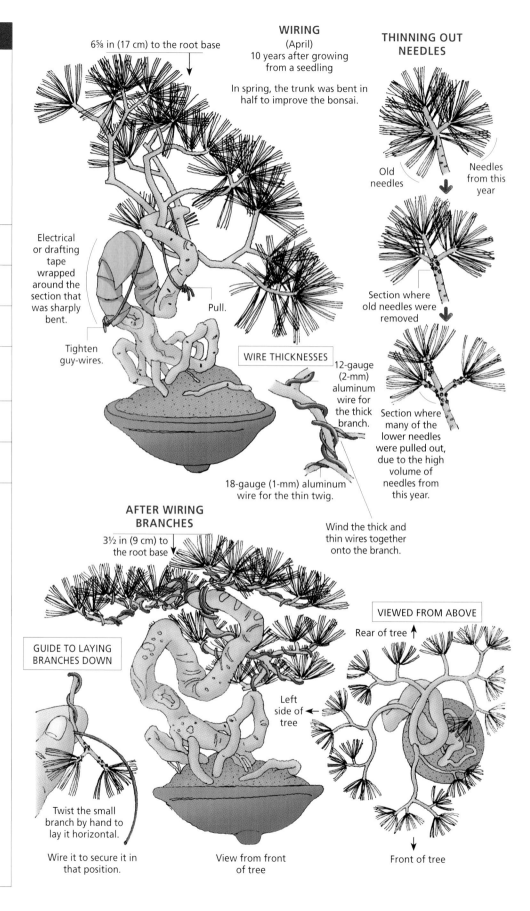

6⅝ in (17 cm) to the root base

WIRING
(April)
10 years after growing from a seedling

In spring, the trunk was bent in half to improve the bonsai.

THINNING OUT NEEDLES

Old needles

Needles from this year

Section where old needles were removed

Section where many of the lower needles were pulled out, due to the high volume of needles from this year.

Electrical or drafting tape wrapped around the section that was sharply bent.

Pull.

Tighten guy-wires.

WIRE THICKNESSES

12-gauge (2-mm) aluminum wire for the thick branch.

18-gauge (1-mm) aluminum wire for the thin twig.

Wind the thick and thin wires together onto the branch.

AFTER WIRING BRANCHES

3½ in (9 cm) to the root base

GUIDE TO LAYING BRANCHES DOWN

VIEWED FROM ABOVE

Rear of tree

Left side of tree

Front of tree

Twist the small branch by hand to lay it horizontal.

Wire it to secure it in that position.

View from front of tree

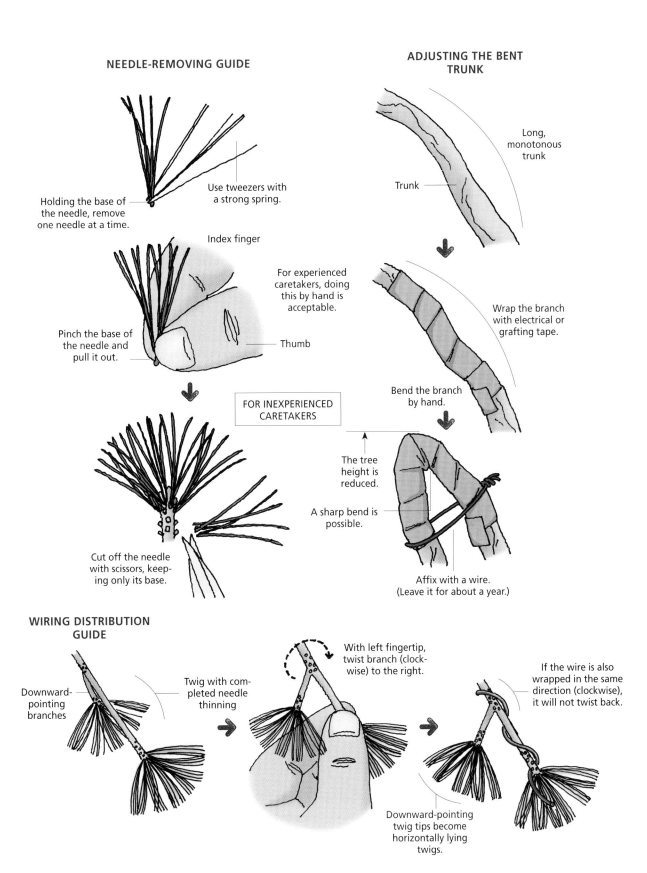

NEEDLE-REMOVING GUIDE

Holding the base of the needle, remove one needle at a time.

Use tweezers with a strong spring.

Index finger

For experienced caretakers, doing this by hand is acceptable.

Pinch the base of the needle and pull it out.

Thumb

FOR INEXPERIENCED CARETAKERS

Cut off the needle with scissors, keeping only its base.

ADJUSTING THE BENT TRUNK

Long, monotonous trunk

Trunk

Wrap the branch with electrical or grafting tape.

Bend the branch by hand.

The tree height is reduced.

A sharp bend is possible.

Affix with a wire.
(Leave it for about a year.)

WIRING DISTRIBUTION GUIDE

Downward-pointing branches

Twig with completed needle thinning

With left fingertip, twist branch (clockwise) to the right.

If the wire is also wrapped in the same direction (clockwise), it will not twist back.

Downward-pointing twig tips become horizontally lying twigs.

157

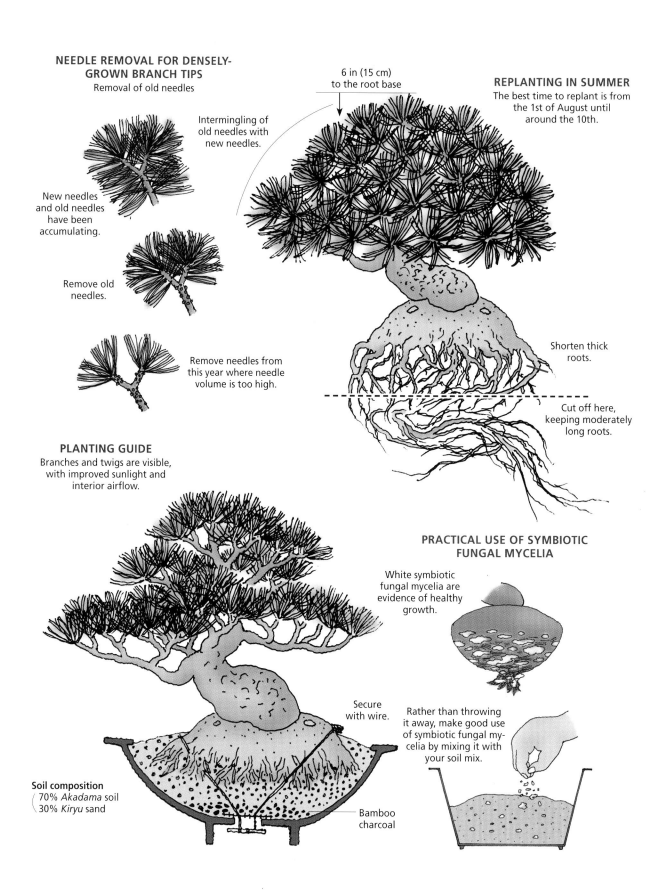

NEEDLE REMOVAL FOR DENSELY-GROWN BRANCH TIPS
Removal of old needles

Intermingling of old needles with new needles.

New needles and old needles have been accumulating.

Remove old needles.

Remove needles from this year where needle volume is too high.

6 in (15 cm) to the root base

REPLANTING IN SUMMER
The best time to replant is from the 1st of August until around the 10th.

Shorten thick roots.

Cut off here, keeping moderately long roots.

PLANTING GUIDE
Branches and twigs are visible, with improved sunlight and interior airflow.

PRACTICAL USE OF SYMBIOTIC FUNGAL MYCELIA

White symbiotic fungal mycelia are evidence of healthy growth.

Rather than throwing it away, make good use of symbiotic fungal mycelia by mixing it with your soil mix.

Secure with wire.

Soil composition
70% *Akadama* soil
30% *Kiryu* sand

Bamboo charcoal

158

SITUATING YOUR BONSAI

Study the tree's native habitat.

In the afternoon, treat your Japanese white pine to a misting and moisten its needles. They prefer moistened needles.

The top of a "monkey pole"* is the most suitable location for Japanese white pine.

Firmly secured

Consider airflow and sunlight in advance.

Japanese white pine

Grows wild on rocky alpine slopes. Prefers extremely well-drained locations.

Make a high shelf for Japanese white pine.

Japanese white pine

Shelf for other trees.

Low shrubs

Ensure that it will not fall.

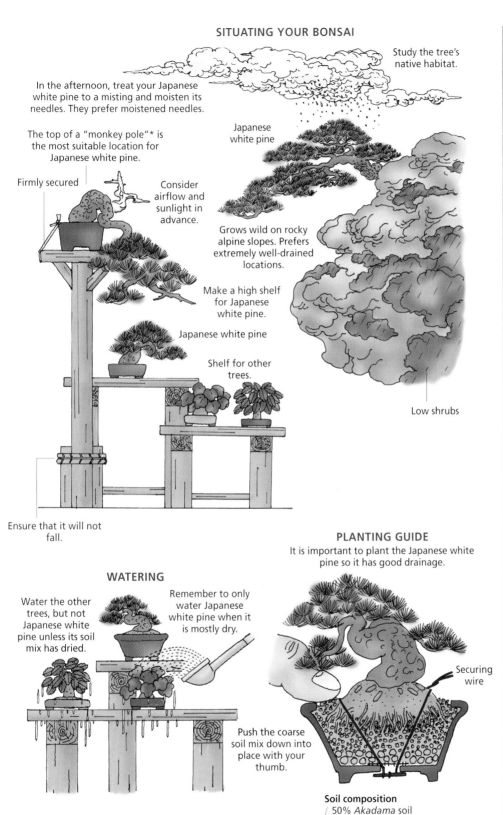

WATERING

Water the other trees, but not Japanese white pine unless its soil mix has dried.

Remember to only water Japanese white pine when it is mostly dry.

PLANTING GUIDE

It is important to plant the Japanese white pine so it has good drainage.

Securing wire

Push the coarse soil mix down into place with your thumb.

Soil composition
50% *Akadama* soil
50% *Kiryu* sand

*A "Monkey pole" is a bonsai stand on a high wooden pillar.

SCHEDULE

Month	Propagating	Watering	Fertilizing	Protection	Shaping	Sterilization	Transplanting	Growth State
January	Grafting	Once a week		Protection room				
February	Seedling	Once a week		Protection room	Winter			Dormancy period
March	Seedling				Pruning			
April		Once daily						
May		Once daily	Add fertilizer		Bud picking			
June	Layering				Bud picking			Growth period
July	Layering	2 times / day	Water & fertilizer					Growth period
August		2 times / day	Water & fertilizer					
September								
October		Once daily	Add fertilizer		Wiring			
November					Wiring	Prime		
December				Winter				

159

Temple Juniper

JAPANESE NAMES
Tosho, muro, nezu,
nezumi sashi

ALTERNATIVE NAME
Needle juniper

SCIENTIFIC NAME
Juniperus rigida

CLASSIFICATION
Cupressaceae (evergreen
conifer / tree)

SYMBOLIC OF
Protection, Salvation

PEAK SEASON
October to November

Both juniper and dwarf
juniper are easily trained.
The wood is dense and
rot-resistant, so *shari*
and *jin* are often created,
and beautifully so. Be-
cause it is difficult to create a taper in the trunk,
let the lower branches
grow out naturally, which
will help thicken the rise
of the lower trunk. Prop-
agating is with cuttings
and air-layering.

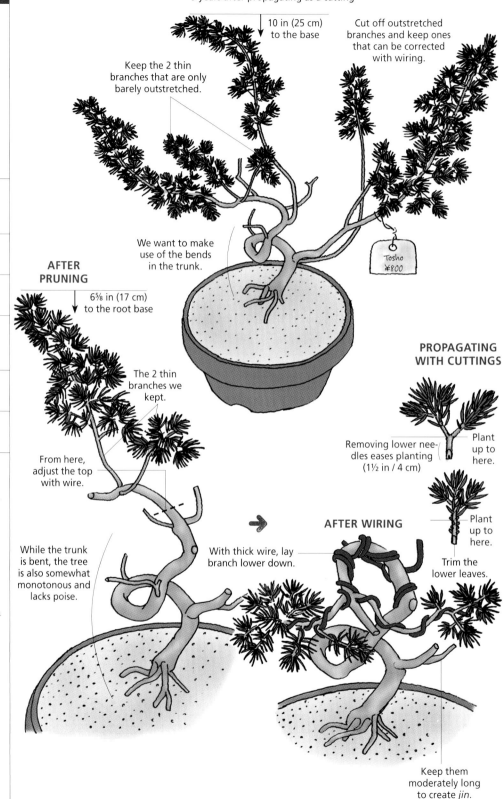

PRIOR TO CARE 1 (March)
5 years after propagating as a cutting

10 in (25 cm) to the base

Cut off outstretched branches and keep ones that can be corrected with wiring.

Keep the 2 thin branches that are only barely outstretched.

We want to make use of the bends in the trunk.

Tosho
¥800

AFTER PRUNING

6⅝ in (17 cm) to the root base

The 2 thin branches we kept.

From here, adjust the top with wire.

While the trunk is bent, the tree is also somewhat monotonous and lacks poise.

PROPAGATING WITH CUTTINGS

Removing lower nee-dles eases planting (1½ in / 4 cm)

Plant up to here.

Plant up to here.

Trim the lower leaves.

AFTER WIRING

With thick wire, lay branch lower down.

Keep them moderately long to create *jin*.

There is a species of tree called "shore juniper" (Juniperus conferta) that has been popular for some time. It is characterized by plump needles in dense clusters that are not as painfully prickly to the touch as some other species of juniper.

AFTER WIRING (VIEWED FROM ABOVE)

FRONT

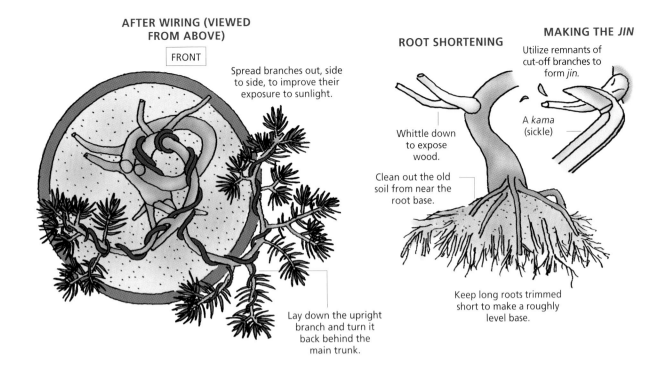

Spread branches out, side to side, to improve their exposure to sunlight.

Lay down the upright branch and turn it back behind the main trunk.

ROOT SHORTENING

Whittle down to expose wood.

Clean out the old soil from near the root base.

Keep long roots trimmed short to make a roughly level base.

MAKING THE *JIN*

Utilize remnants of cut-off branches to form *jin*.

A *kama* (sickle)

AFTER REPLANTING

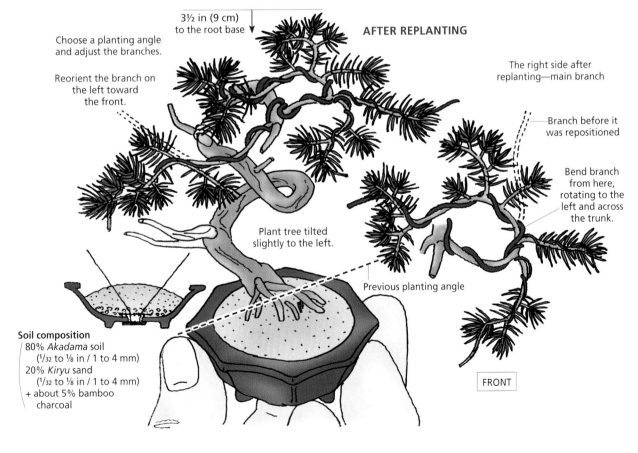

3½ in (9 cm) to the root base

Choose a planting angle and adjust the branches.

Reorient the branch on the left toward the front.

The right side after replanting—main branch

Branch before it was repositioned

Bend branch from here, rotating to the left and across the trunk.

Plant tree tilted slightly to the left.

Previous planting angle

Soil composition
80% *Akadama* soil
(1/32 to 1/8 in / 1 to 4 mm)
20% *Kiryu* sand
(1/32 to 1/8 in / 1 to 4 mm)
+ about 5% bamboo charcoal

FRONT

This bonsai was propagated from a cutting 3 to 4 years ago. Because this species naturally droops as it grows, train each trunk with wire to establish bends.

Pinch off all the new shoots that have grown out.

8 in (20 cm) to the root base

No. 4 pot (4¾ in / 12 cm)

We can make it a "forest" bonsai just as it is.

TRUNK WIRING

While bending each trunk, make sure the overall flow of the entire group is in one direction.

ROOT SHORTENING

When removed from the pot, we see that the red roots have accumulated in every corner of it.

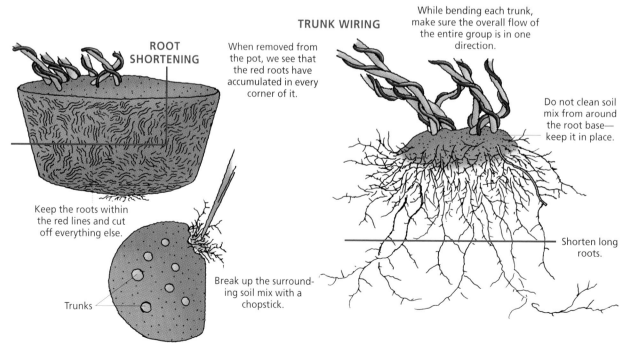

Keep the roots within the red lines and cut off everything else.

Trunks

Break up the surrounding soil mix with a chopstick.

Do not clean soil mix from around the root base—keep it in place.

Shorten long roots.

162

AFTER PLANTING

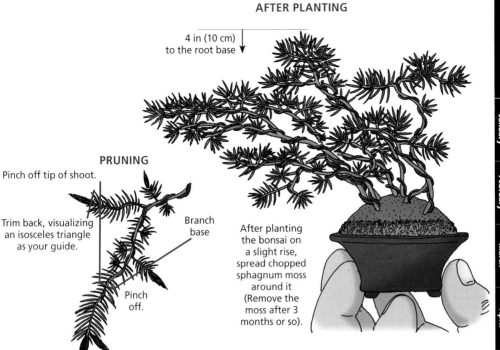

4 in (10 cm) to the root base ↓

PRUNING

Pinch off tip of shoot.

Trim back, visualizing an isosceles triangle as your guide.

Branch base

Pinch off.

Branch tip

After planting the bonsai on a slight rise, spread chopped sphagnum moss around it (Remove the moss after 3 months or so).

HOW THE BONSAI APPEARS AFTER SEVERAL YEARS

After the wiring has been removed, fresh young shoots and short branches appear, and you can enjoy a bonsai with the appearance of a forest.

SCHEDULE

	Growth State	Transplanting	Sterilization	Shaping	Protection	Fertilizing	Watering	Propagating
January							1–2 times/week	
February	Dormancy period		Winter		Protection room			
March								
April	Growth period			Pruning				Cutting • Layering (June–July)
May						Add fertilizer	2–3 times/day	
June		Growth period						
July				Bud picking		Water & fertilizer	3–4 times / day	
August					Shading			
September								
October						Add fertilizer	2–3 times/day	
November					Prime			
December			Winter					

Japanese Cedar

JAPANESE NAME
Sugi

ALTERNATIVE NAMES
n/a

SCIENTIFIC NAME
Cryptomeria japonica

CLASSIFICATION
Cupressaceae (evergreen conifer / tree)

SYMBOLIC OF
Magnificence, Strength

PEAK SEASON
October to November

A conifer native to Japan, These trees have a powerful potential for germinating. The new buds grow gradually until autumn, at which time they can be pinched off. When water and nutrients are scarce, the tree loses strength and the color of its needles becomes pale. Although cold-resistant, being sheltered somewhere not exposed to dry winter winds is essential. Propagating with cuttings is recommended.

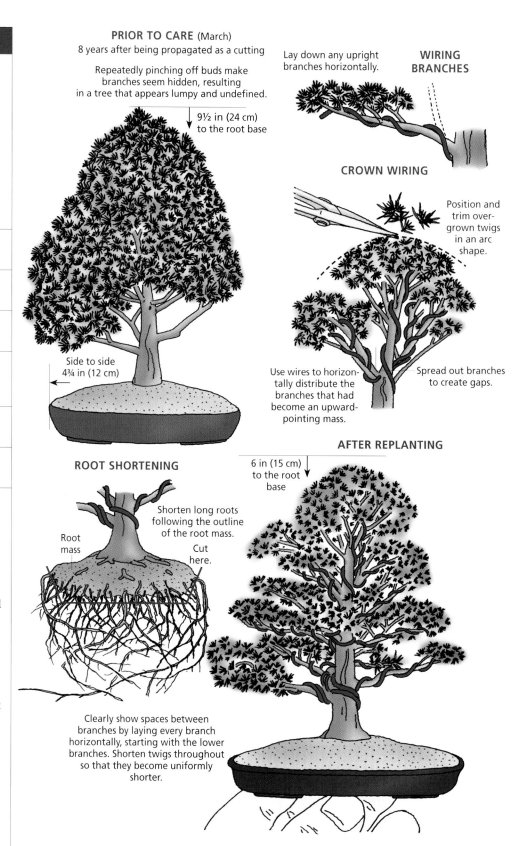

PRIOR TO CARE (March)
8 years after being propagated as a cutting

Repeatedly pinching off buds make branches seem hidden, resulting in a tree that appears lumpy and undefined.

9½ in (24 cm) to the root base

Side to side 4¾ in (12 cm)

Lay down any upright branches horizontally.

WIRING BRANCHES

CROWN WIRING

Position and trim overgrown twigs in an arc shape.

Use wires to horizontally distribute the branches that had become an upward-pointing mass.

Spread out branches to create gaps.

ROOT SHORTENING

Root mass

Shorten long roots following the outline of the root mass.

Cut here.

Clearly show spaces between branches by laying every branch horizontally, starting with the lower branches. Shorten twigs throughout so that they become uniformly shorter.

AFTER REPLANTING

6 in (15 cm) to the root base

PROPAGATING WITH CUTTINGS

If you plant the top of a tree you had trimmed as a cutting for propagation, the cutting will grow straight.

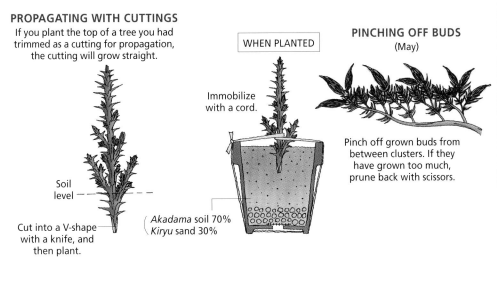

Soil level

Cut into a V-shape with a knife, and then plant.

WHEN PLANTED

Immobilize with a cord.

Akadama soil 70%
Kiryu sand 30%

PINCHING OFF BUDS
(May)

Pinch off grown buds from between clusters. If they have grown too much, prune back with scissors.

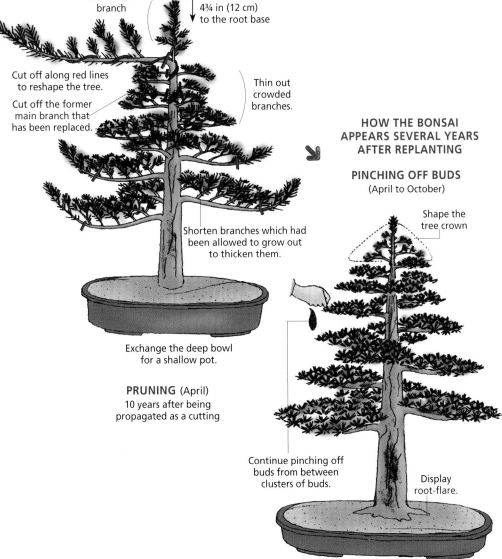

New main branch

4¾ in (12 cm) to the root base

Cut off along red lines to reshape the tree.

Cut off the former main branch that has been replaced.

Thin out crowded branches.

Shorten branches which had been allowed to grow out to thicken them.

Exchange the deep bowl for a shallow pot.

PRUNING (April)
10 years after being propagated as a cutting

HOW THE BONSAI APPEARS SEVERAL YEARS AFTER REPLANTING

PINCHING OFF BUDS
(April to October)

Shape the tree crown

Continue pinching off buds from between clusters of buds.

Display root-flare.

Plant in shallow pot.

SCHEDULE

Month	Growth State	Transplanting	Sterilization	Shaping	Protection	Fertilizing	Watering	Propagating
January	Dormancy period				Protection room		1–2 times / week	
February	Dormancy period		Winter		Protection room		1–2 times / week	Seedling
March	Dormancy period			Pruning	Protection room		1–2 times / week	Seedling
April							1–2 times / day	Cutting
May				Bud picking / Growth period		Add fertilizer	1–2 times / day	Cutting
June	Growth period			Growth period		Add fertilizer	2–3 times / day	Cutting • Layering
July	Growth period					Water & fertilizer	2–3 times / day	Cutting • Layering
August	Growth period					Shading	2–3 times / day	Cutting • Layering
September	Growth period							Cutting • Layering
October	Growth period	Prime				Add fertilizer	1–2 times / day	
November	Growth period	Prime					1–2 times / day	
December			Winter				1–2 times / day	

Chinese Juniper

JAPANESE NAMES
Miyama-byakushin, shinpaku

ALTERNATIVE NAME
True Japanese emperor oak*

SCIENTIFIC NAME
Sabina chinensis

CLASSIFICATION
Cupressaceae (evergreen conifer / shrub)

SYMBOLIC OF
Self-protection

PEAK SEASON
October to November (dormant period)

The trunk appears to be twisting as it grows, and the branches have extended out horizontally. The tree prefers a weak alkaline soil mix, so provide smoked charcoal or similar once a year to prevent acidification. The wood is rot-resistant, so *shari* and *jin* develop beautifully. New buds grow gradually until autumn, and at that time they can be pinched off. Propagation is with cuttings.

PRIOR TO CARE (NOTE TEMPORARY FRONT MARKER)
(March)
12 years after being propagated as a cutting

Cut off at the red lines and reshape the 2 top branches.

8 in (20 cm) to the root base

It has an old *jin*.

Shinpaku ¥5700

Appropriately priced (US$52) for its structure and trunk thickness.

Temporary front marker

No. 4 (4¾-in / 12-cm) unglazed terracotta pot.

Keep overly-long branches trimmed short.

Thick out-stretched branches

Downward-pointing branches

The *jin* looks excellent.

AFTER PRUNING (FROM NEW FRONT VIEW)
Keep just 2 branches, and cut off all the others to whittle down as short *jin*.

The bent trunk clearly displays the flow coming from underneath.

The branch can be usable because it looks straight, so cut it off and use it as *jin*.

PROPAGATING WITH CUTTINGS
Plant your pruned branches rather than throwing them away.

Remove lower needles.

Plant ½ in (1.5 cm) or so into the soil.

Temporary front marker

New front marker

*True Japanese emperor oak: In the bonsai world, this colloquial name is becoming popular.

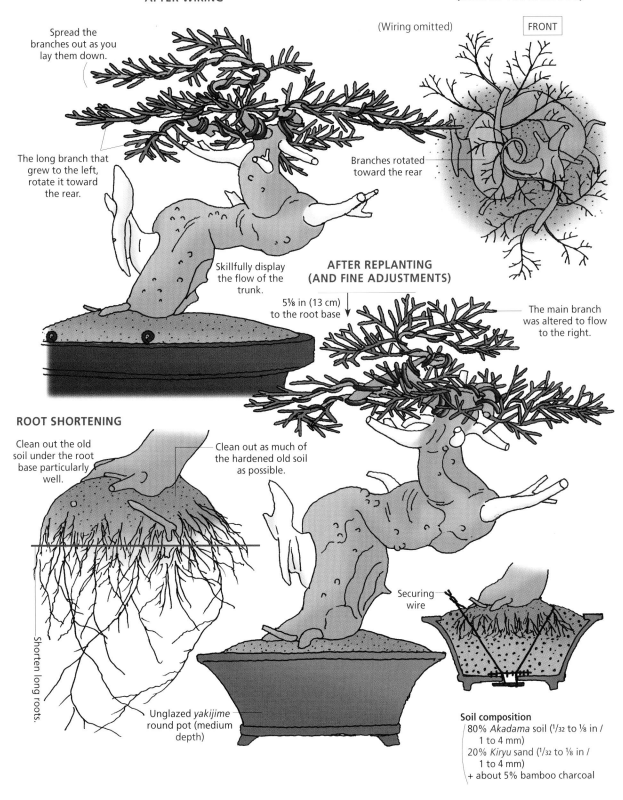

AFTER WIRING

Spread the branches out as you lay them down.

LAYOUT OF BRANCHES (VIEWED FROM ABOVE)

(Wiring omitted)

FRONT

The long branch that grew to the left, rotate it toward the rear.

Branches rotated toward the rear

Skillfully display the flow of the trunk.

AFTER REPLANTING (AND FINE ADJUSTMENTS)

5⅛ in (13 cm) to the root base

The main branch was altered to flow to the right.

ROOT SHORTENING

Clean out the old soil under the root base particularly well.

Clean out as much of the hardened old soil as possible.

Shorten long roots.

Securing wire

Unglazed *yakijime* round pot (medium depth)

Soil composition
80% *Akadama* soil (¹/₃₂ to ⅛ in / 1 to 4 mm)
20% *Kiryu* sand (¹/₃₂ to ⅛ in / 1 to 4 mm)
+ about 5% bamboo charcoal

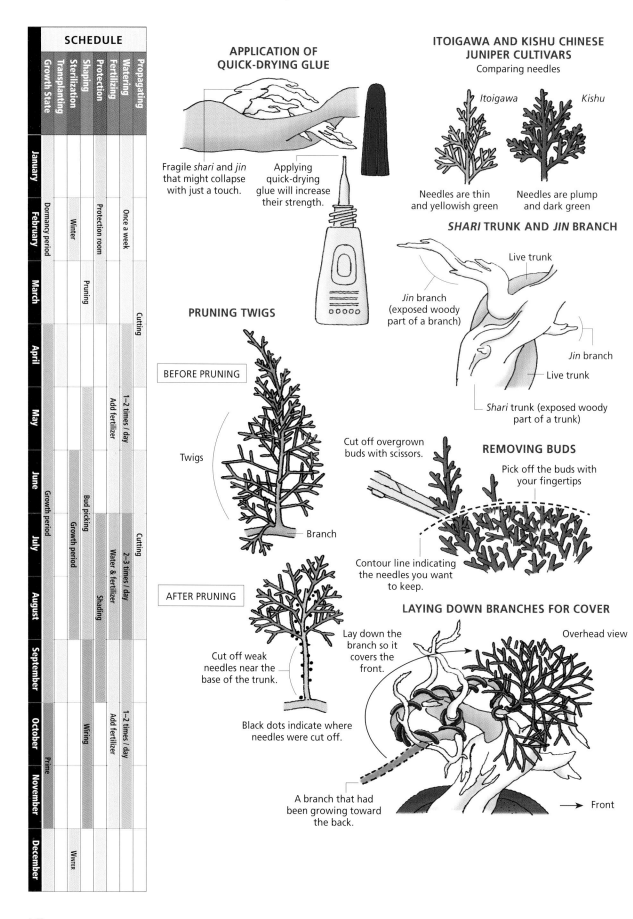

SCHEDULE

Growth State	Transplanting	Sterilization	Shaping	Protection	Fertilizing	Watering	Propagating
January							
February	Dormancy period	Winter		Protection room		Once a week	
March			Pruning				Cutting
April							
May					Add fertilizer	1-2 times / day	
June	Growth period		Bud picking	Shading	Water & fertilizer	2-3 times / day	Cutting
July			Growth period				
August							
September							
October	Prime		Wiring		Add fertilizer	1-2 times / day	
November							
December		Winter					

APPLICATION OF QUICK-DRYING GLUE

Fragile *shari* and *jin* that might collapse with just a touch.

Applying quick-drying glue will increase their strength.

ITOIGAWA AND KISHU CHINESE JUNIPER CULTIVARS

Comparing needles

Itoigawa

Kishu

Needles are thin and yellowish green

Needles are plump and dark green

SHARI TRUNK AND *JIN* BRANCH

Live trunk

Jin branch (exposed woody part of a branch)

Jin branch

Live trunk

Shari trunk (exposed woody part of a trunk)

PRUNING TWIGS

BEFORE PRUNING

Twigs

Branch

AFTER PRUNING

Cut off weak needles near the base of the trunk.

Black dots indicate where needles were cut off.

Cut off overgrown buds with scissors.

Contour line indicating the needles you want to keep.

REMOVING BUDS

Pick off the buds with your fingertips

LAYING DOWN BRANCHES FOR COVER

Overhead view

Lay down the branch so it covers the front.

A branch that had been growing toward the back.

Front

TRAINING BONSAI TO BE HEALTHY WHILE KEPT SMALL
Pruning, Shaping and Shaving Bonsai

With bonsai—unlike potted plants—we can enjoy the look of a large, old tree, even though the plants are small. Toward that end, care suitable to each species is vital.

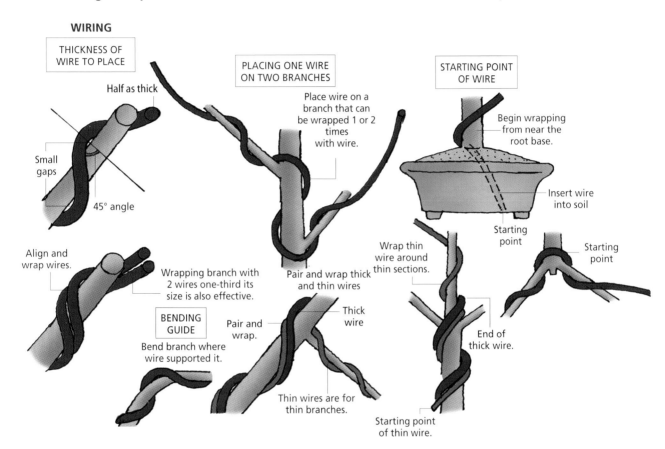

WIRING

THICKNESS OF WIRE TO PLACE

Half as thick

Small gaps

45° angle

Align and wrap wires.

Wrapping branch with 2 wires one-third its size is also effective.

BENDING GUIDE

Bend branch where wire supported it.

PLACING ONE WIRE ON TWO BRANCHES

Place wire on a branch that can be wrapped 1 or 2 times with wire.

Pair and wrap thick and thin wires

Pair and wrap.

Thick wire

Thin wires are for thin branches.

STARTING POINT OF WIRE

Begin wrapping from near the root base.

Insert wire into soil

Starting point

Wrap thin wire around thin sections.

End of thick wire.

Starting point

Starting point of thin wire.

CARE AND TECHNIQUES THAT REVEAL THE EXCELLENCE OF THE TREE

Some bonsai care techniques that are clearly different from those for other garden plants are that branches may be bent with wire or parts of the trunk may be whittled with a blade. One of the most important elements of bonsai viewing is the appreciation for the beauty of the transformations in the tree that have resulted from the passage of time in a harsh natural environment. In order to emphasize that beauty, the branches and trunk are intentionally made to look as if they have been bent by the forces of wind and the weight of snow. Also, some trees may be altered to display sections of bark that have peeled off. These are created as *shari*, in the case of sections of trunk, and as *jin*, in the case of the branches.

Also, in bonsai, newly-grown tips of branches are cut in summer while branches and leaves are cut short during the dormant season from autumn to early spring—pruning, in other words. This is done with the aim of presenting a small tree with the appearance of a grand old tree, but one that does not have long, overgrown or spindly branches, or leaves that appear crowded. At its core, regular pruning is a method of steadily improving the appearance of the tree while keeping the bonsai small for long periods of time.

Why Do We Prune Bonsai?

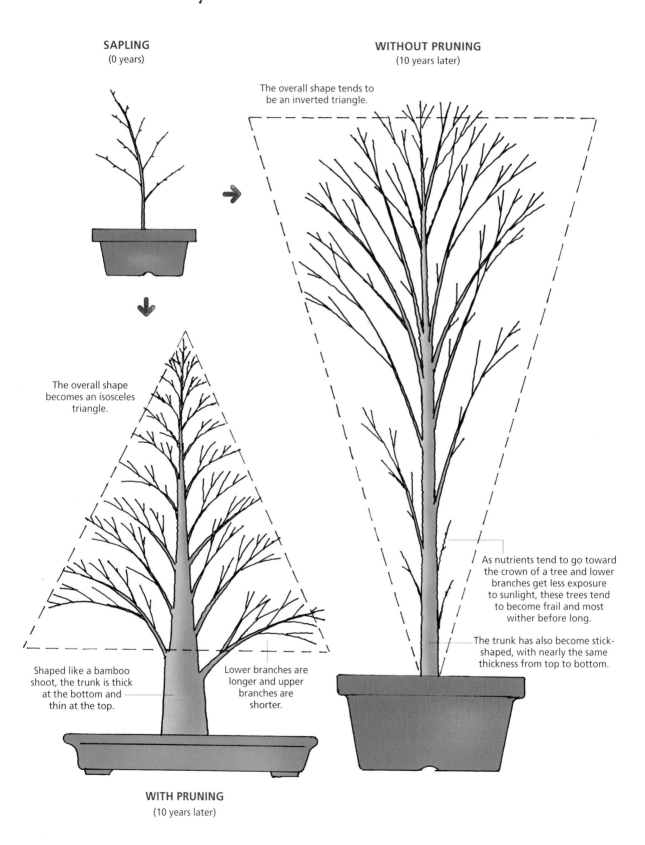

SAPLING
(0 years)

WITHOUT PRUNING
(10 years later)

The overall shape tends to be an inverted triangle.

The overall shape becomes an isosceles triangle.

As nutrients tend to go toward the crown of a tree and lower branches get less exposure to sunlight, these trees tend to become frail and most wither before long.

The trunk has also become stick-shaped, with nearly the same thickness from top to bottom.

Shaped like a bamboo shoot, the trunk is thick at the bottom and thin at the top.

Lower branches are longer and upper branches are shorter.

WITH PRUNING
(10 years later)

Why Do We Bend and Shape Bonsai?

EXPRESS PERSEVERANCE AGAINST THE RIGORS OF NATURAL ENVIRONMENTS

The trunk and branches of the tree have reached the point where they have been flattened by the strong winds that constantly blow.

Rocky alpine slopes and the like

Example: Japanese white pine (*goyomatsu*)

Example: Black pine (*kuromatsu*)

Gravity and the weight of falling rocks and snow have bent the trunk of the tree, and it hangs down.

Example: Japanese maple (*momiji*)

Even on level surfaces, the upper branches look like they have been savaged by the wind, like a torn straw *mino* (traditional Japanese woven raincoat).

Trees, shrubs and so on in public parks

Up to two-thirds of the trunk has grown straight.

Rocky surfaces high up in the mountains, etc.

Why Do We Shave Bark from Bonsai?

JIN AND SHARI

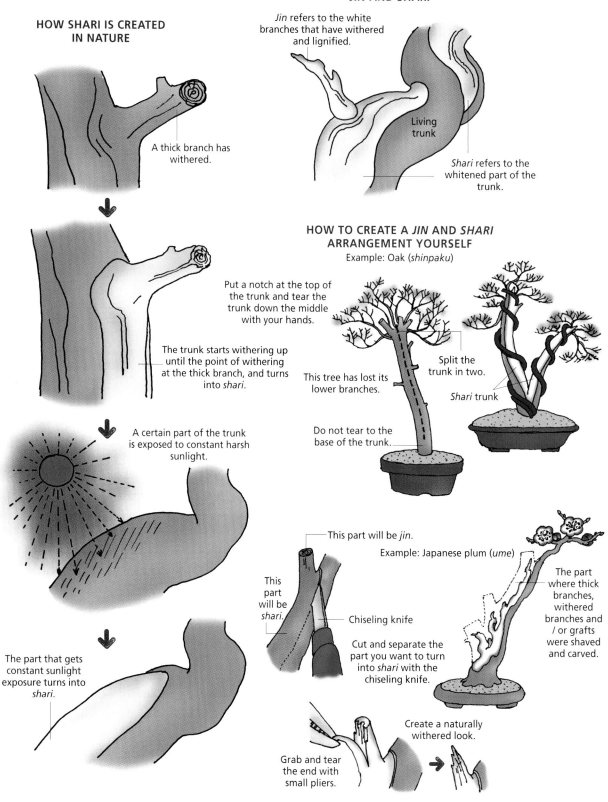

HOW SHARI IS CREATED IN NATURE

A thick branch has withered.

The trunk starts withering up until the point of withering at the thick branch, and turns into *shari*.

A certain part of the trunk is exposed to constant harsh sunlight.

The part that gets constant sunlight exposure turns into *shari*.

Jin refers to the white branches that have withered and lignified.

Living trunk

Shari refers to the whitened part of the trunk.

HOW TO CREATE A JIN AND SHARI ARRANGEMENT YOURSELF
Example: Oak (*shinpaku*)

Put a notch at the top of the trunk and tear the trunk down the middle with your hands.

This tree has lost its lower branches.

Do not tear to the base of the trunk.

Split the trunk in two.

Shari trunk

This part will be *jin*.

Example: Japanese plum (*ume*)

This part will be *shari*.

Chiseling knife

Cut and separate the part you want to turn into *shari* with the chiseling knife.

The part where thick branches, withered branches and / or grafts were shaved and carved.

Grab and tear the end with small pliers.

Create a naturally withered look.

Maintaining Your Bonsai's Health

Similar to trees in their natural environment, even bonsai are constantly at risk from insects, pests and so on. Being knowledgeable about the countermeasures to such problems is essential for bonsai enthusiasts.

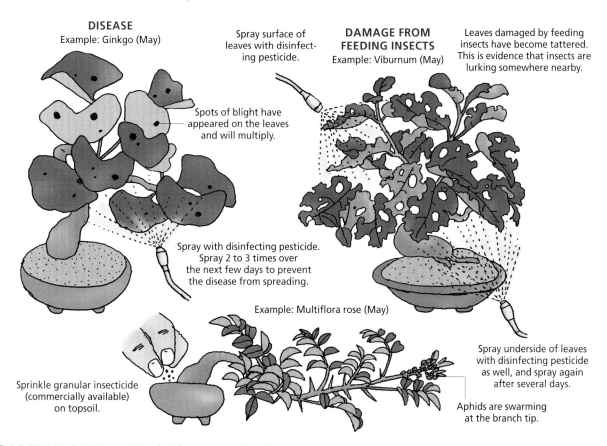

DISEASE
Example: Ginkgo (May)

Spray surface of leaves with disinfecting pesticide.

Spots of blight have appeared on the leaves and will multiply.

Spray with disinfecting pesticide. Spray 2 to 3 times over the next few days to prevent the disease from spreading.

DAMAGE FROM FEEDING INSECTS
Example: Viburnum (May)

Leaves damaged by feeding insects have become tattered. This is evidence that insects are lurking somewhere nearby.

Example: Multiflora rose (May)

Spray underside of leaves with disinfecting pesticide as well, and spray again after several days.

Sprinkle granular insecticide (commercially available) on topsoil.

Aphids are swarming at the branch tip.

CAREFUL DETAILED OBSERVATIONS LEAD TO TAKING THE CORRECT ACTIONS

Throughout the spring and summer in particular, the activities of harmful insects become more vigorous, and outbreaks of pests and disease pose an increasing risk of damage. In order to protect your plants from damage from insects, from spring until autumn you should regularly treat your plants with a disinfecting pesticide and other treatments as a preventative measure.

However, it is difficult for beginners to distinguish these risks, and the most common misunderstanding is to mistake physical damage for pest damage. In the world of bonsai, there are often mystifying questions such as, "Why is my tree is not healthy?" or, "Why is the leaf color dull?" In the majority of cases what has happened to cause these symptoms is root rot appearing in the pot soil. The trouble is that in the case of root rot, symptom onset is slow and thus treatment tends to be delayed. For most pots in which these symptoms occur, the water administered to the bonsai is not draining through the pot. In addition, when the water given to the tree does not evaporate readily, this situation worsens until even the soil on the surface is damp. This is a sign that the soil environment inside the pot has deteriorated, and growing conditions for the roots have become poor. Swift transplanting is the essential response to this problem.

How to Weed and Kill Pests and Germs

Sprayer (hand-operated)

Spray

Holds 3½ cups (1 liter) of solution

Holds 7 cups (2 liters) of solution

Disinfectant for winter

Sprays

Aerosol spray

Powder

Pesticide powder

Emulsions
Insecticide
Disinfectant
Wetting agent

TOOLS FOR DILUTION

Funnel

Measuring cup

Pipette

Chopstick

An insecticide or disinfectant

Water

Pour diluted pesticide or germicide into sprayer and start spraying.

SPRAYING METHODS

On breezy days, avoid physical contact

Be careful not to breathe or consume any of the disinfectant or other chemicals.

Grasses are obstinate and difficult to weed.

WEEDING
Pull out any large weeds by their roots with the edge of a blade.

Tweezers

The Kinds of Fertilizers, and How to Use Them

GUIDE TO MAKING LIQUID FERTILIZER

Bone meal (2 lbs / 1 kg)

WHAT TO PREPARE

Powdered horticultural oil (6½ lbs / 3 kg)

Fish meal (1 lb / 500 g)

Rice bran (from polished rice—1 lb / 500 g)

Note: This step is used to accelerate fermentation process, and it is optional.

FERTILIZING GUIDE

Watering can

Dilute fertilizer between 10x to 100x and apply to surface of topsoil.

Note: Commercial fertilizers are also fine.

Fertilizing after watering is best.

PASTE FERTILIZER

Water

Even after half a day, fertilizer paste will have formed a skin and become difficult to knead.

Powdered horticultural oil 60%
Bone meal 30%
Fish meal 10%

The ratio above is for evergreens and leafy trees. Increase the amount of bone meal for flowering and fruit-bearing trees.

Placing fertilizer immediately after watering is best.

Place a lump of fertilizer paste by pot rim using chopsticks.

DRY PELLET FERTILIZER (COMMERCIAL FERTILIZER)

This fertilizer already contains the proper amounts of nitrogen, phosphoric acid and potassium and can be used immediately.

Horticultural oil (6½ lbs / 3 kg)
Bone meal (2 lbs / 1 kg)
Fish meal (1 lb / 500 g)
Rice bran (1 lb / 500 g)

Stir well with a stick.

Water

12 gallon (45 liter) vessel

Once a month, stir with a stick.

To seal, place plastic between container and lid.

Leave to ferment for about 3 months in winter, 2 months in summer.

Polyethylene bucket

Place fertilizer pellets by pot rim.

Glossary of Bonsai Terms

A

Aburakasu See: Oil cake

Accent decor Scenery decorated with small items and accessories placed alongside the main bonsai tree.

Accent plant Used as an accompaniment. A plant that compliments the main tree in the bonsai viewing area (refer to page 8).

Acidic soil When chemical fertilizers and pesticides are used frequently, the soil is easily acidified. Also, in areas with heavy rainfall, such as Japan, soils tend to be acidic. For neutralization, apply bamboo charcoal.

Adventitious shoots Buds or shoots that emerge from places other than normal, and are found on trees with strong vigor or young trees. Adventitious buds that come from the roots of trees are also called "suckers."

Age determination Determine the age of the tree by counting the number of rings observed in the cross-section.

Air-layering Air-layering refers to peeling off a ring of bark for the purpose of propagation. Adventitious roots will grow quite easily in the section that was peeled.

Akadama soil, red ball earth (akadamatsuchi)
Akadama soil, or red ball earth, is selected from volcanic soil. It takes on a rusty brown color due to iron oxidation. The reddened soil is granulated to maintain its superior water retention and drainage properties. It is used as gardening soil.

Alternating growth Branches and buds alternate from side to side, with no pairing counterpart on the opposite side, as in maples, pomegranates and so on. See page 191.

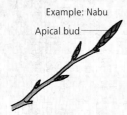

Example: Nabu

Apical bud

Apical bud A bud at the tip of a branch (or stem). The tips will vigorously sprout and grow into branches.

Arakawashou (rough bark appearance) This kind of bark looks rough and has the appearance of the bark on old trees. Arakawashou may also refer to trees that have this characteristic.

Araki (new wood) "New wood" refers to a sapling or some "raw material" that grew from a seed in nature.

Axil The base of the section where a leaf is attached to the stem. Where the leaves are on the join of a section that attaches to a stem, the buds that can be made here are called axillary buds.

Axillary bud (ekiga) axillary buds are buds that grow at the base of a leaf.

B

Ball fertilizer Horticultural oil is kneaded with water, hardened into a ball and dried. The fertilizer is placed atop pot soil. There are many commercial products available.

Bamboo shoot A bonsai tree with a taper that is sharply reduced, like a bamboo shoot from the root to the core.

Bark appearance, rough See: Arakawashou

Bark, appearance of (kawashou) There are many kinds of bark—brocade texture, rough, turtle-shell texture, etc. Rough bark looks like the bark on old trees, which is desirable.

Basin / bowl A porcelain pot for bonsai that is wide and shallow, and often decorated with stones.

Bird's soil (udei) Bird's soil refers to pots that have no glazing, instead capitalizing on the charm of simple clay. They are of a light brown color with a gray tinge. Other unglazed kinds of pots can be made from violet soil, red soil, light crimson soil, green soil, etc.

Blooming, springtime The period of growth produces flowers, and enlarges stems and trunks, and grows branches and leaves.

Bonsai tree A tree that has been well managed, with good shape and organization, and trimmed horizontal branches.

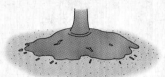

Bound roots A state where the roots grow together and form a clump. This condition is often found in maple and beech trees.

Example: Hanamizuki

When bracts look like the petals of a flower

Real flowers that grow in the middle

Bract Leaves that wrap the buds. Found at the base of flowers and inflorescences.

Branch, lower Among the branches, long and thick branches that harmonize and change the aesthetic of the trees.

Branch growth In the spring, new branches appear and they will remain supple while growing. When the lengthening growth of the branches begins to slow, they will start to become more rigid as they thicken.

Branch insertion (*edauchi*) Branch insertion refers to the way branches are attached to the tree, the way they grow and their thickness. If branch insertion is proper, we call it good branch insertion. This meaning and usage is limited to the world of bonsai! In the Japanese lumber industry, *edauchi* refers to cutting off branches at the trunk.

Branch removal (*edanuki*) Removing branches refers to the action of leaving only branches that are necessary for creating branch training, photosynthesis and oxygen circulation. Also called pruning.

"Broom stand" Tree shape that resembles an inverted broom.

Bud movement Observable signs of budding.

Bud picking A method of picking up new shoots and suppressing overgrowth. Also called "green picking" and "candle picking." The purpose is to have many small branches and small leaves.

C

Example: girdling

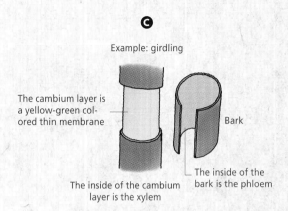

The cambium layer is a yellow-green colored thin membrane

Bark

The inside of the cambium layer is the xylem

The inside of the bark is the phloem

Cambium A layer of meristematic tissue that is associated with the trunk and roots. It exists between the xylem, where water flows, and the phloem, where useful elements obtained through photosynthesis transit, and where cell division thrives the most. Grafting is one of the propagation methods, and a graft will root depending on the connection of the cambium layer of the stock and scion.

Calling A type of grafting, a method of grafting the branches of a tree with roots as scion. The optimum time is spring, and if the side of the branch is scraped off to make a scion and the rootstock with the same side cut is brought into close contact, the callus (fused tissue) will be fused by autumn.

Carbon to nitrogen ratio (C:N) Indicates the ratio of carbon (C) and nitrogen (N) contained in the plant body. The growth rate (nutrition) of young trees is low in carbon and high in nitrogen. During reproductive growth, the carbon rate is high and the nitrogen rate is low. It also changes depending on the season. For example, when 100 grams of carbon and 10 grams of nitrogen are included, the C:N ratio is 10. In the case of bonsai, the carbon rate increases with growth.

Chemical fertilizer (*kaseihiryou*) This kind of fertilizer is necessary for the cultivation of plants. It gives inorganic matter to your bonsai, containing 2 or more of the following: nitrogen, phosphoric acid and potassium. Specific ingredients and content by percentage are displayed in numbers.

Chief branch A strong branch that grows sporadically for many years. Many adventitious buds will develop on such a branch, which can have a major detrimental effect on achieving a pleasing tree shape if left unchecked.

Cliff, hanging One of the basic forms of bonsai. It resembles how a tree grows as it clings to a precipice, and so the bonsai branches and trunk droop down below the pot. If the tree does not droop below the pot and instead sticks out diagonally downward, it is referred to as a "half-hanging cliff." Those that bend sideways are called "windsock." Refer to page 13.

Conifer A tree with needle-shaped or scaly leaves, many of which are evergreens. Common examples are Japanese cedar, *hinoki*, and different cypress varieties.

Core The top of the bonsai. The core of the tree can also be called the "apex of the crown." Refer to page 7.

Cross fertilization Fertilizing with pollen from different trees.

Crossed branches A type of "dreadful branch" that is tangled. Refer to diagram 1, above right.

Cutting A branch to be inserted into the soil for propagation.

Cutting and replanting A breeding method that involves cutting tree branches, leaves, roots, etc., and putting them in the soil for rooting. In this way you can perpetuate the attributes of the donor tree. See page 21.

Cutting buds A breeding method that involves cutting out new shoots of trees and flowers, inserting them into the soil and rooting them. See page 21.

Cypress bonsai Japanese pine, *goyo* pine, juniper, needle juniper and cedar cypress are some of the man varieties. They are known for their strength and perseverance and have thus become the prime examples of bonsai.

D

Defoliation One method of pruning is to remove the leaves to force the tree to produce more numerous, but smaller, leaves. This technique should only be attempted on robust deciduous trees.

Distribution of branches (*edabari*) The stretch of the branch refers to the length and thickness of branches on trees. Alternatively, it refers to the length of the longest branch measured from the ending point of all the other branches.

Division of branches (*edawakare*) The division of branches refers to the way in which branches divide off from the trunk.

Dobuzuke A practice where the entire pot is immersed in water so the plant's root system can absorb the maximum amount of water.

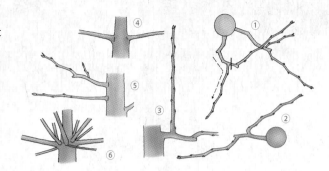

Dreadful branches (*Imieda*) Branches that can easily break the visual harmony and balance of the bonsai are called "dreadful branches." Dreadful branches are pruned.

① Crossed branches (*karamieda*). When branches have grown intertwined.

② Reverse branches (*sakaeda*). Branches usually grow away from the trunk, but reverse branches turn their growth toward the trunk.

③ Standing branches (*tachieda*). Branches that grow upward. Vertical branches.

④ Bar branches (*kannukieda*). Bar branches are pairs of branches that form a continuous visual line from left to right or from the front to the back.

⑤ Parallel branches (*heikoueda*). When multiple branches grow in the same direction close to each other, they become parallel branches.

⑥ Wheel branches (*kurumaeda*). When three or more branches grow from the same spot of the tree and create a spoke-like formation, they are called wheel branches.

Dwarf variety See: *Yatsufusa*

E

Earthenware bowl An unglazed bowl. It is common to plant pines and cypress trees in earthenware bowls because of the acidity of the soil and the attractive color of the bowls.

Edabari See: Distribution of branches

Edaburi See: Shape of the tree

Edanobi See: Extended branches

Edanuki See: Branch removal

Edauchi See: Branch insertion

Edawakare See: Division of branches

Ekiga See: Axillary bud

Evergreens Trees that have green leaves year round. The leaves are glossy due to the cuticular layer. They have glossy leaves or needles. Cypress bonsai fall into this category.

Exposed roots When the roots are visible on top of the soil.

Extended branches (*edanobi*) Extended branches refers to the condition of branches that have been neglected and allowed to grow too long without bud picking and regular pruning. Leaves will only grow at the end of the branch, and there are few forking branches on the middle. This is an undesirable look for bonsai.

F

Fallen branch (*ochieda*) Fallen branches are branches that have been intentionally shaped to droop down. They are important for the visual harmony of the bonsai.

Fertilizing Fortifying the health of the tree and encouraging growth through the addition of artificial fertilizer suitable for the plant.

Fertilizing as a token of gratitude (*oreihi*) Giving fertilizer to a bonsai that has produced flowers or fruit to replenish the bonsai's nourishment and prevent weakening. *Oreihi* is fertilizer with a high amount of nitrogen.

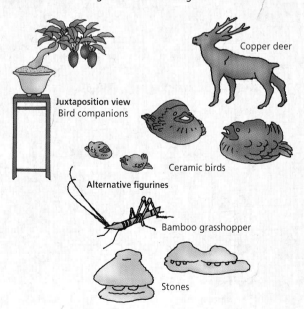

Juxtaposition view
Bird companions

Copper deer

Ceramic birds

Alternative figurines

Bamboo grasshopper

Stones

Figurine An accessory that helps to complete a bonsai arrangement. Common figurines include humans, animals, insects or Buddha statues.

Filament (*kashi*) The filaments are threadlike parts of the flower that support the stamen. Refer to page 190.

First branch (*ichinoeda*) The branch that is closest to the roots. It is often the thickest, longest branch on the bonsai. Going up the tree, the branch that is second closest to the roots is logically called the "second branch" and the branch that is third closest to the roots is called the "third branch."

Fixed bud Top and side buds in fixed positions. Other buds are called "adventitious buds."

Flower bud A bud that becomes a flower. Called a "reproductive bud" in botanical terms.

Flower bud cultivation (*kagabunka*) Cultivation refers to the natural process of specialization of cells, tissues and organs for a specific purpose. In bonsai, flower and leaf bud cultivation usually happens in summer.

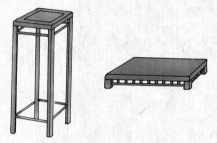

Flower vase stand (*kadai*) Stands are used during viewing sessions.

Flowers, picking The purpose of picking remaining flowers after most of the blooms have wilted is to prevent the decline of tree vigor and pest damage. In order to avoid the decline of the tree due to fruiting, the flowers are picked by pinching the base of the ovary.

Foraging Collecting promising natural trees that are suitable for bonsai growing.

Frog-leg branch (*kaerumata*) The frog-leg branch is a kind of dreadful branch. The division and growth direction of the branch from the trunk looks similar to frog legs.

Front branch Branches that appear at the front of the bonsai. Considered a type of "dreadful branch."

Fruit and flower training Determining where the buds will be allowed to appear on the branches through bud pinching.

Fuji sand A volcanic soil that fosters good water retention and uptake of nutrients. This soil is used when displaying bonsai. It improves the appearance of the bonsai and hides the dirt on the bottom. You can use moss for the same purpose.

Fujimoto See: Vine

Fungicide Pesticides used for disease prevention.

Futokoro The parts of the tree branches that are close to the trunk. If this part of the bonsai is "branchy," the tree is more impressive, but if it gets too crowded, the ventilation and access to sunlight will be poor and the tree shape will be less than ideal.

G

Gakuhen See: Sepal

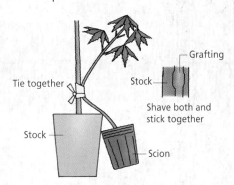

Tie together
Stock
Stock
Scion
Grafting
Shave both and stick together

Grafting A method of propagating in which a non-rooted branch or bud is inserted into the stem of a rooted strain and the formation layers of both are fused. See pages 18–21.

Gravel Also known as "bottom soil," it is the largest-grain used (about ¼ to ½ in / 7 to 10 mm in diameter). It improves drainage at the bottom of the bowl.

Ground plane A board upon which pots and basins are placed when viewing bonsai.

Grouping Planting multiple trees together in a pot to approximate the look of a forest scene.

Growing bud Adventitious buds that grow from the roots of trees. These are likely to develop into trunks.

Growth When the trunk and branches grow to widen and heighten the tree.

H

Haname Flower bud.

Happo root growth A root system that indicates a sense of stability, with roots radiating in all directions.

Height of the tree (Refer to page 7.) The height from the root of the tree to tip of the trunk.

Herbaceous plants Non-woody plants. Those that sprout in the spring and die within that year or the following year are annuals. Perennials live for more than two years. Even if the above-ground part withers, the underground part of a perennial survives for many years. In both cases, the xylem does not develop, and stem enlargement is limited. In other words, it is not a tree.

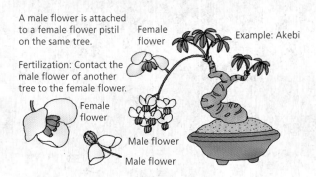

A male flower is attached to a female flower pistil on the same tree.

Fertilization: Contact the male flower of another tree to the female flower.

Female flower

Female flower

Male flower

Male flower

Example: Akebi

Hermaphrodite A plant that bears male and female flowers on the same tree.

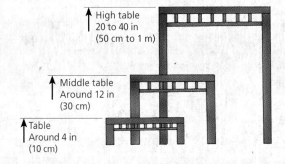

High table
20 to 40 in
(50 cm to 1 m)

Middle table
Around 12 in
(30 cm)

Table
Around 4 in
(10 cm)

Hira Bonsai display platform with legs that serves as a table. Tables that have a height of 4 inches (10 cm) are called "*hira-shoku*." Tables about 12 inches (30 cm) high are called "middle *shoku*." Tables between about 20 to 40 inches (50 cm to 1 m) are called "high *shoku*."

Humus Fallen leaves and twigs that have been placed in a heap and turned into soil through decomposition. This rich soil can be added to depleted soil to make it a better growing medium. You can purchase bagged humus at garden centers.

Husbandry Appropriate management, care and cultivation of bonsai.

Hypertrophy When the trunk or the branches grow to be too thick.

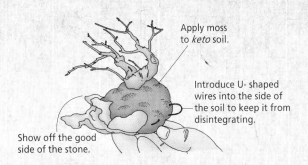

Apply moss to *keto* soil.

Introduce U-shaped wires into the side of the soil to keep it from disintegrating.

Show off the good side of the stone.

Ishizuke (attached to stone) *Ishizuke* is one of the ways in which a bonsai can grow. The bonsai has partially been planted on a stone to add a sense of rustic beauty and natural scenery.

J

Jin When the branch withers and becomes deadwood. For the purpose of showing age in Cypress bonsai, we purposely shave the bark or the skin of the tree. Also, when you take away the unwanted branches, we can leave a bit of the base of the branch and create a *jin*. This emphasizes the aged appearance of the tree. Refer to page 172.

K

Kadai See: Flower vase stand

Kaerumata See: Frog-leg branch

Kaga Flower bud

Kagabunka See: Flower bud cultivation

Kaisaku See: Improving the form

Kajo See: Inflorescence

Kanjouhakuhi See: Air-layering

Kanju See: Tree in winter

Kankouseihiryou See: Long-term fertilizer

Kannukieda Terminology used to describe a bonsai branch that fails to meet the standard of beauty for a bonsai branch.

Kanshoubachi See: Prize pot

Kansui (sprinkling of water) To water the plant.

I

Ichinoeda See: First branch

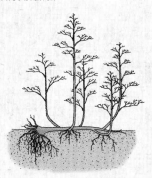

Ikadabuki (raft form) *Ikadabuki* is one of the ways in which a tree can grow. The branches from a tree that has toppled over grow upward, functionally becoming trunks.

Imieda See: Dreadful branches

Improving the form (*kaisaku*) When pruning or layering, we improve the bonsai by adjusting the angle at which branches etc. grow or by improving the way the bonsai looks from the front. We do this often when we have devised a way to create a better look for the bonsai.

Inflorescence (*kajo*) Inflorescence is the appearance of multiple flowers on one flower axis.

Insecticide A chemical application that controls pests.

Inside ridge (*uchien*) This term refers to pots that have their ridge folded over to the inside.

Kanuma soil Kanuma soil is light granular volcanic soil that has been eroded by wind, found in the area surrounding Mt. Akagi, Tochigi prefecture and the coast of Ibaraki prefecture. It has high water retention and breathability. Kanuma soil is used for propagation. It gets its name from its prevalence around the town of Kanuma.

Kataeda See: One-sided branches

Katanebari See: One-sided root settling

Kawashou See: Bark, appearance of

Keto soil A sticky soil formed from plants (mainly phragmites) growing in swamps and rivers. This fiber-rich soil is useful for attaching bonsai plants onto rocks or making moss balls.

Kiryu River sand A type of coarse, grayish, iron-rich soil exported from Kiryu, Gunma prefecture. It is great for drainage and breathability, is water-retentive, and has enhanced drainage capability when mixed with *akadama* soil.

Kisugata The way a bonsai is shaped, the figure of the bonsai.

Knot hole (uro) Holes that occur when scars on the trunk that were made during pruning start to rot, open up and hollow out.

Kuitsukieda A very short branch that appears to be biting onto the tree's trunk. Frequently seen in artistic bonsai creations.

Kuruma eda Branches that grow haphazardly from a single spot.

Kusamono Essentially, bonsai that have been shaped from wild herbs, grasses or flowers. *Kusa* means "grass" and *mono* means "thing" or "material."

Kyokkan A bonsai with a lot of bent branches; an extreme example of a *moyogi*-style (curved) tree.

Kyoku The bent part of the trunk or branch of the bonsai.

Kyoku zuke Using wires to bend the bonsai branches. This is one of the important processes when nurturing a bonsai plant (a tree so wired will be healthy due to receiving a good amount of sunlight and adequate ventilation. Refer to page 171.

L

Lead root Roots growing seed embryos. (See page 188.)

Lead trunk When there are multiple trunks from the root of a tree, the lead is the thickest and tallest of them.

Leaf burn Strong sunshine in summer and high temperatures cause excessive transpiration from the leaves, and some or all of the leaves wither when the water absorption from the roots is insufficient.

Leaf watering The sprinkling of water on the leaves. This has the effect of removing dirt and preventing leaf burn.

Leafiness A term describing leaf properties, including size and gloss, as well as canopy organization. Leafiness is said to be good if the bonsai exhibits attractive organization and bears a proliferation of small, shiny leaves.

Legginess Excessive branch growth. A result of inattentiveness to trimming, it is also affected by lack of sunshine, excessive nitrogen content in the soil, lack of ventilation and crowded buds.

Liquid fertilizer Water containing dissolved fertilizer.

Literati tree A bonsai tree shape with a thin trunk and few branches. The beauty of the tree springs from the rugged sparseness of the unusual tree form. See page 13.

Long-term fertilizer (kankouseihiryou) This kind of fertilizer is usually organic and releases its nutrients over a longer period of time.

M

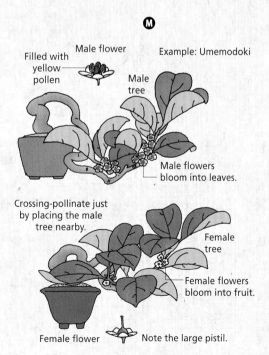

Filled with yellow pollen — Male flower — Example: Umemodoki — Male tree — Male flowers bloom into leaves. — Crossing-pollinate just by placing the male tree nearby. — Female tree — Female flowers bloom into fruit. — Female flower — Note the large pistil.

Male and female mixed stock (dioecious) Plants that have separate male and female trees.

Masaki Bonsai made from seedlings and natural trees, excluding cutting methods, grafting, calling and air-layering. In the bonsai world, it is one of the traditional characteristics of a legitimate bonsai tree.

Material Seedlings or untrained trees that will be made into bonsai.

Midori A pine bud that has not yet opened its needles. Picking these and thus affecting the proliferation of the buds is called "green picking." See pages 152–155.

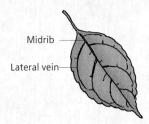

Midrib

Lateral vein

Midrib A large vein running in the middle of the leaf. The vascular bundle of the stem flows into the leaf, and sends water and nutrients from the stem to the leaf, playing a role in sending the carbohydrates made by leaf photosynthesis (carbon dioxide assimilation) to the stem. (Refer to page 191.)

Mini bonsai Bonsai that are smaller than 4 inches (10 cm).

Miscellaneous bonsai Bonsai trees other than pines.

Moss order The "moss order" is said to be good when the tree gradually narrows from the root of the stock toward the upper core. A shape reminiscent of a full size tree is the preferred form.

Moyogi (bending trunk) A tree with a trunk that bends forward, backward, left and right. See page 12.

Mycorrhizae Symbiotic bacteria that proliferate in the root cells, providing nitrogen to the plant in exchange for carbohydrates from the tree.

Nadekaku A bowl shape characterized by rounded corners.

Nanjing Long Bowl

Nanjing bowl A Chinese bowl with glaze over porcelain.

Nearai ("Root washing") After potting, once the roots have grown into the shape of the pot, the plant is removed and allowed to aerate without the pot to keep the roots from adhering to the container.

Needle removal One of the methods for shaping black pine and red pine. In the second bud that has grown after bud cutting, all the old needles are removed during the dormancy period, and particularly thick parts are thinned out in the new needle growth. See pages 154–155.

New branches Branches that have grown from the spring a given year. These are called first-year branches. In the next year, they will be called second-year branches.

New wood See: *Araki*

Nishiki When the bark on the tree exhibits a rough texture.

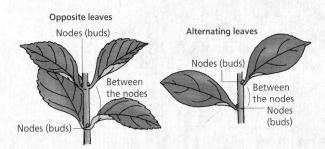

Opposite leaves

Nodes (buds)

Between the nodes

Nodes (buds)

Alternating leaves

Nodes (buds)

Between the nodes

Nodes (buds)

Node Bud growth that will ultimately become branches. Generally, the space between nodes becomes shorter the closer the nodes get to the end of the branch.

Nourishment and growth (*eiyouseichou*) nourishment and growth refers to the process of a plant growing taller and the growth of stems and the trunk, eventually pushing the production of leaves and branches to luxurious growth.

Oblique trunk One of the basic forms of bonsai, with the trunk not standing upright but tilting to the left or right. See pages 12–13.

Oil cake (*aburakasu*) these cakes are made of the dregs of oily vegetables such as soy beans and turnip rapes. They contain a lot of nitrogen. Once they have fermented completely, oil cakes are used in gardening, bonsai, etc.

Old crossing A style of bonsai pot imported from China before the Meiji period. The bowls produced during the Meiji-Taisho period were distinguished as "*Nakawatari*," and those from the end of Taisho until before the war were distinguished as "*Shinto*."

One-sided branches (*kataeda*) When looked at from the front, a bonsai with "one-sided branches" has many branches on one side and few branches on the other. This usually breaks the visual balance, but it can also create a natural windswept look.

One-sided root settling (*katanebari*) "One-sided root settling" occurs when the bonsai's roots settle mostly on the left or right side when viewed from the front.

One-year branches (*ichinenshi*) One-year branches are branches that matured from a shoot but have not seen their second spring yet. One-year branches become two-year branches the following year.

Organic fertilizer Natural fertilizer based on animals and plants. Many exhibit a slow release and are slow acting.

Original fertilizer Fertilizer necessary for growth before transplanting. Slow-acting organic substances are often used.

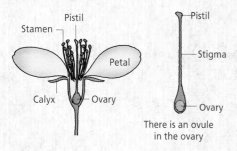

Ovary This is the fruit at the puffy part under the pistil. The ovule in the ovary becomes the seed.

Oven-baked pots Unglazed pots that have been baked at nearly 1,500°F (800°C). It is good for plants to be potted in this type of container because it allows for good drainage.

Over fertilization Excessive fertilizer concentrates in the moist soil around the roots, damaging them and resulting in poor growth.

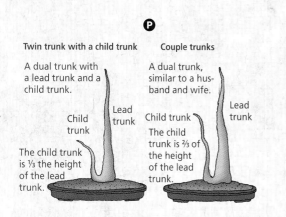

Paired trunks A single base trunk with two main branches. Sometimes referred to as a "couple."

Parallel branches One of the "dreadful branches." See page 178.

Pesticides Granular chemicals that are administered to the soil for the purpose of eliminating pests. The substance will dissolve when the tree is watered and be taken up through the roots. Insects feeding on the sap of a tree that has been treated will ingest the pesticide and die.

Petiole The stem attached to the leaf that serves as a conduit for sap.

pH A symbol indicating the hydrogen ion concentration of soil or water. The middle is pH 7. Acidity is a numerical value less than 7, but the hydrogen ion concentration is high. Alkalinity is a numerical value greater than 7, and the hydrogen ion concentration is low. In general, fertilizers and pesticides continue to be acidic, and when mixed with chalk, plant ash, charcoal, etc., it becomes alkaline. Soil adjustment suitable for the plant is necessary.

Phoenix graft ("*tankuki* bonsai") Live bonsai tree material is rooted to interesting looking deadwood to mimic the appearance of an ancient tree.

Photosynthesis Plants that have chlorophyll will use sunlight to synthesize carbon dioxide from the atmosphere and water absorbed from the roots to create oxygen. The process involves carbon dioxide assimilation.

Porcelain Pale yellow or light gray Chinese earthenware bowl made from clay with low iron oxide content.

Pot spillage When branches and leaves overhand the edge of the bowl, as seen on cliffs.

Potting Moving bonsai that were planted as seedlings in the ground into pots.

Primary branch A branch that is indispensable to the overall composition of the tree.

Prize pot (*kanshoubachi*) A pot is used to display the tree. The tree is moved from an unglazed pot to a temporary pot for viewing, and then to a permanent pot. Refer to pages 22–23.

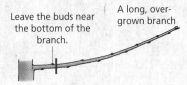

Leave the buds near the bottom of the branch.

A long, over-grown branch

Prune back A pruning technique where the buds near the tip of the branch are cut off, leaving only the buds near the base of the branch. By doing so, one can encourage small branch growth. This is a necessary step to renewing the branches.

Pruning In order to make the bonsai beautiful, make sure to trim the branches when necessary.

Reflection A quality expressed in terms of "good" or "bad" when referring to whether a tree and its bowl exhibit visual harmony.

Reform To attach and string wires on the branches to bend or shape the bonsai tree branches a certain way.

Reproductive growth Growth that produces flower buds, which precedes blooming and fruiting.

Reverse branch One of the "dreadful branches." See page 178.

The rise is ideal.

Rise One of the aesthetic points of good bonsai. The tapering shape between the roots and the first branch.

Root binding When the roots encounter a barrier and become overly dense in the pot.

Root hair A filamentous tissue that grows near the tip of the root and absorbs moisture and nutrients.

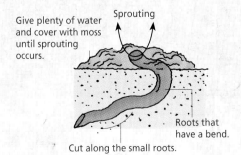

Give plenty of water and cover with moss until sprouting occurs.

Sprouting

Roots that have a bend.

Cut along the small roots.

Root insertion One of the propagation methods, accomplished by cutting the roots and inserting them into the soil.

Root range A tree with multiple standing trunks and connected roots.

Major causes

① Missed replanting for a long time, wrong time, etc.

② The soil is inappropriate and the drainage is bad.

The concentration and number of fertilizer applications are in excess of the needs of the tree.

③ Excessive fertilizer.

Removing dead roots

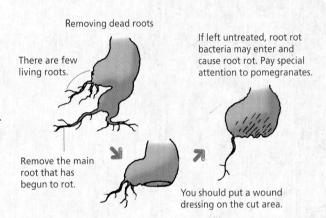

There are few living roots.

If left untreated, root rot bacteria may enter and cause root rot. Pay special attention to pomegranates.

Remove the main root that has begun to rot.

You should put a wound dressing on the cut area.

Root rot This problem may be due to poor drainage, or it may be a sign of too much fertilizer being used. Bacterial infection can also have a detrimental effect on the roots.

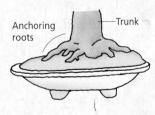

Anchoring roots

Trunk

Rooting One of the ornamental objectives of bonsai is to exhibit the growth of the roots on the surface. It expresses the strength and stability that anchors the tree to the earth.

Rootstock When grafting, the part of the tree that is being inserted.

Rope, decorative A symbolic decoration wrapped around the planting bowl representing purity and protection.

Rounded trunk A round trunk with no scars.

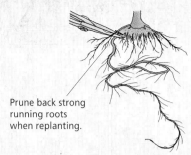

Prune back strong running roots when replanting.

Running root A root that grows extremely long compared to other roots. Shorten when replanting.

Sap-sucking pests Insects such as aphids and scale insects that have needle-shaped mouth parts that they use to suck the sap from plants and trees.

Scion When grafting, young shoots and branches that connect to the rootstock.

Round sea-cucumber bowl

Sea-cucumber bowl Japanese and Chinese bowls with blue and white marbled patterns. The color is derived from indigo glaze.

Seat The roots of a tree, particularly when they have adhered together and become a single lump.

Seedling tree The raw material that is used as the basis for making bonsai. Seed tree.

Self-fertilization Flowers and fruit that supply their own pollen. Pollination and fertilization between the same strain and flowers.

Self-incompatibility Plants that cannot bear fruit using their own pollen. Even if self-pollination occurs, fertilization will not occur, and it will be difficult or impossible for the plant to produce fruit.

Semi-hanging cliff Trees with trunks and branches that do not hang down far below the pot, but instead only dip to near the level of the bottom of the container.

Sepal (*gakuhen*) Parts of the calyx are called sepal. Calyx is a botanical term, referring to the crown of the flower (where the petals are gathered.) Refer to page 190.

Shape of the tree (*edaburi*) The silhouette of the tree and its visual harmony.

***Shari* trunk** A condition where part where the trunk has withered and the woody part is white. It is often found in coniferous pine tree bonsai, and is often created artificially by removing the bark. See page 172.

Shinto pots Pots imported from China during the first half of the Meiji era are called "*towatari.*" Those from the middle of the Meiji era to the beginning of the Taisho era are called "*nakawatari.*"

Short branch A branch with short internodes that grows only slightly year by year. Typically seen in ginkgo, larch and others.

Shrub A tree that has a height of several meters or less, has no clear thickened trunk, but rather many slender stems, such as azalea, Chinese quince, pyracantha, etc.

Single trunk A bonsai with just one trunk.

Small bonsai Normally, trees that are at most 8 inches (20 cm) are called "small bonsai." Bonsai standing at 2¾ to 3⅛ inches (7 to 8 cm) are called "miniature bonsai."

Soil porosity The ratio of the volume of water and air contained in the soil expressed as a percentage.

Sowing Seed planting.

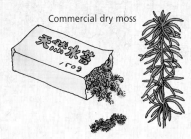

Commercial dry moss

Sphagnum Moss that grows in wetlands. While alive, it is bright green. The sage-colored moss used for horticultural water-retention purposes is simply dried sphagnum moss.

Spiral grain The tendency of the trunk to twist as it grows.

Sprout When the leaf forms, budding.

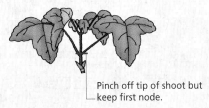

Pinch off tip of shoot but keep first node.

Sprout trimming By trimming off new shoots when they appear, the tree's energy is redirected toward increasing the number of branches while maintaining a limited number of leaves or needles. This is an important task in caring for Japanese black pines. It is also called the "short leaf method." This technique has a variety of purposes and applications. It involves removing the buds that appear in spring, but allowing the second buds that grow later in the year to remain. Essentially, the strong parts are suppressed and weak parts are preserved.

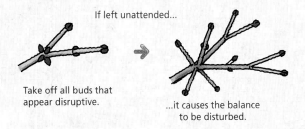

If left unattended...

Take off all buds that appear disruptive.

...it causes the balance to be disturbed.

Sprout (or bud) picking The act of removing superfluous buds.

Example: Japanese zelkova

Seed

Seeds that you can crush with your fingertips are non-germinated. These can be distinguished by the way they float when placed in water.

Sterility The condition of some seeds that are incapable of germination.

Stipule A pair of structures at the base of the petiole, which is said to play a role in protecting young shoots that have just emerged. See page 191.

Stone, attached See: *Ishizuke*

Straight root A young root that emerges from a seed embryo and grows straight down. From there, lateral roots, fine roots and root hairs are produced.

Straight trunk A tree that is straight and upright without bends in its trunk.

Cut-back pruning / halfway pruning (*oikomisentei*) In order to decrease the size of a branch, cut it in the middle.

Successful settling (*katsuchaku*) Successful settling occurs when a bonsai that has been moved from one pot to another successfully settles its root into the new soil. This term can also be applied to the root settling of cuttings, or proper adhesion of the scion in grafting.

Support roots Strong roots that grow in the opposite direction of the slant of the trunk. These provide major support to the trunk.

Surfactant Additive used to facilitate the adhesion of sprayed insecticide to the surface of leaves and stems.

T

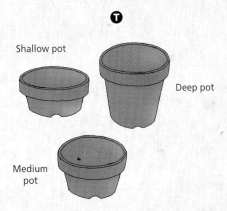

Shallow pot

Deep pot

Medium pot

Tailoring pot A pot for planting a bonsai that is dedicated to the purpose of growing trunk branches more vigorously. Sometimes a weakened tree is transplanted into a "tailoring pot" to help it recover.

Takagi Any tree species that has a crown reaching several meters above the ground. An *Otakagi* (macrophanerophyte) reaches 20 meters or more. For convenience, in horticulture, trees with a height of 3 meters or more are classified as trees, while those under 2 meters are considered shrubs.

Taking root (*uekomi*) Taking root refers to the planting of a bonsai in a pot.

Tanuki bonsai See: Phoenix graft

Tenjin River sand Sand collected upstream of the Tenjin River in Hyogo Prefecture. It has beneficial minerals and excellent air permeability, but weak water retention.

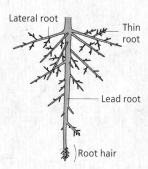

Lateral root

Thin root

Lead root

Root hair

Thin roots Fine roots that originate from the lateral roots. The young root of the seed embryo emerges and grows straight down. From the straight root, lateral roots emerge on the sides, and then fine roots and root hairs are formed to absorb moisture.

Third-year seedlings Seedlings three years after having been sown. These are a recommended as hassle-free starter trees for beginners. However, some may take several years to flourish.

Tightened tree It is a bonsai tree that has been well managed and cultivated for a long time, has a well-shaped trunk, and has no overly-long branches.

To bring in In bonsai nomenclature, the act of tending a tree. For instance, managing a bonsai for 30 years can also be referred to as "bringing in the tree for 30 years."

Example: About ⅜ in (1 cm) of solidified fertilizer

Example: About ⅜ in (1 cm) of commercially available solid fertilizer

About 70% nitrogen
About 20% phosphoric acid
About 10% potassium

Mainly for pine and cedar. No. 3 bowl, one piece in each.

About 35% nitrogen
About 50% phosphoric acid
About 15% potassium

Mainly for flowering and fruiting bonsai. One piece is standard for a No. 3 bowl.

Top dressing Solid fertilizer pellets added topically as a necessary infusion of nutrients each time the tree is replanted and during periods of growth.

Training and grooming Pruning the branches, plucking the leaves, and securing the trunk and branches with a wire. These actions change the shape and posture of the bonsai tree.

Transplanting (*uekae*) The act of removing a bonsai or sapling from its pot, cutting down any roots that have grown too long, placing new soil in the pot and returning the bonsai to the pot again. (Refer to page 18.)

Tree core The trunk. Refer to page 7.

Tree crown In forestry nomenclature, it is the entire canopy of the tree. In the case of bonsai, "crown" refers to only the branches and leaves at the very top of the tree.

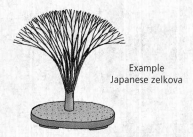

Example
Japanese zelkova

Tree in winter (*kanju*) Deciduous trees lose their leaves in the winter, leaving only the silhouette of the branches. The Japanese zelkova and maples are popular for this look. The thin, bare branch distribution and arrangement specific to the tree species paired with winter buds and the beautiful fallen autumn leaves make for the perfect viewing session.

Tree shape The bonsai's shape, which mimics the shape and appearance of wild trees, and is classified into basic trunks, patterned trees, and cliffs. (Refer to pages 12–13.)

Tree species Trees of a specific type. Males of a given species can pollinate females of the same species.

Tree vigor Growth (health) status of individual trees.

Triple trunk Tree shape with three trunks standing from the root of one tree. Two trunks are "twin-stems" and five or more are "stocks."

Trunk hollow The root forms a single trunk, but due to mishap, disease or pest damage, a hole forms in the middle.

Trunk buds Adventitious buds on the trunk.

Trunk pattern The degree of bending in the trunk.

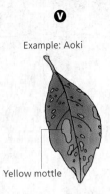

Example: Aoki

Yellow mottle

Variegation When the leaves exhibit patterns in two or more colors.

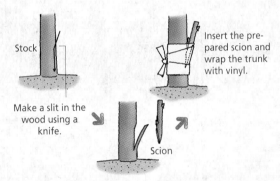

Stock

Make a slit in the wood using a knife.

Insert the prepared scion and wrap the trunk with vinyl.

Scion

Veneer grafting A method to propagate using a graft. Make a slit near the surface of the stock wood and insert graft material (scion) into the slit. Then, wrap vinyl around the trunk.

Vermilion A reddish, unglazed earthenware bowl.

Vine A plant that grows tendrils that become woody, such as Oriental bittersweet, chocolate vine, *Kadsura japonica*, etc.

W

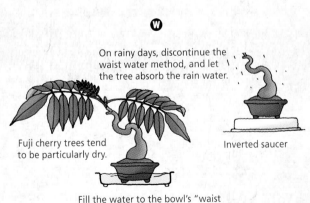

On rainy days, discontinue the waist water method, and let the tree absorb the rain water.

Fuji cherry trees tend to be particularly dry.

Inverted saucer

Fill the water to the bowl's "waist height." By afternoon, the water level should fall below the bowl.

Waist water A method of immersing the entire bowl in a basin filled with water, allowing moisture to be taken up through the hole in the bottom of the bowl. Effective as a dehydration-prevention measure in the summer.

Wakagi An unfinished bonsai that has not yet passed the test of time and does not yet present the appearance of an old tree.

Windsock Said of the shape of a tree with branches and trunk leaning strongly in one direction, as if being swept by the wind. See page 13.

Winter buds Buds that grow over the winter and sprout the following spring.

Wiring Trees tend to grow directly upward if left untended. Bonsai practitioners wrap wire around branches and trunks to improve ventilation and leaf access to sunshine, and also to pleasingly alter the shape and direction of the limbs and trunk. The goal is to train the bonsai and bring forth the appearance of a large old tree. See page 171.

Wound dressing Agents that prevent pruning cuts from being attacked by pathogens and pests, and to promote the formation of *callus* (a tissue that closes over the wound when the plant is damaged).

Y

Yago **bud** Among the adventitious buds, the buds that grow from the base of the trunk. These are liable to become independent trunks.

Example: *Yatsufusa* juniper

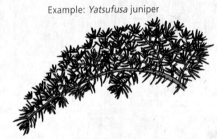

Yatsufusa **(dwarf variety)** A tree with smaller leaves and smaller aspect than a typical tree of the same species. It is common in conifers such as *goyo* pine, spruce pine and temple juniper, but is also found in various other trees.

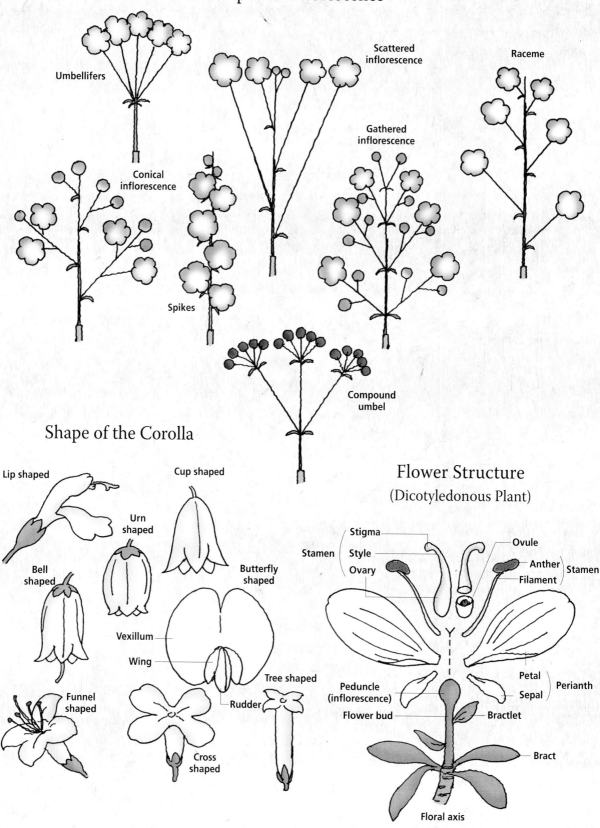

Shapes of Inflorescence

Umbellifers

Scattered inflorescence

Raceme

Conical inflorescence

Gathered inflorescence

Spikes

Compound umbel

Shape of the Corolla

Lip shaped

Cup shaped

Urn shaped

Bell shaped

Butterfly shaped

Vexillum

Wing

Funnel shaped

Rudder

Tree shaped

Cross shaped

Flower Structure
(Dicotyledonous Plant)

Stigma

Stamen — Style

Ovary

Ovule

Anther — Stamen

Filament

Petal — Perianth

Peduncle (inflorescence)

Sepal

Flower bud

Bractlet

Bract

Floral axis

Names of Leaf Parts and How They are Attached

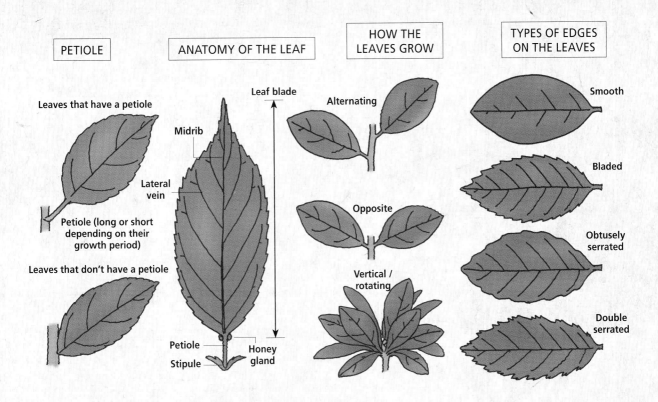

PETIOLE

ANATOMY OF THE LEAF

HOW THE LEAVES GROW

TYPES OF EDGES ON THE LEAVES

Leaves that have a petiole

Petiole (long or short depending on their growth period)

Leaves that don't have a petiole

Leaf blade

Midrib

Lateral vein

Petiole

Stipule

Honey gland

Alternating

Opposite

Vertical / rotating

Smooth

Bladed

Obtusely serrated

Double serrated

Various Shapes of Leaves

Oblong

Lanceolate

Linear

Aciculate

Obovate

Egg-shaped

Elliptic

Various Compound Leaves

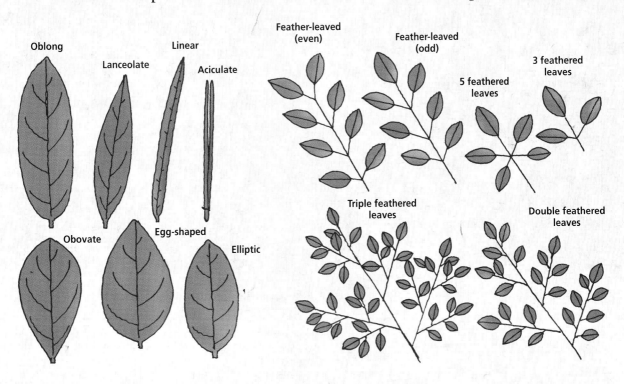

Feather-leaved (even)

Feather-leaved (odd)

5 feathered leaves

3 feathered leaves

Triple feathered leaves

Double feathered leaves

Published by Tuttle Publishing, an imprint of Periplus Editions (HK) Ltd.

ISBN 978-4-8053-1544-6

www.tuttlepublishing.com

NYUMON CHIISANA KI NO BONSAI
Copyright © 2015 SPRESSMEDIA CO, LTD.
Illustration © Kyosuke Gun
English translation rights arranged with
SPRESSMEDIA CO, LTD. through
Japan UNI Agency, Inc., Tokyo

Distributed by
North America, Latin America & Europe
Tuttle Publishing
364 Innovation Drive, North Clarendon
VT 05759-9436 U.S.A.
Tel: (802) 773-8930; Fax: (802) 773-6993
info@tuttlepublishing.com; www.tuttlepublishing.com

Japan
Tuttle Publishing
Yaekari Building, 3rd Floor
5-4-12 Osaki, Shinagawa-ku, Tokyo 141 0032
Tel: (81) 3 5437-0171; Fax: (81) 3 5437-0755
sales@tuttle.co.jp; www.tuttle.co.jp

Asia Pacific
Berkeley Books Pte. Ltd.
3 Kallang Sector #04-01, Singapore 349278
Tel: (65) 67412178; Fax: (65) 67412179
inquiries@periplus.com.sg; www.tuttlepublishing.com

Printed in Malaysia   2108VP
23 22 21   10 9 8 7 6 5 4 3 2 1

"Books to Span the East and West"

Tuttle Publishing was founded in 1832 in the small New England town of Rutland, Vermont [USA]. Our core values remain as strong today as they were then—to publish best-in-class books which bring people together one page at a time. In 1948, we established a publishing office in Japan—and Tuttle is now a leader in publishing English-language books about the arts, languages and cultures of Asia. The world has become a much smaller place today and Asia's economic and cultural influence has grown. Yet the need for meaningful dialogue and information about this diverse region has never been greater. Over the past seven decades, Tuttle has published thousands of books on subjects ranging from martial arts and paper crafts to language learning and literature—and our talented authors, illustrators, designers and photographers have won many prestigious awards. We welcome you to explore the wealth of information available on Asia at **www.tuttlepublishing.com**.